Medieval
French Literature
and Law

Medieval French Literature and Law

R. HOWARD BLOCH

University of California Press

BERKELEY · LOS ANGELES · LONDON

University of California Press
Berkeley and Los Angeles, California
University of California Press, Ltd.
London, England
Copyright © 1977 by
The Regents of the University of California
ISBN 0-520-03230-6
Library of Congress Catalog Card Number: 76-7754
Printed in the United States of America

To the memory of Frank and Bea Varmus

Contents

Acknowledgments

It is, of course, impossible to thank adequately those who have aided me intellectually, morally, and financially in the making of this book. Nonetheless, I would like to express my gratitude to former and present colleagues who have read portions of the manuscript in preparation: Charles Bernheimer, Leo Bersani, Gérard Caspary, Phillip Damon, Eugenio Donato, Robert Edwards, René Girard, Jefferson Kline, Jeffrey Mehlman, and Richard Terdiman. They are responsible for many of the book's strengths, though I alone can answer for its weaknesses. A special note of appreciation is due Joe Duggan, whose sensitive and sensible criticism has provided a constant source of irritation without which the present volume might never have seen the light of day. I would also like to thank: Michel Foucault, whose lectures on Greek law presented at the State University of New York in the spring of 1972 partially reshaped chapters one and three; Jean Frappier, whose encouragement in the beginning makes me regret all the more that he did not live to see the final product; Francis Wilcox, who typed it; Connie Casey, Kathryn Hughes, and Michael Harney, who proofread it; Eric Rutledge, who helped me with translation of quotations; and, finally, the University of California Committee on Research, whose material support has facilitated my research all along the way.

Abbreviations

In order to reduce the number of footnotes I have adopted the following abbreviations for frequently cited texts:

Beaumanoir– Philippe de Beaumanoir, *Coutumes de Beauvaisis*, ed. A. Salmon (Paris: Picard, 1899).

Béroul– Béroul, *Le Roman de Tristan*, ed. E. Muret (Paris: Champion, 1962).

Béthune– *Les Chansons de Conon de Béthune*, ed. A. Wallensköld (Helsingfors: Imprimerie Centrale de Helsingfors, 1891).

Cercamon– *Les Poésies de Cercamon*, ed. A. Jeanroy (Paris: Champion, 1922).

Champagne– *Les Chansons de Thibaut de Champagne*, ed. A. Wallensköld (Paris: Champion, 1925).

Chevalerie Ogier– *La Chevalerie d'Ogier de Danemarche*, ed. M. Eusebi (Milan: Nicola, 1963).

Cligés– Chrétien de Troyes, *Cligés*, ed. A. Micha (Paris: Champion, 1957).

Coucy– *Die Lieder des Castellans von Coucy*, ed. F. Fath (Heidelberg: Gross, 1888).

Courtly Love– Andreas Capellanus, *The Art of Courtly Love*, trans. J. Parry (New York: Norton, 1969).

Erec– Chrétien de Troyes, *Erec et Enide*, ed. M. Roques (Paris: Champion, 1963).

Etablissements– *Les Etablissements de Saint Louis*, ed. P. Viollet (Paris: Renouard, 1881).

Gace Brulé– *Les Chansons de Gace Brulé*, ed. G. Huet (Paris: Firmin Didot, 1902).

[xi]

Girart– *Girart de Roussillon*, ed. M. Hackett (Paris: Picard, 1953).

GC– *Grand Coutumier*, in *Coutumiers de Normandie*, ed. E.-J. Tardif (Rouen: Lestrignant, 1896).

Jostice et Pletz– *Le Livre de Jostice et de Pletz*, ed. P.-N. Rapetti (Paris: Firmin Didot, 1850).

La Mort– *La Mort le roi Artu*, ed. J. Frappier (Geneva: Droz, 1956).

Lancelot– Chrétien de Troyes, *Le Chevalier de la Charrete*, ed. M. Roques (Paris: Champion, 1958).

Leys– *Las Leys d'Amors*, ed. M. Gratien-Arnoult (Toulouse: Privat, 1841–1843).

Marcabru– *Les Poésies de Marcabru*, ed. J. Dejeanne (Paris: Champion, 1909).

Nelli and Lavaud– R. Nelli and R. Lavaud, *Les Troubadours* (Paris: Desclée de Brouwer, 1966).

Quatre Filz– *La Chanson des Quatre Filz Aymon*, ed. F. Castets (Montpellier: Coulet, 1909).

Raoul– *Raoul de Cambrai*, ed. P. Meyer and A. Longnon (Paris: Firmin Didot, 1882).

Renart– *Le Roman de Renart*, ed. M. Roques (Paris: Champion, 1948).

Roland– *La Chanson de Roland*, ed. J. Bédier (Paris: H. Piazza, 1964).

Rose– G. De Lorris and J. de Meun, *Le Roman de la Rose*, ed. F. Lecoy (Paris: Champion, 1965).

Sommer– *The Vulgate Version of the Arthurian Romances*, ed. O. Sommer (Washington: Carnegie Institute, 1909).

TAC– *Très Ancien Coutumier*, in *Coutumiers de Normandie*, ed. E.-J. Tardif (Rouen: Cagniard, 1881).

Thomas– Thomas, *Le Roman de Tristan*, ed. B. Wind (Leiden: Brill, 1950).

Ventadorn (Appel)– *Bernard von Ventadorn, Seine Lieder*, ed. C. Appel (Halle: Niemeyer, 1915).

Ventadorn (Lazar)– *Les Chansons d'Amour de Bernard de Ventadour*, ed. M. Lazar (Paris: Klincksieck, 1966).

Vidal– *Les Poésies de Peire Vidal*, ed. J. Anglade (Paris: Champion, 1923).

William IX– *Les Chansons de Guillaume IX*, ed. A. Jeanroy (Paris: Champion, 1913).

Yvain– Chrétien de Troyes, *Yvain*, ed. M. Roques (Paris: Champion, 1960).

Introduction

This book seeks to define the relation between Old French literature and the judicial transformation of the twelfth and thirteenth centuries. That such a relation exists is not, at first, apparent. We are used to a sharp distinction between the language of literature and that of law, associated historically with separate and sometimes conflicting spheres of human endeavor. The former has, since the Renaissance, become increasingly synonymous with a discourse emanating from and belonging to a personalized self: the product variously of inspiration, imagination, genius, desire, neurosis, and dream. The latter has, since the age of Montesquieu and Rousseau, come to represent the collective discourse governing the relations between individuals or between the individual and the state. Where one stands as a vehicle for the expression of the private and particular, the other serves as a mechanism for their regulation.

Such a distinction would have had less meaning for the literary public of the French Middle Ages. From the appearance of the first works in the vernacular until the era of printing, literature was, to a much greater degree than today, a collective phenomenon whose modes of creation and dissemination involved the community as a whole. Works by identifiable writers were rare before the mid-thirteenth century. Even where origin is ascertainable, little is known about specific authors, scribes, and performers—a Turoldus, Chrétien de Troyes, Marie de France, Thomas, or Béroul—much less about their exact role in the genesis of the manuscripts associated with their names. The literary object was considered to be the product not so much of an individual consciousness as of tradition;

it was appreciated less for its uniqueness than for its conformity to similar efforts in accordance with recognized rules of theme and style.[1] The modern poet may consciously seek to undermine the patterns of a received linguistic medium, to "democratize the word" (Hugo), "to wring the neck of eloquence" (Verlaine), "to purify the words of the tribe" (Mallarmé). The medieval poet set a humbler task: to renew the inherited materials—the *topoi*, rhetorical figures, proverbs, or oral formulae—at his disposal. The notions of personal authorship, authenticity, and originality remained essentially foreign to the literary temper of the post-feudal age.

More important, manuscripts produced before the fourteenth century were, almost without exception (bestiaries and lapidaries?), intended for oral presentation.[2] They were designed to be read aloud, recited, or sung. Solitary readers were uncommon until the end of the Middle Ages; and the chief means of literary diffusion, the performance, was, by definition, a public collective affair. The medieval text, like the participatory "happenings" of the present day, functioned as a periodically repeated expression of an assumed rapport between a singer (or reader) and the listeners to whom his song was addressed.[3] As such, it implied a complicit act of self-definition on the part of audience and performer. This is especially true given the economic dependence of poets upon patrons and the homogeneity of at least one segment of the literary public: the seigneurial courts of Normandy, Champagne, Flanders, and the South. For the aristocracy of the feudal era, the "performed" text represented a locus in which shared values were publicly—orally and ritualistically—communicated and affirmed.

The affirmation of shared ideals within the context of public perfor-

---

1. R. Dragonetti, *La Technique poétique des trouvères dans la chanson courtoise* (Bruges: De Temple, 1960), pp. 539ff.; N. Regalado, *Poetic Patterns in Rutebeuf* (New Haven: Yale University Press, 1970), pp. 3–4, 196, 311–312; P. Zumthor, *Essai de Poétique médiévale* (Paris: Seuil, 1972), pp. 44, 117.

2. P. Gallais, "Recherches sur la mentalité des romanciers français du moyen âge," *Cahiers de Civilisation Médiévale* 7 (1964): 479–493; 13 (1970): 333–347; Zumthor, *Essai*, pp. 37, 41, 340.

3. H. Brinkmann, *Zu Wesen und Form mittelalterlicher Dichtung* (Halle: Max Niemeyer, 1928), pp. 18–26; H. Emmel, *Formprobleme des Artusromans und der Graldichtung* (Bern: Francke, 1951), p. 11; R. Hanning, "The Social Significance of Twelfth-Century Chivalric Romance," *Medievalia et Humanistica* 3 (1972): 13; W. Kellermann, *Aufbaustil und Weltbild Chrestiens von Troyes im Percevalroman* (Halle: Max Niemeyer, 1936), pp. 7, 156, 172; Zumthor, *Essai*, pp. 31–32, 37–44, 112.

mance is a fact of great importance for any culture in which tradition is the prime element of law and in which the law is itself transmitted orally. It confers upon the literary object—or event—a legal status otherwise ✓ unattainable. During and long after the experience of European feudalism, traditional usage, as preserved in memory and habit, alone constituted law. Though Latin documents were edited throughout the Dark Age of legal learning, these were divorced from the everyday practices of the feudal court in much the same way that Latin literature was isolated from a vital creative context. Possessed of the letter but not the spirit of the law, the written record was not legally binding; it was, in fact, considered an inferior judicial product subordinate to the living verbal expression of communal legal feeling. The function of the feudal court was essentially commemorative. Its public, oral, and formulaic procedures were designed to recall the practices of the past in order that they might be applied to a situation in the present. They were in no way intended to judge an individual cause according to its particular merit and according to criteria external to the act of judgment itself. In cases of disputed possession or privilege, for example, the court met to determine what rights had historically prevailed. In cases of criminal infraction its members assembled to insure that traditional methods for the determination of guilt—trial by oath, combat, or ordeal—were implemented as they had always been.

Based upon formula, gesture, and ritual, the procedures of the feudal ⌐ court resembled more than superficially the literary performance. Both fulfilled in different ways a common purpose—the affirmation of an acknowledged set of shared beliefs and aspirations through the articulation of a collective history as prerequisite to the constitution of the legal and social community. But with this essential distinction: where the judicial court confirmed its corporate identity through an immediate and physical power exerted upon those it judged, the literary *séance* achieved a similar effect through the mimetic and mediated forms that it engendered. The literary performance stood as a sporting version of trial—a ceremonial demonstration of the principles by which the community defined itself, at once the code and the inventory of its most basic values.

If the feudal court and the literary performance enjoyed a common and inherently legal function, respectively the articulation and the enforcement of a sanctioned code of conduct, our only access to the plethora of possible codes is through the written traces that they have left. On the one hand, a body of poetic texts, manuscripts dating for the most part from the thirteenth and fourteenth centuries, give some indication of the performances of an earlier age. Whether these were originally simple transcriptions of actual performances or consciously created texts intended to serve as the mnemonic tool of oral presentation is a much debated question, whose resolution varies according to genre and carries us beyond the scope of the present discussion. On the other hand, some documentary material—chronicle accounts, charters, records of rights and homage, statutes—survived the long night of legal feudalism. In addition, the *coutumiers* which began to appear in the early 1200s in the regions of Normandy, Brittany, Orléans, Beauvais, and Anjou afford a comprehensive glimpse of the legal practices of the preceding period. The customal represented an attempt to collect and codify prevailing usage by writing it down. Unlike the more theoretical discussions of law by late thirteenth-century jurists such as Beaumanoir, the oldest customary compilations served as a supposedly accurate transcription of that which was assumed to have always been in the hopes that it might continue to be.

While the literary and legal languages of poem and customal seem to be unconnected, they are, in fact, surprisingly similar. Both involved the elevation to written status of a primarily oral linguistic function.[4] Both can be situated within the context of a preexisting Latin tradition. The early French text appeared against the background of a continuous production of Latin works; the secular court functioned alongside and sometimes even along with its ecclesiastical counterpart, possessed of written canonical collections throughout the Middle Ages.

The discourse of the literary text and that of the customal demonstrate a degree of thematic and stylistic commingling that cannot be ignored. There are few sustained narrative works belonging to the twelfth and thirteenth centuries that do not contain a trial. From the *Chanson de Roland* to the epics of the feudal cycle, from the romances of Chrétien and Béroul to the prose continuations of the mid-1200s, from the initial branches of the *Roman de Renart* to the last, the inclusion of at least one scene of judicial combat, oath, or ordeal appears to have been a *sine qua non* of poetic production. Conversely, the customals, manuals of procedure, and court records from the postfeudal era seem to possess an autonomous narrative structure closer to that of the literary text than to

4. See P. Zumthor, *Langue et technique poétiques à l'époque romane* (Paris: Klincksieck, 1963), pp. 31, 68.

[4]

the law books of a succeeding age. The compilations belonging to the thirteenth century do not contain abstract and systematic discussions of legal theory based upon example and precedent. Devoid of an explicit philosophy of law, the early customal is dominated by the relation of particular situations. For instance, the author of the *Grand Coutumier de Normandie*, in delineating the general formula of accusation for murder, adopts specific characters and a semiliterary tone: "Richard accuses Thomas of murdering his father, who was born under God's and the Duke's Peace. . . . Thomas, however, denies this word for word and offers to defend his wagers of battle" (*GC* 167). Saint Louis is unable to explain what constitutes intentional criminal infraction without conferring upon his definition the structure—setting, dramatic progression, and resolution—of a story:

Se aucunes gens avoient empris à aler tuer I home ou une fame, et il fussent pris en la voie, ou de jorz ou de nuiz, et l'en les amenast à la joutise, et la joutise lor demandast que il aloient querant, et il deïssent que il alassent tuer I home ou une fame, et il n'aüssent riens plus meffait, ja, por ce, ne perdroient ne vie, ne manbre.

If any have undertaken to go kill a man or woman, and they be taken en route, day or night, and led to justice, and the judge asks them what they were going to do, and they say they were going to kill a man or woman, and they have not otherwise wronged, they will lose neither life nor member.

(Etablissements 2:55)

The medieval jurist writing in the vernacular often had difficulty presenting a legal point—outlining a formula of accusal or defining the moral element of wrongdoing—without at the same time "telling a story." Thus, in perusing the customal, the reader frequently has the impression of a distinctly literary legal document; and in studying the more conventional poetic forms, he becomes aware of the documentary nature of the literary text.

The present study was originally intended as a reading of medieval French literature in terms of early customary material. There is, to my mind, little doubt that familiarity with specific procedures and situations whose legal ramifications would have been apparent to even the rudest medieval audience is essential to an historically informed appreciation of some of the most important passages in Old French. It was my hope that such a reading would also serve to redirect the recent detour away from history—the tendency on the part of specialists either to be overly formalistic (concerned with literature as a self-referential system) or to minimize the relation between the literary text and its historical context. This trend is, of course, a matter of critical balance and is most apparent in work dealing with the least representational of medieval genres, the courtly novel and lyric. The epic has remained the object of serious historical treatment by modern scholars such as Bezzola, Calin, Adler, Bender, and Matarasso; but the courtly forms, whose origins and social function are perhaps less accessible, have, since Erich Köhler's ground-breaking thesis (1956), received relatively short shrift. The essay which follows is, then, conceived as a reminder of the importance of the historical background of courtliness as against those who would ignore, deny, or simplify it.

Several complications lurk unavoidably in the background of such an endeavor. Medieval studies suffer generally from a lack of information about the composition, diffusion, and uses of literature within a fundamentally oral culture. Documents detailing the everyday interaction of poet and public are relatively rare. Such records as Gui de Ponthieu's chronicle account of the poet Taillefer's role at the Battle of Hastings (*Carmen de Hastingae Proelio*) and the Provençal *vidas* and *razos* of the troubadours (as problematic as they may be) are truly exceptional. In most cases there is little to be learned from documentary sources about the conditions of poetic creation in postfeudal France. We are particularly ill-informed about the historical status, or even the existence as a social phenomenon, of courtly love, since no mention can be found in the historical writings of the twelfth and thirteenth centuries.[5] Most evidence remains internal to the text and must either be gleaned from dedications, prologues, and authorial asides or be deduced from the thematic and structural character of the works themselves. Recent studies of the oral, formulaic discourse of the epic, for example, have permitted much informed conjecture about the origins and mode of composition of the early *chanson de geste*.[6]

Our relative ignorance concerning the social situation of medieval

5. For a particularly incisive discussion of this question see J. Benton, "Clio and Venus: An Historical View of Medieval Love" in *The Meaning of Courtly Love*, ed F. X. Newman (Albany: State University of New York Press, 1968), pp. 19–42.

6. See J. Duggan, *The Song of Roland: Formulaic Style and Poetic Craft* (Berkeley: University of California Press, 1973); A. Lord, *The Singer of Tales* (New York: Atheneum, 1965), pp. 202–207; J. Rychner, *La Chanson de Geste: essai sur l'art épique des jongleurs* (Geneva: Droz: 1955). For a similar treatment of internal evidence of composition within romance see P. Gallais's two part article cited in note 2.

French literature is compounded by a corresponding lack of precise information about the workings of the feudal court. It is a commonplace to point to the paucity of historical documentation during the period under consideration. Not only is feudalism practically synonymous with a general declivity of the written word—a decline in the rate of literacy, literary production, and the administrative uses of writing; but much of the material that does exist comes from the pen of those who had learned to write in monasteries or episcopal schools and who remained in the service of the Church, men, in other words, whose view of the world around them—the perception of what constituted relevant events as well as their interpretation—was informed by ecclesiastical precept.

To the clerical bias implicit in much medieval historiography can be added one further complication: a great deal of that which is known about the society which existed prior to the oldest French texts is itself derived from the more representational literary genres. The epic, in particular, serves, alongside more properly historical material, as a valuable source of information about feudalism. Despite the tendency toward exaggeration which is its hallmark, the Old French *chanson de geste* offers a panoramic view of contemporary institutions: solemn oaths of homage and breaches of troth, enfeoffments and disputed heritages, expiatory pilgrimages and pious donations, crusades and vendettas.[7] Filled with the detailed descriptions of weaponry, fortification, and tactics, accompanied by explanations of the justifications of war and the means to peace, the epic represents a virtual catalogue of medieval military practice. It is, in fact, this appearance as the literary form of social history which has led historians to read epic poetry "as if it were true" and which presents a special dilemma for the literary critic. For any reading of poetic works according to secondary sources—works about feudalism—involves a methodological tautology: an interpretation based upon historical accounts which are themselves based in part upon the original objects of inquiry. This is why I have relied as heavily as possible upon the primary material contained in customary compilations. Even here, however, a certain degree of caution is warranted, since both the literary work and the customal reflect the image of a social reality which had begun to disappear by the time of the earliest poetic text and which was certainly tainted—

7. The actual historical events contained in the epic often hark back to a much earlier period.

mixed with elements of learned tradition—by the time of the earliest *coutumier*.

In recognizing the customal and the early literary work as the written traces of a world in transition, we touch upon their most intimate relation: both were the products of a period of intense social transformation of which they were the reflection and in which they also played a determining role. Each represents a source of information about an historical crisis of which it was itself an integral part.

The century and a half between the reign of Philip the First and that of Saint Louis was an era of crucial importance for the development of the French state, the first in a series of discontinuous stages in France's growth as a nation. This period witnessed a general increase in the population of Western Europe, a demographic shift toward larger rural centers, the rise of towns along with the gradual revival of a money economy, and the steady progress of the French monarchy at the expense of feudal aristrocracy—a trend which by the mid-1200s affected even the most powerful feudatory princes, those who had been kings in their own right. Although many of the gains of royalty were later lost by the sons and grandsons of Louis IX, the time between the First and Fourth Crusades stands as an age of rapid political centralization.

The expansion of the royal domain and power in the twelfth and thirteenth centuries can, in part, be attributed to military conquest. Philippe-Auguste's campaign in Normandy, Louis VIII's incursions into the region of Poitou and Toulouse, Saint Louis's ventures into Brittany and Burgundy were determining factors in the annexation of diverse geographic regions by the Crown. They were not, however, the sole factors. Despite the numerous and important victories of the late Capetians, theirs was a world of mounting crisis at the very center of the military ideal—a world in which, for political and technological reasons, war was becoming increasingly difficult. This crisis, which, as we shall see, is chronicled in the epic, was closely connected to a fundamental shift in judicial institutions.

Though the initial gains of monarchy were the result of conquest, the long-term domination of conquered territories depended more upon effective administration than upon war. In fact, the customals, which—like the Germanic laws of the fifth and sixth centuries—were often compiled in the wake of victory, attest to the flexibility of royal policy concerning annexation. While the king installed his own judicial officers, *prévôts* and *baillis*, in newly acquired lands, he permitted the diverse regions under his control to be governed according to the practices that had traditionally prevailed. Hence the necessity of fixing such practices in writing and hence the heterogeneous nature of French law up until the seventeenth century.

At the same time, the Crown, joined at first by canonical jurists and later by its own secular bureaucratic personnel, attempted a slow, sometimes halting, but startling substitution. While pursuing their own wars both at home and abroad, the kings of France struggled, from the time of Philip the First onward, to suppress legally all but royal or holy wars. In place of the feudal system of private wars of vengeance and nobility's traditional right to bear arms, monarchy sought to substitute a system of national conscription (a goal that was not achieved until the late fourteenth century). More important, the Crown attempted, with varying success, to replace a judicial system whose chief function was the cessation of an armed fight between private parties with a system adequate to the everyday governance of a burgeoning domain. That attempt involved not only the legal suppression of private war, but the replacement of the feudal procedure of trial by combat with the Frankish and canonical procedure of inquest. Monarchy undertook to substitute for the physical violence of an immanent ordeal the mediated verbal violence of disputation; in place of the oral public mechanism of the feudal court, it strove to impose a secretive legal apparatus dependent upon a series of written operations—statutory legislation, letters of request, transcribed testimony, archival documentation, records of previous judgments, and, eventually, the *lettres de justice* that constituted legal currency until the time of the Revolution. In addition, the establishment of a system of appeal with the Parliament of Paris at its center helped to secure for royalty what it might never have obtained by force alone: the absorption of a multiplicity of petty suzerainties by the centralized administrative arm of a strong civil authority. Through a gradual shift in judicial institutions monarchy gained mastery over the language as well as the institutions of law.

The legal revolution of the High Middle Ages, which was also accompanied by the renewed study of Roman law at Europe's nascent universities, might hold less interest for the literary specialist were it not for a contemporaneous revolution in the cultural uses of writing among those most affected by the winds of change. For despite its tremendous wealth and power in an age in which war constituted a major factor of economic and political life, France's military aristocracy had been divorced from an intelligible literary tongue since the end of the Roman Empire.[8] This situation began to shift in the late eleventh century. It was, in fact, at the very moment at which its position of dominance was threatened—by monarchy from above, by a growing bourgeoisie from below—that nobility appropriated to itself a literary language in which to articulate the crisis of its own changing status. This articulation was, of course, by no means uniform, varying according to poet, genre, date and place of origin. Nonetheless, we begin from the premises that all of the major "aristocratic" forms—epic, courtly novel, and lyric—are deeply rooted in the evolving legal ethos of their time and that many of the essential distinctions between them may be interpreted as divergent responses to a common legal crisis. The epic, for instance, reveals a conscious attempt at representation of judicial procedures and the tension between monarchy and aristocracy, as if the text referred to a corresponding set of acknowledged practices and a *de facto* political situation outside of itself. The tendency toward representation of a recognizable social reality is less apparent in romance. Although Béroul, Marie de France, Chrétien de Troyes as well as his continuators do rely upon trials by combat and ordeal for the construction of major dramatic episodes, the inclusion of historically accurate judicial material remains in the background of the fairylike world of courtly narrative.[9] It is even further attenuated in the courtly lyric, which despite the semantic infusion of feudal terminology—terms associated with economic exchange, legal procedure, military service—seems to refuse the recreation of any specific historical context.

All of which changes somewhat our original project of reading the literary work in the light of the customal. For the initial stages of this endeavor were marked by a discovery which prevented any simplistic concept of their affinity and which thus affected my own critical strategy toward the problem of their relation: that is, while the vernacular text appears to integrate within its overall design themes which are historically

8. See E. Auerbach, *Literary Language and its Public in Late Latin Antiquity and in the Middle Ages* (New York: Pantheon, 1965), pp. 269ff.

9. See G. Cohen, "Le Duel judiciaire chez Chrétien de Troyes," *Annales de l'Université de Paris* 8 (1933): 510–527; E. A. Francis, "The Trial in *Lanval*" in *Studies in French Language and Mediaeval Literature Presented to Mildred K. Pope* (Manchester: Manchester University Press, 1939), pp. 115–124; P. Jonin, *Les Personnages féminins dans les romans français de Tristan au XIIᵉ siècle* (Aix-en-Provence: Orphys, 1958), pp. 107–138; J. Rychner, *Le Lai de Lanval* (Geneva: Droz, 1958), p. 78.

[10]

verifiable according to the descriptions found in customary material, the institutions portrayed are shown time and time again to be legally and humanly deficient. From Charlemagne's difficult prosecution of Gane-lon, to Lanval's near conviction on false charges, to Iseult's subversion of the ordeal by oath, to the judicial shenanigans of Isengrin and Renart, and to the tragic legal dilemmas of the feudal epic cycle, the text which seeks to reproduce the practices of the "first feudal age" offers a persistent image of their inadequacy. Conversely, to the extent to which the literary work—and especially the courtly work—seems to resist an explicitly mimetic function, its own formal apparatus tends to resemble the increasingly dominant procedure of inquest. More precisely, both the courtly novel and lyric respond to the dilemmas posed within the epic (and to a certain degree within romance) in much the same way that an inquisitory judicial system responded to the faltering institutions of the late feudal world.

From this perspective, the task ahead is less one of trying to understand the poetic text in terms of its judicial counterpart than one of assessing the parallel evolution of contemporaneous literary and legal forms. Thus, we shall, first of all, explore some of the poignant literary reflections of the legal upheaval which began in France toward the latter half of the eleventh century. Second, we shall trace the shift in judicial procedures from those of the feudal court to those adopted by monarchy as part of a prolonged effort to undermine the sovereignty of aristocracy. Third, we shall follow a corresponding shift in literary forms from epic to courtly genres. While the Old French epic served to define a profound crisis in the institutionalized violence of the feudal era, the solutions which it offers are rarely viable. Courtly literature, on the other hand, crystallizes much that remains implicit in the *chanson de geste* and, as we shall see, points in the direction of an enduring change in the inferred relation between individual, clan, and state. Finally, we shall situate the evolution of poetic theme, structure, and convention within the shifting historical pattern. This last consideration leads, inevitably, to the question of literature and political ideology in the High Middle Ages, which is the subject of our conclusion. Only by addressing this issue is it possible to arrive at a global historical explanation for the sudden appearance of the vernacular literary tongue, as well as for the social function of its dominant distinctive types.

Countless facets of medieval usage, as well as countless literary texts, fall within the purview of a subject whose universality has necessitated a number of crucial choices. I have, for instance, selected the thirteenth-century *Mort Artu*, rather than the more familiar *Chanson de Roland*, *Lanval*, *Roman de Tristan*, or romances of Chrétien de Troyes, for a discussion of the judicial duel and capture in the act. These works have been treated elsewhere, and I have referred the reader to appropriate secondary material where relevant. Moreover, the prose text serves as a more satisfactory introduction to the workings of the feudal trial. Many of the issues raised by the author of *La Mort Artu*—questions of criminal intent, the role of the medieval judge, physical might as opposed to judicial right—emphasize the epistemological weakness of feudal procedure, which is the major topic of the first chapter. I have also concentrated in the second chapter upon four epics of the cycle of the rebellious barons—*Raoul de Cambrai*, *La Chevalerie Ogier*, *Les Quatre Filz Aymon*, and *Girart de Roussillon*—in order to illustrate a more pervasive military and political crisis. Among the lyric poets, I have relied heavily upon the troubadours William IX of Aquitaine, Marcabru, Bernard de Ventadorn, Cercamon, and Peire Vidal, as well as the *trouvères* Conon de Béthune, Le Châtelain de Coucy, Gace Brulé, and Thibaut de Champagne. Andreas Capellanus's *Art of Courtly Love* along with the Provençal *Leys d'Amors* (Laws of Love) are, of course, essential to a treatment of the legal aspects of courtly tradition.

Bearing in mind the obvious difficulties of any attempt to link literary superstructure to social substructure as well as the limitations imposed by the above choices, I am still convinced that a fuller appreciation of the legal context of France's earliest poetic monuments might prove useful to both the historian and the critic. To the former it offers a means of understanding the literary artifact as an organic part, and not just the reflection, of a broad social mutation. To the latter it offers one possibility of getting beyond the dogged question of origins, of identifying the indigenous social roots of artistic production and of determining their relation to poetic form during one of Europe's formative and most intense periods of creative activity.

CHAPTER I

Trial by Combat and Capture: Twilight of the Arthurian Gods[1]

For a novel that begins in earthly splendor and spiritual plenitude *La Mort le roi Artu* ends in a curious spectacle of chaos and decline.[2] The final sequel of the enormous thirteenth-century Lancelot Prose Cycle contains what should have been the golden era of Arthur's court, knighthood having regained the native soil of Camelot after the distant Grail Quest. Instead, it proclaims the twilight of the Arthurian world, the steady disintegration of the courtly and chivalric ideals that are the very stuff of romance. Of the hundred thousand knights who gather for the last battle of Arthur's reign—*la derreniere qui i sera au tens le roi Artu*—only four survive the end of an empire and the end of an age:

Einsi commença la bataille es pleines de Salesbieres dont li roiaumes de Logres fu tornez a destrucion, et ausi furent meint autre, car puis n'i ot autant de preudomes comme il i avoit eü devant; si en remestrent aprés leur mort les terres gastes et essilliees, et soufreteuses de bons seigneurs, car il furent trestout ocis a grant douleur et a grant haschiee.

Thus began the battle on Salisbury Plain through which the realm of Logres was turned to destruction, and so were many others, for after there were not so many valiant men as there had been before; after their death the lands remained waste and devastated, and lacking in good lords, for they were all killed in great pain and in great slaughter.

(La Mort 232)

1. Parts of this chapter appeared under the title "From Grail Quest to Inquest" in *Modern Language Review* 69 (1974): 40–55.

2. I have used the term "novel" instead of "romance" because the universe of *La Mort le roi Artu* is closer to that of the modern novel than to the romances of the twelfth century; that is to say, it is a universe from which the gods have withdrawn and immanence has become problematic; see below pp. 26–46.

The wasting of Logres and the depletion of its ruling class of *preudomes* and *bons seigneurs* is, to a limited extent, attributable to those who least desire it. Lancelot's adultery with the queen, Gawain's madness, Arthur's blindness and weakness, all contribute to the chain of catastrophe that drives the novel toward its apocalyptic finale. And yet none justifies, ultimately, the collapse of a kingdom, its noble families, its ruler, and all that surrounds them. Rooted far deeper than personal foible or folly, the disintegration of Arthur's world reflects a crisis of values and institutions which is traceable to the rapidly evolving history of France in the century and a half preceding the prose novel's composition (ca. 1230). Logres is, politically speaking, a model of the feudal world: a collection of independent states linked by ties of fealty, clannish loyalty to family as part of a vendetta ethic, judicial practices of trial by combat and private war. A system that offers little distinction between private and public domains, Arthurian kingship resembles the feudal monarchies of the late Carolingians and early Captians as seen from the increasingly national perspective of a Philippe-Auguste or Saint Louis. From this point of view, the death of Arthur and the destruction of the Round Table along with its baronage of *bons seigneurs* look like the failure of feudal organization to deal with the problems of a new, more centrally-oriented era.

Accusal

The first real test of the strength of the realm comes about unexpectedly. At dinner one evening Gawain's enemy Arvalan prepares a piece of poisoned fruit which he offers to Guinevere, thinking that she will, in turn, offer it to Gawain. To Arvalan's surprise the queen hands the fatal dessert to a third knight, Gaheris de Karaheu, who dies "as soon as it passes his neck": *et si tost comme il en ot le col passé, il chaï morz erranment voiant la reïne et touz cels qui furent a la table.*[3] Arthur reacts to Gaheris's death with astonishment and sadness but takes no cognizance of the event in terms of criminal action. Arvalan disappears entirely from the tale. The queen, in spite of the fact that many have witnessed her part in the deed, is not indicted; and Gaheris, after an honorable burial, is soon forgotten. Forgotten, that is, by all except his brother Mador de la Porte. Upon arrival in Camelot for the next assembly, Mador stumbles upon the

---

3. And as soon as he had swallowed it, he fell dead immediately within sight of the queen and all those who were at the table (*La Mort* 76).

tombstone attesting both to Gaheris's death and to the guilt that Guinevere, by common consent, is felt to bear.[4] He verifies by hearsay the inscription on the stone and then proceeds to Arthur's court, where, long after the infraction has taken place, he is the first to mention redress in connection with Guinevere's crime. Mador, as the victim's brother, first reminds Arthur of his duty as king and judge:

Roi Artus, se tu es si droituriers come rois doit estre, tien moi a droit en ta cort, en tel maniere que, se nus m'i set que demander, g'en ferai droit a ton plesir, et se ge sai que demander a ame qui i soit, droit m'en face l'en einsi comme la cort esgardera.

King Arthur, if you are as just as a king should be, hold me in the justice of your court, in such a way that, if anyone has reason to accuse me, I will do just as you please, and if I have reason to accuse whomsoever it might be, justice will be granted me as the court will decide.

(La Mort 84)

In the demand for recognition Mador stresses the obligation of the feudal ruler to provide justice at his vassal's request as well as the vassal's obligation to submit to pleas proffered against him. As was customary, the plaintiff renounces fealty to Arthur, pronounces publicly a formal accusation of murder, and tenders the required wager of battle:

Sire, or vos requier ge comme a roi que vos me faciez droit de la reïne qui en traïson a ocis mon frere; et se ele le velt noier et mesconoistre, que ele traïson n'ait fete et desloiauté, je seroie prez del prouver contre le meilleur chevalier que ele i vodra metre.

Sire, I ask that you, as king, grant me justice for the queen, who killed my brother treasonably; and if she wishes to deny and not to recognize that she acted in treason and disloyalty, I shall be ready to prove it against the best knight she would place before me.

(La Mort 85)

The accusation is repeated before the queen, who agrees to judgment according to the custom of the court.[5] Arthur informs his wife that if convicted she will be "in sorry straits"—vos est alee. The court then adjourns for a period of forty days during which time she is free to seek a

---

4. Gaheris's tombstone reads as follows: "ICI GIST GAHERIZ DE KARAHEU, LI FRERES MADOR DE LA PORTE, QUE LA REINE FIST MORIR PAR VENIM." "Here lies Gaheris of Karaheu, the brother of Mador de la Porte, whom the queen killed with poison" (La Mort 84).

5. "Sire, ge vos pri que vos me teingniez a droit selonc l'esgart de vostre cort." "Sire, I pray that you judge me according to the decision of your court" (La Mort 86).

champion: *aucun preudome qui por vos entrast en champ et qui vos deffendist de ce dont vos estes apelee.*[6]

The criminal procedure under which Guinevere is indicted for the murder of Gaheris is not unknown within Western legal tradition. Prevalent in Greece and Rome, it disappeared during the latter days of the Empire and reappeared on the Continent in Germanic feudal custom; portions are preserved in the judicial institutions of England and the United States. According to this and similar "accusatory" methods of prosecution, a criminal action can be initiated only by the victim of an offense or, as under feudal law, the family or liege lord of the offended party. Under an accusatory mode of indictment, everyone is eligible to become the plaintiff in a judicial proceeding; but no action can be undertaken independently of private pleas for recognition. In other words, neither the civil apparatus of the state nor its representative agent, the judge, had the power to proceed against offenders like Guinevere without the formal appeal of a Mador to the justice of Arthur's court.[7]

For the well-armed and well-trained warrior aristocracy of the feudal era, trial automatically implied physical combat. As long as the accused denied the charges against him and the parties involved did not agree to arbitration, almost any accusation punishable by mutilation or death featured the judicial duel as its primary mode of proof.[8] Even in minor actions, where testimony was sometimes permitted, the only means by

6. Any good man who will enter the field and defend you against that of which you are accused (*La Mort* 86).

7. The *Assizes de la Cour des Bourgeois* stipulates that even though the civil authorities may hold a man in prison for a year and a day, someone must step forward with a formal accusation before the court can proceed against the prisoner: "La cour attendoit le clamant quant il voudroit venir poursuivre son clain, et avoit liberté de non venir clamer ce tant come à luy plairet et le visconte ne la court ne le doivent esforcier de venir porsuivre son clain." "The court waited for a plaintiff who wanted to pursue his accusal, and he had the liberty of not stepping forward for as long as it pleased him, and neither the viscount nor the court could force him to pursue his claim" (*Abrégé du livre des Assizes de la Cour des Bourgeois*, ed. A.-A. Beugnot [Paris: Imprimerie Royale, 1841], p. 320); see also Beaumanoir 1: 917: 463; *Etablissements* 2: 386.

8. According to the *Grand Coutumier de Normandie*, cases involving loss of life or injury that could lead to corporal punishment or execution—Pleas of the Sword—automatically led to battle if the plaintiff refused to accept payment for the injury done him (*GC* 166). See also Y. Bongert, *Recherches sur les cours laïques du Xe au XIIIe siècle* (Paris: Picard, 1948), p. 238; A. Canel, "Le Combat judiciaire en Normandie," in *Mémoires de la Société des Antiquitaires de Normandie* 22 (1927): 575; A. Esmein, *Cours élémentaire du droit français* (Paris: Sirey, 1930), pp. 253, 415; A. Esmein, *A History of Continental Criminal Procedure* (Boston: Little Brown, 1913), p. 59.

[16]

which testimonial evidence might be contested was by challenging the witness to battle. In both cases the burden of proof rested upon the shoulders of the defendant, who was forced either to accept the challenge or stand guilty as accused. Arthur explains the situation to Mador and the queen:

> Mador, la querele la reïne doit estre menee a fin par tel maniere que, s'ele en ce jor d'ui ne trueve qui la vueille deffendre, l'en fera de son cors ce que la cort esgardera. Or remanez ceanz jusques a eure de vespres; et se dedenz celui terme ne vient avant qui por lui empraigne ceste bataille, vos est quites de l'apel et ele est encolpee.

> Mador, the dispute with the queen must be brought to an end in such a way that, if today she finds no one who will defend her, she will be dealt with as the court shall decide. Remain here until the hour of Vespers; and if in that time no one comes forth who will undertake this battle for her, your accusation is upheld and she is found guilty.

> *(La Mort* 103)

As far as Guinevere is concerned, the absence of a champion is tantamount to conviction.

Mador's charge, which works by definition against the accused, conforms historically to the procedure of indictment in use well after the novel's composition.[9] Beaumanoir outlines in the *Coutumes de Beauvaisis*, a manual of judicial practice compiled in the late 1200s, the correct method of accusal:

> De tous cas de crime l'en puet apeler ou venir a gages se l'acuseres en veut fere droite acusacion selonc ce qu'apeaus se doit fere, car il convient que cil qui est apelés s'en defende ou qu'il demeurt atains du fet du quel il est apelés.

> In all cases of crime one can accuse or come to wagers if the accuser wishes to make just accusation as charges should be made, for it is fitting that he who is accused defend himself or stand guilty of that of which he is accused.

> (Beaumanoir 2: 1710: 375)

For Beaumanoir, as for Arthur, accusation—*apeler*—is equivalent to a wager of battle—*gages*—as long as the proper judicial formula—*droite acusacion*—has been observed. Failure to defend oneself or to provide for representation carries the force of confession.[10]

Despite the obvious seriousness of arriving for trial without a defender,

---

9. This is generally more true of criminal than of civil proceedings.
10. Bongert, *Recherches*, p. 45; L. Halphen, "Les Institutions judiciaires en France au XIe siècle: région angevine," *Revue Historique* 77 (1901): 290.

Guinevere experiences a great deal of difficulty in locating a champion. Because of the clear and evident nature of her offense—*il chai morz erranment voiant la reïne et touz cels qui furent a la table*—none of the knights who would have undertaken her cause ordinarily will do so against Mador. Lancelot's clan is absent from court. Arthur is prohibited by his role as judge from openly advocating her defense, though he does later seek a supporter on her behalf. Both Arthur and Guinevere have lost all hope of finding an advocate by trial time, when Lancelot, having heard meantime of the queen's predicament, arrives at court, defeats Mador and simultaneously redeems the defendant's honor and regains her favor. Lancelot's victory and vindication of his mistress correspond generally to our own ideas of justice. The passage from false accusation to acquittal serves to reaffirm the efficacy of a judicial system in which the innocent are cleared in the end, despite intervening moments of hesitation or doubt. Yet the seemingly just correlation of innocence and acquittal obscures a number of logical dilemmas concerning Arthur's support of the queen, Lancelot's espousal of her cause, and the impunity with which the true culprit escapes. Instead of assuring the integrity of the feudal mode of justice, Guinevere's exculpation calls into question the philosophic and pragmatic bases of trial by battle.

The Judgment of God

The judicial duel belongs to the series of ordeals common to any primitive sense of justice in which legal process remains indistinguishable from divine process, human will from godly will, positive law from divine law. Historically, it came to France from the Germanic tribes mentioned by Tacitus and Caesar, although there is some evidence of its practice by the Gauls before the northern invasions.[11] Opposed at times by the Church, the ordeal of battle was eventually Christianized by its opponents; it was prohibited periodically by the civil authorities, the larger feudal territories, northern municipalities, and royalty, but survived the efforts of Carolingian, late Capetian, and Angevine rulers to control its use. In fact, the principle of the duel as a private means of resolving personal disputes, *affaires d'honneur*, has persisted in England and France well into the twentieth century.

11. R. Ruggieri, *Il Processo de Gano nella "Chanson de Roland"* (Florence: Sasoni, 1936), p. 25.

The efficacy of the *judicium Dei* rests upon a belief in the immanence of supernatural powers within the natural sphere. As in the *Chanson de Roland*, where the battles between Charlemagne and Baligant, Thierry and Pinabel, are clearly linked to a transcendent contest between good and evil, all physical combats between mortal opponents reflect a super-human struggle. For Homer, the immanence of justice was often the result of capricious disputes between semihuman divinities; medieval man was much more likely to picture the judicial duel in terms of a conflict between the forces of Satan and those of a Christian God. Underlying both views is the assumption that the natural universe remains incapable of indifference to the outcome of earthly events and that the judicial process represents but one expression of a constant dialogue between nature and man.

Within an immanent universe the world accessible to the senses is, as Marc Bloch observed, a "mask behind which the truly important events take place."[12] Visible objects are mere reflections of a presence exterior to themselves, degraded images of the godhead who alone endows them with meaning. They exist only in so far as they partake of his existence. Every event represents an expression of the divine will in which provi-dence, justice, and history are combined. Chance has no place in such a world, for it is assumed that God remains essentially watchful of men's actions and that everything that occurs within the human sphere has the status of godly intention. As in the Old Testament, what appear to be the quirks of history or the accidents of fortune are ultimately manifestations of divine favor or retribution. Justice is always temporal. Punishment for transgression takes place immediately and automatically in the here and now; reward for virtue works in similar fashion. Both are determined by the inner moral states of those involved, states not always evident to the mortal eye, yet nonetheless subject to the omniscient eye of God. In a universe which places little value upon individuality or interiority, the assumed targets of divine judgment—inherent innocence or guilt—can never be known directly. They become apparent only through the sec-ondary effects, recompense or penalty, which they engender.

Paul Rousset has amply documented, in a long article on immanent justice during the feudal era, the direct relationship between a wide range of natural phenomena and the intrinsic moral condition of those affected

12. M. Bloch, *Feudal Society* (Chicago: University of Chicago Press, 1966), 1: 83.

by them.[13] Catastrophes—sickness, death, imprisonment, defeat in battle —offer certain proof of inner vice. Collective ills such as plague, flood, and famine are the result of guilt shared by the community as a whole. For instance, Saint Bernard blamed the unsuccessful military ventures of the Second Crusade upon the prideful actions of the crusaders, who were punished by defeat. Chroniclers do not hesitate to attribute inexplicable disasters to the sinful conduct of the victims. Raoul Glaber considered the famine of 1033 to be an act of divine retribution: *peccatis hominum exigentibus.*[14] Foucher de Chartres traced the massacre of crusaders in Hungary to the numerous personal faults of the men involved: *sed quia peccaverunt, fere perierunt.*[15] Even the defeat of Pope Leon's troops by the Normans in 1054 served, for Hermann de Reichenau, as an unmistakable indictment of the misdirected religious leader who declared war upon his fellow Christian: *Normani Dei judicio extitere victores.*[16] In a letter dated March 17, 1151, addressed to the Archbishops of Cologne and Treve, Eugene III blamed a recent fire at the monastery of Remiremont upon the relaxed morals of its inhabitants.[17] Joinville attributed the death of six knights to their impious behavior in church the preceding day: *Et Diex en fist tel vengeance que l'endemain fu la grans bataille dou quaresme-prenant, dont il furent mort.*[18] Benevolent events—recovery from sickness, victory in battle, escape from captivity—were, on the other hand, indications of inner moral strength justly rewarded by divine approval. Everything that happens within an immanent system of belief becomes intelligible in the light of an absolute but invisible rapport between the signs of nature and man, who is the interpreter of signs according to their predetermined metaphysical, moral, or historical significance. History, from the early medieval perspective, is infinitely recuperable in terms of God's providence, which alone knows the "hows" and "whys" of everyday events.

13. P. Rousset, "La Croyance en la justice immanente à l'époque féodale," *Le Moyen Age* 54 (1948): 225; see also G. Duby, *Le Dimanche de Bouvines* (Paris: Gallimard, 1973), p. 146.

14. An expulsion of the sins of men (Rousset, "Justice immanente," p. 241).

15. But those who sinned perished altogether (*Ibid.*, p. 227).

16. By God's judgment the Normans were victorious (*Ibid.*, p. 229).

17. C. Oulmont, *Les Débats du clerc et du chevalier dans la littérature poétique du moyen âge* (Paris: Champion, 1911), p. 57.

18. Joinville, *Histoire de Saint Louis*, ed. N. de Wailly (Paris: Firmin Didot, 1874), p. 164.

Under an immanent legal mode, the role of human judgment in criminal actions is reduced to a bare minimum; the assumption being that God alone judges and that men, having acted in either innocence or guilt, then become the passive objects of divine scrutiny.[19] The cognitive decisions that we associate with the active binding authority of the Roman *praetor* or the modern magistrate had little meaning for the feudal judge. Prohibited by the threat of open reprisal from denying justice, he enjoyed none of the autonomy of later monarchs to accept or to refuse at will pleas like that of Mador: *Et li rois, qui trop est dolenz de cest apel, a ce qu'il ne puet noier qu'il ne face droit au chevalier. . . .*[20] Unable to disregard the law and unable to indict of his own accord, the feudal judge presided only to pronounce sentence and to insure the fairness of the proceedings. Much like the referee in a sporting event, he possessed sufficient discretionary power to apply the rules that had applied in the past but had no authority to change them through the precedent of his decisions.

Free to fix the fine details of Guinevere's trial, the forty day adjournment, Arthur is obliged to establish the conditions under which a direct encounter between plaintiff and defendant can take place.[21] That encounter, the judicial ordeal, represents an attempt to elicit supernatural intervention in human affairs. The unilateral ordeals of trial by fire, water, burning oil, coal, or iron and also the bilateral ordeals of the cross and combat seek to force God to show his hand in cases where the righteousness or culpability of the parties is not apparent. In the phrase of a Carolingian capitulary, "Let doubtful cases be determined by the judg-

19. The *Burgundian Code* contains the following passage: "If the party to whom oath has been offered does not wish to receive the oath, but shall say that the truthfulness of his adversary can be demonstrated only by resort to arms, and the second party (the one accused) shall not yield (the case charged), let the right of combat not be refused; with the further provision that one of the same witnesses who came to give oath shall fight, God being the judge" (*Burgundian Code*, ed. and trans. K. F. Drew [Philadelphia: University of Pennsylvania Press, 1972], p. 52).

20. And the king, who is very sad at this accusation, in that he cannot refuse to give justice to the knight. . . . (*La Mort* 85).

21. "On peut expliquer ainsi la position du juge: d'une part le duel était incontestablement pour lui la solution la plus facile et la plus avantageuse, lui évitant tout travail et lui permettant de garder une prudente neutralité entre les plaideurs; d'autre part la conciliation était préférable, quoique moins avantageuse du point de vue pécuniaire, car elle le mettait à l'abri de toute contestation et plus particulièrement de l'appel de faux jugement qui se réglait aussi par le duel" (Bongert, *Recherches*, p. 234). Forty days was the standard period (*essoine*) between accusation and judgment under Frankish law (F. L. Ganshof, *La Preuve dans le droit franc* [Brussels: Société Jean Bodin, 1965], p. 75).

ment of God."[22] Justice becomes manifest through the burns that either heal or fester, the accused who floats or sinks, the bearers of the cross who endure or falter, the combatants who kill or are killed—the entire process dependent upon the theoretical premise that the Lord does not abandon the just man and that he punishes those who have failed him. According to the Charlemagne of *Huon de Bordeaux*, the judicial duel constitutes a "miracle made visible."[23] Similarly, the heroine of *Guillaume de Dole* prays for an "open miracle" in the Senechal's trial: *Qu'il i face miracle aperte.*[24] In *Roland* the emperor's struggle against Baligant provokes a divine intrusion (v. 3608). Later, the formal judicial encounter between Thierry and Pinabel will be decided by another manifestation of God's abiding presence in the affairs of men. Pinabel deals his rival what would have been the death blow if the designation of guilt under the *judicium Dei* were any less than a matter for divine concern:

> L'osberc desclot josque par sum le ventre,
> Deus le gaurit, que mort ne l'acraventet.

> * * * * *

> Escrient Franc: "Deus i ad fait vertut!
> Asez est dreis que Guenes seit pendut."

> The hauberk split open to the top of the belly
> God protected him from being struck dead.

> * * * * *

> The Franks cried: "God has manifested his power!
> It is just that Ganelon be hanged."
>
> (*Roland* v. 3922)

Although Pinabel and Charles both are physically weaker than their opponents, they win because of the essential righteousness of their cause and because justice—*dreis*—within an immanent universe is more closely linked to the idea of God's power—*Deus i ad fait vertut*—than to the idea of physical might. For Chrétien de Troyes, God and right are one and the same: *Et Dex et droiz a un s'an tienent.*[25] On two occasions in *La Mort Artu*

---

22. Cited H. C. Lea, *The Ordeal* (Philadelphia: University of Pennsylvania Press, 1973), p. 4; see also J. Gaudemet, *Les Ordalies au moyen âge: doctrine, législation et pratique canoniques* (Brussels: Société Jean Bodin, 1965), pp. 103–105.

23. *Huon de Bordeaux*, ed. P. Ruelle (Brussels: Presses Universitaires de Belgique, 1960), v. 1959.

24. Let him work an open miracle (J. Renart, *Guillaume de Dole*, ed. G. Servois [Paris: Firmin Didot, 1893], v. 4974).

25. God and right are one (*Yvain* v. 4439); see also *Quatre Filz* v. 8839; *Girart* v. 4227; *Raoul* v. 4964.

Gawain expresses his faith in the unerring justness of trial by battle. First to the messenger who carries his challenge to Lancelot: *Mes ce sevent bien tuit que torz et desloiautez feroit del meillor chevalier del monde mauvés, et droiz et loiautez feroit del plus mauvés et seür et preu.*[26] And then to Yvain just prior to combat:

Or ne vos esmaiez, messire Yvain, fet missire Gauvains, que ge sei veraiement que li droiz est miens et li torz siens; por ce si me combatrai plus asseür encontre lui, s'il estoit mieudres chevaliers a doubles qu'il n'est.

Now don't be alarmed, Sir Yvain, said Sir Gawain, for I know truly that right is mine and wrong is his; for this reason I would fight him more assuredly than if he were twice as good a knight as he is.

(*La Mort* 193)

Whether or not Gawain's cause is, in fact, just, he believes that right and force are sufficiently allied to insure judicial fairness.

The strictness of the rules governing combat and the obligation on the judge's part to apply them are meant to facilitate God's work in making his judgement evident. The accusation and denial, acceptance of the wagers of battle, and swearing of oaths that accompany the physical match are conducted according to precise formulas whose slightest infraction can invalidate the entire proceeding.[27] By the twelfth century the ritual of judgment had been Christianized to such an extent that trial had the appearance of a sacrament.[28] At the end of *Roland* Thierry and Pinabel visit church, hear mass, go to confession, and offer pious gifts before battle (v. 3858). Huon de Bordeaux recounts the entire passion story, finally begging God for victory, prior to his encounter against Amauri.[29] Chrétien's Lancelot submits to a three day fast before meeting Méléagant (*Lancelot* v. 3524). The Lancelot of *La Mort* confesses his sins

26. But all know well that wrong and disloyalty will make the best knight in the world bad, and right and loyalty will make the worst sure and valiant (*La Mort* 183).

27. Yvonne Bongert expresses a certain amount of scepticism with regard to the formalism of feudal procedure; she is, however, an exception (*Recherches*, p. 183).

28. Gaudemet, *Les Ordalies*, p. 114; Lea, *The Ordeal*, p. 30; The *Grand Coutumier* requires combatants to testify to their belief in God before entering battle: "Post hec autem pugiles ad campum evocentur, et jurent per verba de duello recitata, flexis ambobus genibus, et tenebunt se per manus, appellator a dextris et defensor a sinistris. Interragato ab utroque nomine quo denominatur in baptismo, et utrum credat in Patrem et Filium et Spiritum Sanctum, et utrum teneat fidem quam sancta conservat Ecclesia." "Afterwards, the champions are called to the field, and they swear the words of battle; and they kneel holding each other by the hand, the accuser on the right and the defendant on the left. Each is asked his baptismal name and if he believes in the Father and Son and Holy Spirit, and if he keeps the faith of the Church" (*GC* 170).

29. *Huon de Bordeaux*, v. 1558.

in an all night vigil preceding the contest against Gawain (194). The assumption that God judges according to the comparative moral status of the two contestants makes it a matter of utmost importance to enter combat as free as possible from any trace of lingering sin. The judicial combatant was no different, in this respect, from the crusader who practiced similar purification rituals—pious processions, prayers, fasting and *aumônes*—both prior to and at decisive moments of the fray.

During the Frankish period knights about to face each other in battle were made to swear purgatory oaths upon their weapons. By the feudal era religious relics had replaced the sacramental arms that gave the ordeal its authenticity. For Iseult's trial at the Gué Aventuros Marc assembles the most precious relics of the land (Béroul v. 4129). The author(s) of *Le Roman de Renart*, which is filled with the satire of feudal judicial procedure, do not spare the ritual relics from barbed attack.[30] Belin, the lamb-chaplain of King Noble's court, supervises the swearing of oaths before Renart meets Isengrin (vv. 8334, 8359). Beaumanoir specifies almost a century later that participants in judicial encounters are obliged to swear upon the Bible and the saints as to the righteousness of their cause; vestiges of the sacramental oath—*Se Dieus m'aït*—and the courtroom Bible still constitute a part of our own legal procedure:

> Cil qui apele doit jurer premierement seur saintes evangiles et dire: *Se Dieus m'aït et tuit li saint et les saintes et les saintes paroles qui ci sont,*—et doit tenir la main seur le livre.

> He who accuses must first swear on the Holy Bible and say: *So help me God and all the saints and the sacred words which are here*—and must keep his hand on the book. (Editor's italics)

> (Beaumanoir 2: 1839: 431)

Ritualization—blessing of relics and arms, swearing of oaths, hearing of mass, confession, donation, and prayer during combat—is aimed, ultimately, at establishing a direct rapport between the divine judge and the human instruments of his judgment. As the author of *Huon de Bordeaux* notes, they inextricably bind the perjurer to his fate: *Les sains fist on aporter et venir / Que li parjures ne puist del jor issir.*[31] Cases are submitted to God for his decision, *per duelli probationem*; the ceremonial

---

30. For a discussion of judicial procedure in the *Roman de Renart* see J. Graven, *Le Procès criminel du Roman de Renart: étude du droit féodal au XIIe siècle* (Geneva: Georg, 1950).

31. The saints were made to be brought forward/That the forsworn might not outlive the day (*Huon de Bordeaux* v. 1606).

trappings insure his participation. Thierry declares to Pinabel, *Deus facet hoi entre nus dous le dreit!*[32] Harold is said to have decreed before the Battle of Hastings, *Dominus inter me et Willelmum hodie quod justum est decernat.*[33] Henry I, prior to meeting Robert Curthose at Tinchebray in 1106, is purported to have asked God "to grant victory to whomever he elects to procure peace and to protect his people." And according to the chronicler Guillaume le Maréchal, Philippe-Auguste at Bouvines reminded God that he had protected his Church in the past and therefore deserved to emerge victorious from the encounter.[34] Both literary character and historical figure are aware that God alone judges the petty quarrels of men and that his judgment often surpasses their understanding.

Champions

Representation in battle by a champion was an ancient Germanic prerogative—*sunnis* or *avoué*—by which direct participation of the parties involved in litigation could, under certain circumstances, be waived. Provisions for substitution in the judicial duel were a constant feature of medieval procedure and were mentioned in the Frankish capitularies as well as in the sixth-century *Lex Burgundionum*. In *Roland* representation is automatic: the outcome of Ganelon's trial hinges upon the appearance of Thierry to substantiate Charlemagne's accusation. According to Beaumanoir, if a defendant is missing a limb, is over sixty years of age, has a sickness that prevents excitement or a chronic illness (*quartaine* or *tierçaine*), he has the right to find a champion to fight in his place. The *Coutumes de Beauvaisis* also contains a specific proviso for women: *li quins essoines, si est se fame apele ou est apelee, car fame ne se combat pas.*[35] Hence, Arthur, as judge, is perfectly warranted in permitting Guinevere a stand-in for the actual trial by battle. His position becomes considerably less tenable, however, through his active solicitation of support. Where the queen acquiesces to the lack of a champion, Arthur first turns to the knights of the Round Table who balk at the idea of defending a cause in

---

32. May God do justice between us today! (*Roland* v. 3898).

33. Today God will decide what is just between William and myself (Rousset, "Justice immanente," p. 234).

34. Duby, *Bouvines*, pp. 54, 150.

35. The fifth exception is if a woman accuses or is accused, for women do not fight (Beaumanoir 2: 1713: 377).

which defeat is a foregone conclusion: *car il sevent bien que la reïne a tort et Mador a droit.*[36] He next approaches Gawain, who refuses on the grounds that no loyal knight would enter combat with the knowledge of his party's fault, "not even if the party were his own mother": *car nos savons bien que la reïne ocist le chevalier dont ele est apelee.*[37] With Gawain's refusal, Arthur urges the queen, on the eve of trial, to solicit help from Boort and Hestor: *Toutevoies vos lo ge, fet li rois, que vos en requerez l'un et l'autre.*[38]

What stands out most clearly in Arthur's attempt to find a champion for Guinevere is his hesitancy to let the process of divine justice run its natural course. The king is not content to trust the matter of God's judgment to the invisible mechanism of infallible providence but feels compelled to hasten the progress of providence with his own interventions. Nor is he secretive about his reasons for wanting to protect the queen:

Certes, dame, ge ne sei que dire de vos; tuit li bon chevalier de ma cort me sont failli; por quoi vos poez dire que au jor de demain recevroiz mort honteuse et vileinne. Si volsisse mieuz avoir perdu toute ma terre que ce fust avenu a mon vivant; car ge n'amai onques riens el siecle autant com ge vos ai amee et aing encore.

Surely, Lady, I know not what to say of you; all the good knights of my court have failed me; for which reason you may say that tomorrow morning you will receive shameful and villainous death. I would rather have lost all my lands than that this should occur in my lifetime; for in my time I have never loved anything as much as I have loved you, and love you still.

(*La Mort* 101)

Arthur's personal commitment to the woman he loves leads him to disregard her evident guilt. And whereas the judge within an immanent accusatory system should remain neutral once he has established a direct confrontation between parties, Arthur confuses his public role as justiciar with his private role as husband. Mador accuses him after the trial of having manipulated the proceedings: *Sire, vos m'avez deceü qui encontre moi avez mis monseigneur Lancelot.*[39]

In the long run, the efficacy of the judicial duel depends upon the faith

36. For they knew well that the queen was wrong and Mador was right (*La Mort* 100).
37. For we know well that the queen killed the knight, for which she is accused (*La Mort* 100).
38. Anyway, I advise you, said the king, to ask them both (*La Mort* 101).
39. Sire, you have deceived me in placing Sir Lancelot against me (*La Mort* 106).

of those who participate in it, a faith that God's will eventually protects the innocent and punishes those who perjure themselves in his presence. The fear of perjury in the name of a bad cause explains Gawain's and the other knights' reluctance to respond to Arthur's call for help. Lancelot, however, reacts differently to the news of the queen's dilemma. Fully aware of her guilt, he nonetheless consents to champion what is commonly acknowledged to be a faulty cause:

Certes, fet Lancelos, s'ele me devoit haïr a touz jorz et en tel maniere que ge ne trouvasse jamés pes a li, si ne voudroie ge pas qu'ele fust deshonoree a mon vivant; car c'est la dame del monde qui plus m'a fet d'enneur puis que ge portai armes; si me metrai en aventure por li deffendre, non mie si hardiement come j'ai fet en autre bataille, car ge sei bein veraiement, a ce que g'en ai oï dire, que li torz en sera miens et li droiz Mador.

Certainly, said Lancelot, even if she should hate me always in such a manner that I should never find peace with her, I would not want her to be dishonored in my lifetime; for in all the world she is the woman who has done me the most honor since I have carried arms; I will risk myself to defend her, though not so hardily as I would do in another battle, for I know quite truly, from what I have heard of it, that the wrong will be mine and the right Mador's.

(*La Mort* 97)

Lancelot's acceptance has been attributed to shock and momentary weakness.[40] Yet his decision seems more a conscious act than a transitory slip. He states explicitly that he will defend the queen not because he believes in her essential righteousness, but because of her past reputation. In reflecting upon his choice Lancelot accepts the prospect of entering battle "half-heartedly" due to the certainty of her guilt: *car ge sei bien veraiement. . . . que li torz en sera miens et li droiz Mador*. And in so doing, the greatest knight of Logres shows himself clearly willing to undertake what amounts to an adequate, but not wholly valid, judicial cause.

Lancelot's readiness to perjure himself and thus to compromise with the *sine qua non* of feudal justice, a belief in the omnipotence of the divine judge, has far-reaching implications. For Lancelot the absolute certainty of God's vengeance no longer poses a serious threat. His attitude is much closer to an Aristotelian vision of a universe created by God, but existing apart from his continual presence, than to an immanent universe in which the divine being penetrates every object and event. Alfred Adler has

40. J. Frappier, *Etude sur "La Mort le roi Artu"* (Geneva: Droz, 1961), p. 340.

argued convincingly that *La Mort Artu* contains multiple levels of moral value and that disparate levels of meaning seem to exist side by side.[41] What Adler refers to as the "incongruity between legal and poetic justice" suggests a vision in which the positive values of moral stature, physical prowess, and friendship occur within the degraded context of adultery, hatred, and pride. In this light, Lancelot's espousal of a sufficient judicial cause, instead of the right one, points to a crisis of belief that runs deeper than the manipulation of justice by Arthur or the difficulty experienced by an innocent woman in finding a defender; it is more subversive, even, than the escape of the true offender. Lancelot's action implies a world in which human and divine wills function independently of each other, a world from which the gods have withdrawn, leaving humans responsible for the consequences of their deeds. When Arthur later blames Lancelot, and not "God's justice," for the death of his nephews and the downfall of his kingdom—*Ceste perte ne m'est pas avenue par la justise Damledieu, mes par l'orgueill Lancelot*—he has assimilated, both literally and figuratively, the meaning of Lancelot's gesture.[42] The loss of valuable members of the king's entourage does diminish the strength of the realm. Duplicity with regard to the *judicium Dei*—acceptance of relative innocence and adequate cause—undermines the only judicial procedure at Arthur's disposal and hence his entire political base. Ironically, what Arthur unknowingly seeks, in soliciting support for his wife, is the subversion of the chief judicial institution of the Arthurian-feudal court.

Criminal Intent

Further doubt concerning the efficacy of the immanent legal mode emanates from the trial itself. According to the *judicium Dei*, every effort is made not only to force the parties into a situation of direct confrontation, but to establish a clear-cut contradiction between their respective allegations, the assumption being that one of the two will be guilty of perjury.[43] Accusations are therefore pronounced orally, public-

41. A. Adler, "Problems of Aesthetic versus Historical Criticism in *La Mort le roi Artu*," *PMLA* 68 (1953): 930.

42. This loss has not come to me through the justice of the Lord God, but by the pride of Lancelot (*La Mort* 133).

43. The Charlemagne of *Huon de Bordeaux* is aware of the necessity of perjury before God as an essential part of the judicial duel: "Et Dix de glore en doinst le droit veïr, / Que li parjures soit hui cest jor honnis." "And let glorious God make right known, / So that the perjurer will today be shamed" (v. 1597).

ly, and according to set formula. Beaumanoir outlines the prescribed pattern for an accusal of murder:

Qui droitement veut apeler, il doit dire ainsi, se c'est pour murtre: *Sire, je di seur tel*—et le doit nommer—*qu'il, mauvesement et en traïson m'a murtri tele personne* —et doit nommer le mort—*qui mes parens estoit, et par son tret et par son fet et par son pourchas.*

He who wishes to accuse justly, must speak thus, if it concerns murder: *Sire, I say of so-and-so*—and should name him—*that he evilly and in treason killed such a person*—and should name the deceased—*who was my relative, by his instigation and his deed and by his effort.* (Italics his)

(Beaumanoir 2: 1711: 376)

Denial also takes place according to fixed formula requiring first a counter-accusal of perjury—*Et quant il a ce dit, cil qui est apelés doit dire: "Je vous en lieve comme parjure"*—and then a verbatim refutation of the charges.[44] The *Grand Coutumier de Normandie* (ca. 1260) provides for a direct contradiction between plaintiff and defendant, beginning with public accusation—:

Sequela autem de multro facienda est in hac forma: *Ricardus queritur de Thoma, qui patrem suum nequiter in pace Dei et ducis multrivit, quod paratus est probare et facere ei recognoscere una hora diei*

—followed by denial and wagers of battle: *Thomas autem hoc negat verbo ad verbum, et offret vadium suum ad defendendum.*[45]

At Guinevere's trial Mador repeats the allegation originally pronounced upon arrival in Camelot. Lancelot refutes it word for word:

Sire chevaliers, ge sui prez de prouver qu'ele desloiaument et en traïson a ocis mon frere.—Et ge sui prez, fet Lancelos, del deffendre qu'ele n'i pensa onques desloiauté ne traïson.

Sir knight, I am ready to prove that she killed my brother disloyally and in treason.—And I am ready, said Lancelot, to defend that she never intended disloyalty or treason.

(*La Mort* 104)

Although Mador's assertion conforms almost to the letter to the formula of accusation outlined by Beaumanoir, and Lancelot's denial fulfills the

44. And when he has said this, the accused should say, "I challenge you as forsworn" (Beaumanoir 2: 1839: 432).

45. An accusal of murder takes the following form: "Richard accuses Thomas of murdering his father, who was born under God's and the duke's peace, and he is prepared to prove and make him recognize it at an agreed upon time. . . . Thomas, however, denies this word for word and offers to defend his wagers (of battle)" (*GC* 167).

required contradiction, both carry us a long way from Gaheris's death and the common knowledge of the queen's part in it. Mador maintains that Guinevere not only killed his brother, but that she did so knowingly and treacherously: *desloiaument et en traïson a ocis mon frere*. The formulary accusation opens the delicate question of intention behind wrongdoing and the adequacy of the judicial duel to determine criminal intent.

In fact, the accused at no point denies having handed the fatal piece of fruit to Gaheris, despite her disavowal of any knowledge of the poison. At the time of the victim's death she professes the innocence of her intentions (77). Upon indictment, she questions Mador's use of the word *traïson—Conment, fet ele, dites vos donc que ge vostre frere ocis en traïson et a mon escient?*[46] And before the duel begins, the queen reasserts the purity of her intent: *Sire, fet ele, Dex en soit au droit si veraiement comme ge n'i pensai desloiauté ne traïson.*[47] In spite of his initial concern about the motive surrounding Guinevere's act, Arthur seems singularly indifferent to the notion of intention. Having called the queen to account for the poison and heard her denial—*se ge cuidasse que li fruiz fust desloiaus, je ne li eüsse donné por demi le monde*—he quickly excludes any possible distinction between unconscious and purposeful misdeed:[48]

Dame, fet li rois, comment que vos li donnissiez, l'ouvraigne en est mauvese et vileinne, et ge ai moult grant doutance que vos n'en soiez plus corrouciee que vos ne cuidez.

---

46. What, she said, are you saying then that I killed your brother treacherously and wittingly? (*La Mort* 85).

47. Sire, she said, God be with the just, for truly I never thought disloyalty or treason (*La Mort* 105).

48. If I had believed the fruit to be poisoned, I would not have given it to him for half the world (*La Mort* 77). The king's inattentiveness to motive is especially apparent when contrasted with Malory's *Morte Arthur*. In the fifteenth-century version Arthur's awareness of the distinction between his role as judge coupled with his conviction of the defendant's innocence leads to a troubling dilemma: " 'Fayre lordys,' seyde kynge Arthure, 'me repentith of thys trouble, but the case ys so I may nat have ado in thys mater, for I muste be a ryghtfull juge. And that repentith me that I may nat do batayle for my wyff, for, as I deme, they dede com never by her. And therfor I suppose she shall nat be all distayned, but that somme good knyght shall put hys body in jouperté for my quene rather than she sholde be brente in a wronge quarell.' " The question of intention is raised by Mador himself. The court remains divided, however, some believing the queen to be guilty and others looking beyond the deed itself to secondary causes: " 'And therfor I beseche you that ye be nat displeased, for there ys none of all thes four-and-twenty knyghtes that were bodyn to thys dyner but all they have grete suspeccion unto the quene. What sey ye all,' seyde sir Madore. Than they answerde by and by and seyde they coude nat excuse the quene for why she made the dyner, and others hit muste com by her other by her servauntis" (*The Works of Sir Thomas Malory*, ed. E. Vinaver [London: Oxford University Press, 1959], p. 748).

Lady, said the king, however you may have given it to him, the deed is evil and villainous, and I fear greatly that you will be more afflicted by it than you believe.

(*La Mort* 77)

Arthur says nothing when Mador first accuses the defendant of willful murder, nor when she questions her accuser's use of legal terminology. He remains silent at the time of the acceptance of the wagers of battle along with the repetition of the original charge. It is not until the final accusation has been pronounced and the combatants have left for the battlefield that the error becomes apparent; by that time it is too late. Gawain points out to Arthur, as an afterthought, the weakness of the plaintiff's allegation:

> Or creroie ge bien que Mador fust en mauvese querele; car comment que ses freres moreust, je jurroie seur seinz au mien escient qu'onques la reïne n'i pensa desloiauté ne traïson; si l'en porroit tost max avenir, se li chevaliers avoit en lui point de proesce.

> Now I would well believe that Mador is wrong in this dispute; for however his brother may have died, I would swear on saints that to my knowledge the queen never thought disloyalty or treason; the worst may come to him if this knight has in him any prowess.

(*La Mort* 104)

With Gawain's sudden awareness of the inaccuracy of Mador's charge, the queen's originally indefensible position becomes justifiable once again. Lancelot's cause, through the unconscious mishandling of judicial formula, unexpectedly becomes the right cause, as Mador's carelessness with words during the proceedings neutralizes Arthur's negligence prior to trial.

The outcome of Guinevere's case points to a judicial system that succeeds despite itself. Its fragile triumph, coming as it does after a series of fortunate errors of judgment and procedure, can be attributed to Lancelot's willingness to risk perjuring himself and to Mador's misconception of the events surrounding Gaheris's death. At root, the weakest point in the entire process centers on the issue of motive; for the circumstances surrounding the queen's infraction, coupled with her repeated renunciation of premeditated guilt, give every indication of a cause that should have been eminently defendable. Yet Guinevere's case hinges upon a distinction between intentional and unintentional wrongdoing, a difference that escapes the ken of archaic legal methods and one that becomes especially muddled in the judicial apparatus of Camelot.

[31]

Arthur's court, like its feudal counterpart, does not possess an adequate investigatory mechanism—a system of inquest, testimony, witnesses, written proof, and documentary evidence—to determine the motivation behind infraction, much less to apprehend the offender when his action is not apparent. Nor would such techniques have been of much use: under a system of immanent ordeal it is God, and not man, who alone is capable of assessing intent. Once the conditions of confrontation have been established by the necessarily circumscribed power of the feudal judge, the process of judgment shifts to the shoulders of the divine arbiter; His infallible designation of guilt precludes the need for human inquiry.

Guinevere's offense constitutes what in modern jurisprudence is a case of accident or neglect, a special category of infraction under medieval law. For the jurist of the Middle Ages, the perpetrator of a criminal act, however innocent his intentions, was nonetheless liable for his misdeed. As the compiler of the *Leges Henrici* (Laws of Henry I) states, in adapting an Old English proverb, there is no distinction between the material and moral elements of infraction, between fact and intent: *Legis enim est qui inscienter peccat, scienter emendet.*[49] Negligence as we know it did not enter the picture. Harm done a stranger with unguarded weapons was, under Anglo-Saxon law, attributable to the owner of the arms. Borrowing or stealing weapons was a frequent means of obscuring evidence and thereby deflecting guilt. The armorer himself received them only after pledging to assume responsibility for their safekeeping and return free from unlawful use. The medieval law of *deodand*, showing traces of the Roman noxal actions, specifies that where injury is inflicted, the nearest object—animate or inanimate—bears the blame and should by rights be handed over to those obliged to avenge the crime. In England, for instance, if two men are at work in a forest and one lets a tree accidentally fall upon the other, the tree belongs to the victim's kin, provided that they claim it within thirty days. When injury occurs under the jurisdiction or protection of the king's forest, the blameworthy object is automatically transmitted to the royal agent of justice.[50] Both cases acknowledge that where one brings about the death of another he is, like Guinevere, liable regardless of intent.

Damage done to humans by dogs or other animals is, under both Old

49. According to the law, he who unwittingly sins, knowingly makes amends (cited F. Pollock and F. Maitland, *The History of English Law* [Cambridge: Cambridge University Press, 1923], 1: 54).

50. *Ibid.*, 1: 55; 2: 471.

English and Continental law, ascribable to the owner. In cases of dogbite, Aethelbert of Kent provides for payment by the master "according to a scale of compensation increasing after the first bite." The *Coutume de Tourraine et Anjou* prescribes a fine of 100s. 1d. payable directly to the injured party's family by the owner of an animal that causes the death of a man.[51] Trials of barnyard animals were not uncommon. Under the assumption that the responsibility of domestic animals is identical to that of humans, the *Registre Criminel de Saint-Martin* reports the case of a sow which, having killed a young child, was executed at Noisi according to the procedure reserved for murderers.[52] This particular register also details the trial, dragging, and execution *in absentia* of a horse responsible for the death of a man residing in Bondis. It seems that the owner, anxious not to lose the animal, removed it from the court's jurisdiction and then, as was customary, paid the family of the victim a sum equivalent to its value. They, in turn, allowed an effigy of the guilty horse to be hanged in its place.[53] Although Beaumanoir condemns the trial of animals on the grounds that it represents a waste of justice and that beasts are unable to distinguish good from evil, he nonetheless recognizes the prevalence of what seems, from the modern perspective, like the enactment of certain scenes from *Le Roman de Renart*.[54]

Pragmatic to an extreme and sometimes absurd degree, feudal law punished misdeeds of a general kind without regard to the motivation or circumstances surrounding wrongdoing. Harm inflicted upon one's fellow man constituted criminal action, but where no harm was done no crime had been committed. As the thirteenth-century *Livre de Jostice et de Pletz* specifies, the thoughts of a man were not to be tried: *Nus hom ne doit soffrir painne de sa pensée.*[55] Nor was attempted offense any offense at all. Saint Louis stipulates that even if a man confesses to plotting the murder

51. P. Viollet, *Introduction aux Etablissements de Saint Louis* (Paris: Renouard, 1881), 1: 233.

52. See Y. Bongert, *Cours d'histoire du droit pénal français de la seconde moitié du XIIIe siècle à 1493* (Paris: Cours de Droit, 1970), p. 350.

53. *Ibid.*, p. 351.

54. "Li aucun qui ont justices en leur terres si font justices de bestes quant eles metent aucun a mort: si comme se une truie tue un enfant, il la pendent et trainent, ou une autre beste. Mes c'est nient a fere, car bestes mues n'ont pas entendement qu'est biens ne qu'est maus, et pour ce est ce justice perdue." "Some who judge hold beasts accountable when they kill a human: for example, when a sow or any other animal kills a child, they hang and drag it. But this should not be done, because dumb beasts have no way of telling good from evil, and for this reason justice is wasted upon them" (Beaumanoir 2: 1944: 481).

55. No man should suffer penalty for his thoughts (*Jostice et Pletz* 277).

of another, he shall not be prosecuted unless he has actually carried his plan to completion (*Establissements* 2: 55; see Introduction, p. 5). Under feudal law the idea of guilt does not exist apart from actual infractions against specific individuals. Courts had no concept equivalent to the Roman *culpa* or the modern sense of negligence within the criminal sphere. On the contrary, feudal justice had little use for such abstract precepts, its immediate goal being the cessation of hostilities between private parties; its long-range aim, the prescription of indemnities to be paid the injured party or his family. Without injury there was no need for reparation; and where retribution was required, the amount of compensation was determined by the victim's social status and the fixed tables of payment, the *wergeld* or *relief d'homme*. In neither case did the need arise to consider the offender's motive or intent.

Although archaic Germanic law provided for only one degree of homicidal guilt, with little distinction between premeditated and accidental manslaughter, it did possess limited means of differentiating a few cases of aggravated slaying known as *morth* (Lat. *murdrum*, O.F. *murdre*). The term *morth* designated an unemendable crime involving concealment of the victim's body and requiring, consequently, an augmented *wergeld*. Salic law, for example, specified that if a dead man's corpse had been hidden in a well or in the branches of a tree, the deed fell into the category of *morth*, or *homicide odieux*. Otherwise it constituted plain manslaughter, *homicide simple*, for which the tariff of compensation was considerably lower. The *Lex Salica* sets the price for murder at three times that of an ordinary slaying, while Allemand and Frisian law prescribe a payment of nine times the normal amount: *Si quis hominem occiderit et absconderit, quod mordritum vocant, novem weregeldos componat.*[56]

The essential distinction between homicide and murder hinged, from the feudal period until the fourteenth century, upon the idea of open, as opposed to hidden, misdeed. Originally, *mordritum* denoted a slaying for which there was no witness other than the slayer or his accomplice; this original meaning was preserved by later jurists. Glanvill defines *murdrum* as a "killing seen by none": *Duo autem sunt genera homicidii. Unum*

---

56. He who kills a man and disappears, which is called murder, shall pay nine times the *wergeld* (cited Viollet, *Introduction aux Etablissements*, 1: 236).

est quod dicitur murdrem, quod nullo vidente, nullo sciente clam perpetratur. . . .[57] Bracton concurs:

Nunc autem dicendum de homicidio quod nullo praesente, nullo sciente, nullo audiente, nullo vidente clam perpetratur, quod dicitur murdrum.

Now we must turn to homicide committed in secret, in no one's presence, to no one's knowledge, and in no one's sight or hearing, which is called murder.[58]

The *Très Ancien Coutumier de Normandie* (ca. 1200) classified murder, along with arson, among the unemendable crimes occurring under the cover of darkness:

De larrecin, de murtre, de traïson, d'arson de meson par nuit, de roberie ne puet nule pes estre fete o ceus qui en sont convaincu; mes se il sont pris, il soient pandu.

There can be no pardon for those convicted of theft, murder, treason, arson of houses at night; but if they are captured, let them be hanged.

(*TAC* 28)

The *Livre de Jostice et de Pletz* is even more precise; slayings carried out at night automatically constitute murder: *homicide fet nuitantre fet murtre.*[59] Beaumanoir combines the idea of aforethought with that of covertness: murder involves premeditated ambush—*aguet apensé*—committed between sunset—*soleil esconsant*—and sunrise—*soleil levant* (1: 825: 429). Thus for Germanic custom, Glanvill, Bracton, the *Très Ancien Coutumier, Jostice et Pletz*, and Beaumanoir, the notion of murder is equivalent to deception, either because of an attempt to hide wrongdoing after the fact or because of an inferred malice in its enactment. It necessarily implies treachery, a killing in which the guilty party, through ruse or surprise, knowingly takes unfair advantage of his victim.[60] The *Livre de Jostice et de Pletz* again makes the connection that is only suggested in the Norman customal's

---

57. There are two kinds of homicide. One is called murder because it is seen by none and no one can knowingly lodge a claim. . . . (Cited Pollock and Maitland, *English Law*, 2: 486).

58. Bracton, *De Legibus et Consuetudinibus Angliae*, ed. S. Thorne (Cambridge: Harvard University Press, 1968), p. 379.

59. Homicide done at night makes murder (*Jostice et Pletz* 290).

60. In his accusal of Huon de Bordeaux, Amauri emphasizes the necessary link between murder, premeditation (*a ensciant*), and the attempt to hide the deed (*par couvreture*): "Par traïsson le tue et mourdri, / A ensciant le tue et ocist, / Par couvreture vint fuiant a Paris." "You killed him treacherously and you murdered him, / You killed him knowingly, / By ruse you came fleeing to Paris" (*Huon de Bordeaux*, v. 1626); see also *Quatre Filz*, v. 9722.

juxtaposition of *murtre* and *traïson: Et totes traïsons mellées à homecide fet le murtre.*[61]

By far the most curious category of premeditated homicide, under customary medieval law, is that of suicide. Since the killing of oneself necessarily implies aforethought, the victim, quite independently of ecclesiastical sanction against taking one's own life, was tried posthumously for murder. The *Très Ancienne Coutume de Bretagne* prescribes hanging and dragging, punishments ordinarily applied in cases of *homicide odieux*, for the man who kills himself.[62] *Le Livre Roisin*, a thirteenth-century collection of the customary laws of the city of Lille, distinguishes between the fate reserved for male suicides and that suitable for females; each submits to the penalty normally affixed by sex to the "proved murderer of another."[63] Beaumanoir stipulates that the only circumstance under which the suicide might escape trial and his body might be returned to his kin for burial is if madness can be proved as the cause of death. Otherwise, evidence that implies intent represents sufficient proof of "self-murder" and leads automatically to posthumous prosecution (Beaumanoir 2: 1948: 482).

Treacherous homicide comprises, on the one hand, any slaying not enacted openly, that is not the result of direct conflict between the slain man and his slayer: *Nus murtres ni est sans traïson.*[64] Saint Louis incorporates both the concept of nighttime deed and that of unfair advantage in the definition of murder found in the *Etablissements*. For Louis, murder was synonymous with death in bed, "or in any way that does not involve a fight": *Murtres si est d'ome ou de fame quant l'en la tue en son lit, ou en aucune meniere por coi ce ne soit en mellée.*[65] Murder entails trickery, the denial of a fair chance at self-defense; *poi de disference a entre tricheeur et traiteur.*[66] It elicits an automatic death sentence without the obvious benefit of trial to the killer. All that Louis required in order to admit the

61. Treachery and homicide combined constitute murder (*Jostice et Pletz* 290); Malory understood the archaic meaning of treason, as is evident in his version of Mador's accusal: "And ever sir Madore stood stylle before the kynge and appeled the quene of treson. (For the custom was such at that tyme that all maner of (s)hamefull death was called treson)" (*Morte Arthur*, p. 748).

62. *La Très Ancienne Coutume de Bretagne*, ed. M. Planiol (Rennes: Plihon et Hervé, 1896), p. 277.

63. *Le Livre Roisin*, ed. R. Monier (Paris: Domat-Monchrestien, 1932), p. 109.

64. There is no murder without treachery (Beaumanoir I: 827: 430).

65. It is murder of a man or woman when one kills him in his bed, or in any way so that there is no fight (*Etablissements*, 2: 37).

66. There is little difference between a trickster and a traitor (Beaumanoir 1: 992: 502).

possibility of legal process was that the slayer show, by the presence of scars inflicted prior to the victim's death, proof that open conflict did, in fact, occur (*Etablissements* 2: 44). Beaumanoir concurs, emphasizing the necessity of trial to determine where the fault lies in a quarrel that results in injury or death (2: 1946: 484).

The notion of murder comprehends, on the other hand, the idea not only of treachery, but of surprise. A murdered man has been taken unawares, either in his sleep or in a contest without formal challenge or equality in the means of confrontation. As the *Jostice et Pletz* delicately phrases it, the murder victim "does not see the blow coming" (*Jostice et Pletz* 289).

In a literary example from Chrétien, Laudine accuses Yvain of having murdered her husband treacherously, without his having seen his slayer prior to death (*Yvain* v. 1232).[67] Accused of treason at the end of *La Chanson de Roland*, Ganelon denies the charges on the grounds that his challenge of Roland was made publicly and not in secret.[68] First, the accusal:

---

67. Gawain finds himself charged with "treacherous" homicide at the end of *Perceval*. Guigambresil accuses him of having slain without warning:

> Ainz l'apele de felonnie
> Et dist: "Gavains, tu oceïs
> Mon seignor, et si le feïs
> Issi que tu nel desfias.
> Honte et reproce et blasme i as,
> Si t'en apel de traïson.

> Thus he accused him of felony
> And said: "Gawain, you killed
> My lord, and you did it such
> That you did not challenge him.
> You bear the reproach and the blame for this
> And I accuse you of treason.

(*Le Roman de Perceval*, ed. W. Roach [Geneva: Droz, 1959], v. 4758).

Similarly, in the late twelfth- or early thirteenth-century *Perlesvaus*, Clamadoz's appeal of murder constitutes a textbook example of premeditated slaying: "Dame, fet Clamadoz, il ocist mon pere en la Forest Soutaine, sanz defiance, et lança .i. javelot parmi le cors comme traïtre, ne je n'ere jamés a ese si l'avrai vengié; si l'apel en vostre cort de murtre et de traïson." "Lady," said Clamadoz, "he killed my father in the Soutaine Woods without challenging him, and hurled a javelin through his body like a traitor; I will never be at ease until I have avenged him; I accuse him in your court of murder and treason" (*Perlesvaus*, ed. W. A. Nitze and T. A. Jenkins [Chicago: University of Chicago Press, 1932], p. 153).

68. Yvonnes, Renaud de Montauban's son, makes a similar claim in *Quatre Filz*, vv. 16, 811, 17, 291; the Bernier of *Raoul de Cambrai* makes a point of challenging Raoul openly in order to avoid the subsequent charge of murder:

"Seignors barons," dist Carlemagnes li reis,
"De Guenelun car me jugez le dreit!
Il fut en l'ost tresqu'en Espaigne od mei,
Si me tolit .XX. milie de mes Franceis
Et mun nevold, quo ja mais ne verreiz,
Et Oliver, li proz e li curteis;
Les .XII. pers ad traït por aveir."

"Barons," said Charlemagne the king,
"Judge Ganelon for me according to the law!
He went with the army into Spain with me,
He took away from me 20,000 of my Franks
And my nephew, whom I shall never more see,
And Oliver the valiant and courtly;
He betrayed the twelve peers for wealth."

(*Roland* v. 3750)

And then the refutation:

Dist Guenelon: "Fel sei se jol ceil!
Rollant me forfist en or e en aveir,
Pur que jo quis sa mort e sun destreit;
Mais traïsun nule n'en i otrei."

       * * *

Jo desfiai Rollant le poigneor
E Oliver e tuiz lur cumpaignun
Carles l'oïd e si nobilie baron.
Venget m'en sui, mais n'i ad traïsun.

Said Ganelon: "May I be accounted a traitor if I dissemble!
Roland wronged me in gold and in goods
For which I sought his death and his woe;
But I admit no treason in it."

       * * *

I defied Roland the warrior,
And Oliver and all their companions

Il prent .iij. pox de l'ermin qu'ot vesti,
Parmi les mailles de l'auberc esclarci,
Envers Raoul les geta et jali;
Puis li a dit: "Vassal, je vos desfi!
Ne dites mie je vos aie traï."

He took three pieces of the ermine he was wearing,
Among the links of mail on his shining hauberk,
Toward Raoul he threw them with force;
Then he said to him: "Vassal, I challenge you!
Never say that I betrayed you."

(*Raoul* v. 2314)

Charles heard it, and his noble barons.
I avenged myself, but there's no treason in it.

(Roland vv. 3757, 3775)

Significantly, Ganelon's response to Charles does not contain the usual word-for-word denial of the charges; it is based upon the medieval formula of *exceptio* by which a defendant can refuse to answer an accusal directly, questioning instead the propriety of the allegation.[69] For Ganelon the difference between treason, a punishable misdeed, and vengeance, a justifiable one—*Venget m'en sui, mais n'i ad traïsun*—centers on the visible nature of his action. Challenge to the emperor's nephew took place in the open, that is to say, within the hearing range of all concerned: *Carles l'oïd e si nobilie baron.* Instead of denying the accusation, Ganelon makes a virtue out of the overtness of the deed, which, by feudal standards, did not constitute a criminal offense.

Traditional feudal law recognized only two kinds of homicide, overt and covert slaying. It was not until later in the twelfth century that jurists, influenced by theological discussions of the intentionality and the mental elements of sin, began to discern diverse degrees of criminal guilt according to individual cases. Then, and only then, was renewed emphasis placed upon the psychic components of crime. The canonical courts, which on more than one occasion throughout the Middle Ages shaped the development of their secular counterparts, were the first to formulate legal doctrines for various shades of responsibility based upon the crime itself and attached to an appropriate penalty. Unlike the archaic *wergeld*, which was fixed according to the victim's social status, canonical sentence depended increasingly upon the nature of the infraction and upon a gradual scale of punishment, ranging from life imprisonment to disqualification from further promotion within the ecclesiastical hierarchy. The cleric who killed accidentally could be acquitted if the act that resulted in death was itself lawful and performed with due care.[70] Twelfth-century jurists like Glanvill began to contrast civil and criminal cases, to speak of the difference between the Roman *dolus, culpa,* and *casus.* Bracton, a century later, specifies that homicide becomes justifiable only under certain conditions: in execution of a legal sentence of death, in slaying a known outlaw or a thief who resists, and in self-defense. Even here, however, pardon was by no means automatic. In France and England

---

69. Pollock and Maitland, *English Law*, 2: 587.
70. *Ibid.*, 2: 477.

[39]

royal letters of grace were required for the remission of penalty, and accidental homicide could still lead to *deodand* if no human agent were involved, or to pardon where human action was present. The fine distinctions that Glanvill and Bracton draw between various shades of homicidal guilt—the circumstances which bestow upon each infraction its particular character—were, at any rate, entirely absent from customary Germanic practice. Within the legal limits of feudal procedure observance of the rules of public challenge sufficed to render homicide lawful, and all killings conducted properly were essentially redeemable. It mattered little why one man killed another, but how he did it:

Homicides si est quant aucuns tue autrui en chaude mellee, si comme il avient que tençons nest et de la tençon vient laide parole et de la laide parole la mellee par laquele aucuns reçoit mort souventes fois.

Homicide is when someone kills another in heated fighting, as happens when a dispute arises and from the dispute comes injurious words and from the injurious words the fight through which someone is often killed.

(Beaumanoir 1: 828: 430)

Beaumanoir acknowledges that even though the distance between words —*la laide parole*—and act—*la mellee*—may be short indeed, as long as speech precedes death, the offense reverts to a case of homicide and not murder.

Treason, under Germanic law, meant either aiding the enemies of the warrior group, the *comitatus*, or flight from battle. Both required successful completion of an act of military betrayal or cowardice, breach of troth or *Treubruch* (Frankish *herisliz*). Only with the renewed interest in Roman law of the twelfth and thirteenth centuries did treason again become associated with the crime of *laesae maiestatis*, an infraction directed against the more abstract and extended political body of the state, or its representative, the king.[71] It was, moreover, not until the middle of the fourteenth century that war against the monarch constituted treason and that misdeeds of this type were officially considered political crimes against the state. Unlike the feudal notion of *traïson*, that of *maiestas* did not imply only actual betrayal, but comprehended potentially harmful acts of disloyalty as well—plotting or scheming against the king's life or the realm. This shift from the necessity of material action—*traditio*,

71. A. Dessau, "L'idée de la trahison au moyen âge," *Cahiers de Civilisation Médiévale* 3 (1960): 23; S. Lear, *Treason and Related Offenses in Roman and Germanic Law* (Houston: Rice Institute, 1955), p. 32.

seditio—to the sufficiency of endangering thought means that infraction no longer resided in the criminal act itself, but in the endeavor to commit it. As innovative as Saint Louis had been just a century earlier, he was still so steeped in traditional patterns of legal thought that he would have had trouble understanding the idea of harm done by words or thoughts rather than deeds. The complex notion of the potential criminal, the accessory before the fact, escaped entirely the cognizance of the feudal court, which only admitted the possibility of premeditation once wrongdoing had occurred.

When Mador accuses Guinevere of having killed his brother treacherously—*ele desloiaument et en traïson a ocis mon frere*—he is, in effect, accusing her of premeditated murder in the limited Germanic sense. According to his allegation, she must have been aware of the poison hidden in the piece of fruit and intended to trap Gaheris with her gastronomic deceit. Yet the reader knows what Lancelot only suspects: that the queen is completely innocent of premeditation and that her part in the slaying is the product of accident or chance. Not even a case of archaic manslaughter, her crime constitutes what today is considered involuntary manslaughter, an ambiguous mixture of guilt in deed and innocence of intent which defies the legal mechanism of Arthur's court. Structured around a well-defined and undeviating series of binary options, feudal procedure had no means of assimilating events like Gaheris's murder, which could not be reduced to a strict "either/or" proposition. In the first place, there was no regularized method of prosecution, a fault shared by all purely accusatory systems. Guinevere either escapes public notice of her act, as during the period prior to Mador's arrival in Camelot, or she finds herself charged with intentional wrongdoing; she either eludes prosecution altogether, or is indicted for murder with evil intent. Second, although Mador's accusal and Lancelot's denial are both meant to be truthful statements about a past event that has left no trace in the present, neither accurately or wholly describes the original deed. Plaintiff and defendant alike are forced, by the judicial formulas at their disposal, into contradictory positions, each of which is assumed to describe adequately the issue under dispute. Neither, however, represents the comprehensive truth—Guinevere's material guilt and moral innocence—visible only from the reader's privileged perspective. Whereas the author of *La Mort* possesses a language in which to recount happenings as ambiguous as accidental death, Arthur's court has no legal language in which to couch such equivocal phenomena. The formula of accusation, together with the inflexible denial, discloses the insufficiency of a judicial process that has no way of affirming the reality of an event, its simple occurrence, without at the same time confirming conscious motivation, an act of will on the part of those involved. The failure of the justice of the Round Table reaches far beyond a mere lack of familiarity with problematic criminal action to a lack of discourse by which to assimilate partial, relative, nonexclusive half-truths and therefore to give adequate legal meaning to Guinevere's misdeed.

A Second Trial

The breakdown of procedure during the queen's trial would not offer such incontrovertible evidence of a more general crisis of legal institutions were it not for the novel's second judicial combat—that which pits Lancelot against Gawain before the walls of Gaunes. Here, trial by combat has been agreed upon as a suitable means of resolving the blood-feud between the sons of Ban and those of Uterpandragon following the death of Gawain's three brothers. Gawain, like Mador, adopts the standard accusatory formula under which all homicide becomes premeditated homicide:

Lancelot, fet messire Gauvains, messires le rois est ci venuz por fere ce que vos m'avez requis; vos savez bien que entre moi et vos avons emprise une bataille si grant comme de traïson mortel por la mort de mes freres que vos oceïstes en traïson, desloiaument, ce savons nos bien tuit; si en sui apelerres et vous deffenderres.

Lancelot, said Sir Gawain, the king has come here to do what you have required of me; you know well that between you and me we have undertaken a great battle of mortal treason for the death of my brothers whom you killed treacherously, disloyally, this know we all well; I am the accuser and you the defendant.

(*La Mort* 189)

Lancelot responds in the appropriate manner, with a direct denial of the charges: *vos jurrai sur seinz que onques au mien escient n'ocis Gaheriet vostre frere.*[72] Once again the question put to legal test is not whether the accused did, in reality, perpetrate the act of which he stands accused, but whether his actions were intentional. Gawain insists upon the premedi-

---

72. I swear to you on saints that never did I knowingly kill your brother (*La Mort* 191).

tated quality of the deed—*vos oceïstes en traïson*—while Lancelot disavows any conscious intent—*au mien escient n'ocis vostre frere.*

The issue under judicial dispute occurs during the quarrel over Guinevere's pending execution after her capture in *flagrante delicto.* In the struggle to save her, Lancelot's men kill Gawain's brothers. Boort maintains that the conflict took place "openly, in an area where there were more than one hundred knights," and that the resulting deaths were therefore justified: *onques en traïson n'oceïstes ses freres, mes en apert, en tel leu ou il avoit plus de cent chevaliers.*[73] Lancelot's cousin thus establishes the traditional opposition between treacherous and overt wrongdoing; as long as the slaying does not involve stealth, it does not represent criminal infraction. Lancelot's other cousin, Lionel, adopts a different and quite sophisticated legal tactic. He dismisses Gawain's accusation on the grounds that the plaintiff's suicidal folly, and not his righteousness, motivates the accusal of murder (*La Mort* 185). In suggesting that Gawain's assertions do not constitute a *bona fide* accusal because they are the product of extreme sorrow, Lionel, like Ganelon, refuses the plea in favor of the *exceptio* (see above, p. 39). He does not, however, contest the circumstances surrounding the original act, resorting instead to an even rarer category of exception, the plea of hate and spite—*de odio et atia.*[74] Through Lionel's counteraccusation, intention is again introduced at the level of common sense, while, at the same time, the archaic ordeal of battle provides no means of integrating such subtle psychological distinctions. In this, Lionel's response resembles Gawain's recognition of the queen's innocence only after the first judicial duel has reached the point of no return, only after it is too late to reconcile legal and moral fact.

A close look at the incident under consideration reveals that Lancelot did, in fact, literally ambush the party accompanying Guinevere to the stake. As the queen's escort approaches the place of execution he waits, hidden in the woods, for a message from court: *Tant alerent parlant entre Agravaïn et Gaheriet qu'il aprouchierent del feu. Et Lancelos, qui fu enbuschiez a l'entree de la forest a toute sa gent....*[75] When Lancelot hears that his

73. You never killed his brothers treacherously, but openly, in a place where there were more than a hundred knights (*La Mort* 185).

74. Pollock and Maitland, *English Law,* 2: 587.

75. Agravain and Gaheriet rode along talking till they came near the fire. And Lancelot, who was in ambush with all his men at the edge of the forest.... (*La Mort* 123).

mistress has been condemned to die he singles out Agravain, the man responsible for the entrapment of the lovers, as the prime target of attack:

Seigneur, fet il, or del monter! Que tel i a qui la cuide fere morir qui ainçois en morra. Or doint Dex que, s'il onques oï priere de pecheeur, que ge truisse premierement Agravain qui m'a cest plet basti.

Sirs, said he, now mount! May those who think to kill her [Guinevere] die first. Now grant God, if ever he heard the prayer of a sinner, that I find Agravain first, who set the trap for me.

(*La Mort* 123)

Lancelot's lying in wait in the forest—*enbuschiez a l'entree de la forest*—bears the mark of the original sense of ambush (Ital. *imboscare*) implying a concealed attack "from the woods." His designation of Agravain as the object of assault—*que ge truisse premierement Agravain*—betrays a degree of premeditation that cannot be denied. The crime of which Gawain accuses Lancelot combines the Roman notion of aforethought with the Germanic concept of surprise attack, *guet-apens* or "thoughtful watch." It appears in every way an exemplary illustration of first-degree murder as later defined by article 296 of the French Penal Code: *Tout meurtre commis avec préméditation ou de guet-apens est qualifié assassinat.*

Thus Gawain's accusation, unlike that of Mador, has a strong basis in fact. Lancelot did kill his brother with harmful intent and in a deceitful manner. The episode in question reveals none of the uncertainty that surrounds Guinevere's case; and yet the outcome is even more ambiguous. Lancelot wins the judicial duel, but he wins on the grounds of a technicality long after his opponent has, for all intents and purposes, been physically vanquished. Arthur, acting in his capacity as judge and upon an appeal from the defendant, puts an end to the fight:

Quant il rois, qui bien conoist que messires Gauvains estoit au desouz, entent la deboneretè Lancelot, il li respont: "Lancelot, Gauvains ne lera pas la bataille, s'il ne li plest; mes vos la poez lessier, se vos voulez, car ja est eure passee; si avez bien fet ce que vos devez.

When the king, who well knew that Sir Gawain was beaten, heard Lancelot's good will, he replied, "Lancelot, Gawain will not leave off battle, if he does not want to; but you can leave off, if you wish, because the time has now passed; you have certainly done what you ought.

(*La Mort* 202)

Through his reference to the "hour that has come"—*ja est eure passee*—the Anglo-Norman author of *La Mort* invokes the regional judicial custom according to which any defendant who manages to fend off his accuser until evening stands acquitted. The *Grand Coutumier de Normandie* defines the *terminus ad quem* of combat with the appearance of stars in the sky: *Si autem defensor usque ad stellas in celo de nocte apparentes poterit se defendere, victorie retinet dignitatem* (*GC* 171).[76] Lancelot sets the limit at the hour of vespers in a last minute plea to end the struggle, for, as he explains, "anyone who accuses a man of treason should have decided his dispute and won his battle before vespers, or he has lost it by law" (*La Mort* 201). Lancelot scores, then, what amounts to a technical knockout in a present-day prize fight. His victory is neither complete, as against Mador, not produced by his efforts alone, since, with Arthur's intervention, the application of human procedure, positive law, succeeds where divine justice has failed.

Having undertaken what was a dubious cause in Guinevere's defense and a patently poor cause in his own case, Lancelot emerges victorious from both encounters. The first can be justified in terms of a sudden reversal due to an inappropriate judicial formula; the second, however, can only be explained as the triumph of superior physical force. Gawain's certainty that right resides with him—*ge sei veraiement que li droiz est miens et li torz siens*—is countered by Yvain's recognition that might makes right:

Sire, pour coi avés vous ce fait? Haés vous si durement vostre vie, qui avez emprise bataille encontre le meillour chevalier del monde, vers qui nus hom ne pot onques durer en bataille qui ne fust honnis au daerrain?

Sire, why have you done this? Do you hate your life so much, that you have undertaken battle against the best knight in the world, against whom no man can last in battle who is not shamed in the end?

(*La Mort* 192)

Thus, a lack of faith in the immanence of divine justice, a crisis of belief that allows Lancelot to support a merely sufficient cause on the one hand and an indefensible suit on the other, finds articulate expression in Yvain's

76. In *La Chevalerie Ogier* Charlot reminds his opponent Sadone: "Ains que soit vespres ne li solaus escons, / Vus quit je metre a grant confusion." "Before vespers or sunset, / I intend to confound you utterly" (*Chevalerie Ogier*, v. 1928); Gautier taunts Bernier in similar fashion: "Ains q'il soit vespres t'arai ci justicié." "Before vespers I will have conquered you" (*Raoul*, v. 5004); Amauri swears before battle that he will conquer Huon before vespers: "Se li ferai par le geule gehir / Ains qu'il soit vespres, s'ensanble sommes mis, / Que le dansel malvaisement mordri." "I will make him admit / Before vespers, if we are put together / That he killed the knight treacherously" (*Huon de Bordeaux*, v. 1635).

reproach. Unlike *La Chanson de Roland*, where God intervenes at crucial moments to save the hero and thus to reaffirm men's faith in His abiding presence, the two trials of *La Mort* serve only to undermine credence in the fundamental tenets of feudal justice: that the righteous man, though not necessarily the most powerful, emerges victorious and that human error and chance play no part in the working of the judicial process. Whereas the ordeal can function only under the assumption that any sufficiently polarized conflict might be resolved if put to the test, here accident and ineptitude belie its basic effectiveness. Chance has entered the breach where providence once stood. The *judicium Dei* no longer punishes wrongdoing, nor does it vindicate injury swiftly and clearly. It has failed in its chief capacity, which is the designation of intrinsic but unobvious guilt through an irreducible contradiction of parties. Trial by combat has ceased, even, to distribute justice fairly. Arvalan and Lancelot, the guilty parties in the two legal actions, elude prosecution; Mador and Gawain fail to obtain redress.

Feudal Justice and Truth

The ineffectiveness of trial by combat can, in Mador's case, be ascribed to the formulary weakness of the system, and, in Gawain's, to the substantive failure of the duel itself. A more inherent defect lies at the epistemological root of immanent justice. Stated simply, the outcome of combat exists independently of the notion of cognitive truth. The justice of Camelot, and of the feudal court in general, depends exclusively upon the observance or nonobservance of a series of fixed rules which have little to do with substantive issues of judgment. The *Grand Coutumier*, to take but one example, gives some indication of the preciseness of procedural detail surrounding the duel itself (*GC* 168–170). First the court must decide whether or not an infraction has actually occurred and whether or not combat represents the appropriate method of proof. The judge then accepts the wagers of battle from both parties, who pledge to respect the law of the court. Plaintiff and defendant find themselves henceforth confined to the duke's prison unless they can produce pledges willing to guarantee their appearance "dressed for combat" on the prescribed day. The guarantor swears, in turn, to protect the life of his party and to fight in his stead, suffering his penalty, if he does not appear as agreed.

On the day of assignation the combatants are obliged to make their presence known shortly after noon. Once the formulary accusal and denial

[46]

have been pronounced, precise gestures enacted according to prescribed form set the stage for battle. Participants may be armed only with a shield and a stick curved at one end. The shield and other protective armor—tunic or leg-guards—can be made out of cloth, leather, wool, or cotton padding, but all other materials will be disqualified. Combatants may grease their bodies if they wish. Their hair must be cut above ear-level. Once they have passed inspection, the court scribe reads aloud the allegation and terms of confrontation to the satisfaction of plaintiff and defendant. The adversaries are then led to the battlefield by four knights who have been designated as referees. They swear, along with the rest of the witnesses seated around the area of combat, not to assist—by word or deed—either party.[77] When the entire gathering has so sworn, the champions kneel holding hands before the judge who, with the accuser on his right side and the accused on his left, asks each to respond to his baptismal name and to confirm his belief in the Father, Son, Holy Ghost, and the dogma of the Church. The defendant repeats the original denial of accusal and sacred oath, which is followed by the plaintiff's affirmation of the original allegation, accompanied this time by the additional charge of perjury. Before the weapons are delivered the combatants are obliged to swear individually that they possess no instrument of sorcery or magic to influence the outcome of the proceedings. Finally, prayers are offered by both sides and combat ensues until one knight wins or, as in the case of Lancelot and Gawain, "stars appear in the sky."

From the prescription for duels contained in the *Grand Coutumier* it is evident that the regulations governing combat—formulas of accusation and denial, solemn oaths of faith and honesty, codes for representation, surety, dress, hair length, wagers, and termination of struggle—count much more than the collection and assessment of information surrounding the criminal act. The customal is even more precise: the only elements that distinguish one trial from another are the identities of the parties involved and the nature of the charge:

Et hec forma in omni duelli sequela est attendenda, hoc sane intellecto quod juramentum debet fieri de verbis de quibus duellum vadiatum fuerit et retractum.

And this form must be kept in all battles, except that the oath should be composed of the words with which the battle was wagered

(*GC* 171)

---

77. It is, in fact, the interference of witnesses that disrupts the judicial duel between Bernier and Gautier (*Raoul*, vv. 4525, 4609).

The question of judicial proof—*preuve*—is never really posed at the level of demonstration, only at that of ordeal or *épreuve*. A deductive test of physical strength takes precedence over any more inductive effort to determine rationally where guilt lies. Under the *judicium Dei* every procedural detail prepares and converges upon the final *épreuve de force*. Until the actual moment of battle there can be no departure from the invariable steps leading to it; there is, in other words, no possibility of testing the validity of respective allegations. In fact, within a feudal accusatory system, the only means of challenging the truthfulness of the proceedings is to prove that the rules have not been applied with sufficient rigor—that the judge has either refused to hear a case brought before him, or that he has mishandled the precepts at his disposal. Both require an additional wager of battle, tendered this time against the judge by the party which questions his probity. Neither involves reference to the original deed, whose truth or falsity is never really examined.

Arthur initiates no investigation at the time of Guinevere's crime; he calls no witnesses, and holds no inquest during her trial; nor does anyone present at the initial accusation raise the question of what, in point of fact, occurred at the time of Gaheris's death. Mador has, furthermore, built his case upon the thinnest of evidential givens: the commonly admitted truth of the queen's guilt verified by hearsay. Gawain, too, depends upon casual rumor and the second-hand testimony of the crowd of mourners, the *menu peuple* of Camelot that greets him, as if by chance, with the news of his brother's slaying (*La Mort* 130). He has not witnessed the deed of which he accuses Lancelot but relies instead upon the opinion of the crowd confirmed this time by Mordret's report of what took place. Again, no effort is made during the preliminary discussions of battle to reconstruct the events surrounding Gaheriet's death and thus to determine without recourse to physical combat whether the accused is guilty or not. The attempt to recreate faithfully the reality of past events remains a nonessential concept within the feudal legal system, whose only concern is the prevention of their recurrence. At best a means of regularizing and codifying single hand-to-hand conflicts, the judicial duel represents a symbolic reenactment of the original deed brought before the court. It can in no way be confused with the endeavor to recapture the truth of the crime: the coherence of its etiology, strategy, and resolution.

Founded upon the weakest of fragmentary evidence, the 'truth of infraction stands, under the procedure at Arthur's disposal, only loosely bound to the process of rational human thought. Judicial truth, that involved in the trial itself, is witnessed by the presence of the barons at court, affirmed by the judge, who receives accusations and pronounces sentence, and risked by the parties who expose themselves to divine wrath. The barons are, in this respect, a repository of collective truth, the customs of the community as expressed by the judge. Their attendance validates the entire proceeding, and no legal action can officially be admitted without them. This is why Mador, upon learning of Gaheris's death, does not rush immediately to court but waits until the appropriate moment—until Arthur has sat down to dinner among his vassals—in order to publicly register his plea.[78] It also serves to explain why Charlemagne summons his barons to Aix before opening Ganelon's trial (*Roland* vv. 3741, 3748). At the end of Béroul's *Roman de Tristan* King Marc sends for Arthur's court as well as his own. All three literary trials tell us something fundamental about the nature of feudal justice and the relation of justice to law. For the Germanic court, the Frankist *placitum* or *mallus*, legal power resided, at least theoretically, in the community as a whole. Law originated in the living conviction of the group as validated by use and common consent. The decisions of the Arthurian court, like those of the Germanic *mootcourt* or the Anglo-Saxon *holimote*, were based upon the traditional customs and practices of Logres—*us ne coustume en cest païs*—as preserved in the memory and legal feeling of the lawful men of the realm.[79] The presence of numerous court officials—the Merovigian

---

78. "Moult fet Mador grant duel de son frere et demeure illuec tant que la grant messe fut chantee; et quant il sot que li rois fu assis au mengier, il se parti de la tombe son frere tout en plorant et vint en la sale devant le roi, et parole si haut que tuit cil de leanz le porent entendre." "Mador grieved greatly for his brother and remained there while the high mass was sung; and when he knew that the king was seated at dinner, he left his brother's tomb crying and came into the hall before the king, and spoke so loudly that all who were within could hear him" (*La Mort* 84).

79. "Here we touch upon a concept which lay at the heart of all medieval thinking about law, and was nowhere more powerful than in its influence on the structure of rural society. Traditionalists to the core, medieval men could be said with slight (very slight) exaggeration to have ordered their lives on the assumption that the only title to permanence was that conferred by long usage. Life was ruled by tradition, by group custom. (. . . .) Custom might sometimes find written embodiment in charters, legal decisions, seigneurial inventories drawn up with the help of inquest proceedings; but in the main custom continued to be purely oral. In short, human memory was the sole arbiter. If a certain institution was known to have existed 'time out of mind,' then it was assumed to be good and sufficient" (M. Bloch, *French Rural History* [Berkeley: University of California Press, 1966], p. 70). See also L. Buisson, *König Ludwig IX, der Heilige, und das Recht* (Freiburg: Herder, 1954), p. 9.

rachimburgii or Carolingian *scabini*—merely insured the application of the truths that had always applied in the past. The memory of the judge represented, in turn, a storehouse of appropriate rules intended to provoke a manifestation of higher truth. Unlike his canonical counterpart or civil successor, the feudal justiciar presided not to decide which cases were admissible to court, nor to draw up the appropriate articles for consideration, nor to distinguish, finally, innocence from guilt. The difference between the judge and the members of his court was one of quantity and not of quality. He possessed few skills to differentiate him, even, from those he judged. His knowledge of gesture, ritual, and tradition set him above the parties under his jurisdiction; this knowledge, however, hardly differed from that of the other credible men of the community, whose tacit consent or dissenting clamors endowed tradition with the force of law. The feudal *comes* was more of a spokesman for the *boni homines* of the court, a functionary of the *mallus*, than an autonomous agent for the designation of judicial truth.

Logically, the process of judgment breaks down as follows: an accusal and wager of battle, once pronounced, could be either accepted or refused; if rejected, the accused party stood guilty as charged (see above, p. 17). Assuming that the accusation were true, then the defendant would supposedly lose the judicial duel; and if it were false, then, and only then, would the wrath of the gods fall upon the accuser, who would undergo, ordinarily, the same penalty risked by his adversary were the outcome reversed. The genesis of a judicial action looks like this:[80]

Deed (occurred or not)

Accusal (with offer of battle)

Refusal of Battle   Acceptance of Battle
(avowal of guilt)   (denial of accusal)

True Accusal   False Accusal
(plaintiff wins combat)   (defendant wins combat)

Under an immanent accusatory system the act of accusal, coupled with the oath which establishes the conditions of combat, stands at the center of

---

80. I would like to thank M. Michel Foucault for the diagram, suggested during a series of lectures on Greek justice delivered at the State University of New York at Buffalo in the spring of 1972.

trial. The opposition between falsehood and truth is relegated to a secondary position within the proceedings, coming into play only at the
conclusion of battle. It is not until the final stage of judgment that a
distinction is theoretically made between innocence and guilt and that the
court can distinguish the truth of the outcome from the formulaic observance of judicial ritual. In the absence of any concept of abstract justice,
truth for the feudal *mallus* exists independently of any uniform criteria by
which to judge all cases. That which corresponds not to the facts but to
the rules of procedure is just, and any departure from the precepts
belonging to the community constitutes an abrogation of justice. Barring
abrogation, there is, in effect, no way for the court to judge falsely and,
hence, no principle exterior to itself by which it may judge truly. In this it
is the opposite of the modern court, for which the uniform application of
objective standards and the abstract principle of equity define the parameters of judicial truth.

In Guinevere's case the deed of which she is accused did take place,
although her indictment is, strictly speaking, false because of the innocence of her intentions. The wager of battle is accepted by Lancelot,
who, as defendant, defeats Mador:

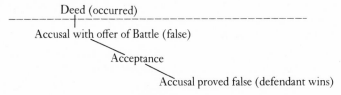

In the second judicial test the infraction did again occur, but the accusal is
essentially true this time, since Lancelot killed Gaheriet with evil intent
according to the medieval formula for *traïson*. Once more the defendant,
Lancelot again wins the duel:

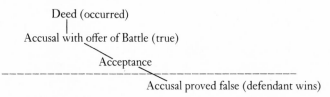

Thus both trials of *La Mort* begin from the same initial premise: the
occurrence of the act submitted to judicial scrutiny. Yet in both cases the

link between the truth of wrongdoing and the outcome of the *judicium Dei* is at some point severed (see dotted horizontal lines). Mador disturbs the progression at the outset through the inaccuracy of his accusal; from that moment onward it is no longer a question of the veracity of the events surrounding the queen's misdeed, but of the veracity of her intent, something that the feudal court had no means of measuring. In Gawain's suit the alliance of justice and truth is not disrupted until the battle itself, when the plaintiff loses, despite the truth of his allegations. Here, the victory of a defendant faced with a true accusation leads to far greater consequences—of a cosmic nature—since it can be taken only as a failure of divine judgment and, hence, of the entire set of assumptions underlying immanent procedure.

Despite its obvious dangers and inadequacies, trial by ordeal was, up until the thirteenth century, the only public means by which a man who felt wronged by another and could not come to terms with him might seek justice for the offense. Short of recourse to war, it remained the only formal procedure by which a member of the feudal warrior aristocracy might bring legal suit against the party who had caused him wrong and refused to recognize his guilt. By today's standards the duel would hardly constitute public redress; it seems, rather, to be the private resolution of a personal quarrel in which the public organ of justice, the state, plays a relatively minor role. All of which is true: except for Arthur's personal interest in the outcome of the first trial, the state stands neither to gain nor to lose in the two claims against Lancelot. It serves merely to establish the proper conditions under which a plaintiff can settle his quarrel without further extension of the conflict. The judicial duel represents an implicit assertion on the part of the combatants of the right to reconcile their difference independently of the prevailing civil authority. And yet they still bring their dispute to court, allowing the judge to regulate the formal aspects of settlement according to commonly accepted procedure. The parties still face each other in the presence of the barons, who, along with the judge, authenticate the entire proceeding. Even though it would have been relatively easy for a plaintiff like Mador or Gawain to take matters into his own hands, to pursue on his own what he considers to be just retribution, neither chooses to do so. As required under feudal law, each takes his quarrel to his lord, whose jurisdiction in the disputes of his vassals constitutes the sole legal means by which an accuser can meet his adversary in battle. Both pass through the only existent public mechanism,

[52]

however rudimentary, by which the state controls the settlement of personal grievances. The duel represents a minimal quantity of civil jurisdiction within the private sphere.

Capture in the Act

Medieval law did provide for two cases in which the normal procedure for public resolution of private disputes might be waived in favor of a more expeditious solution. The first involves the murder of a man who was himself an outlaw, who was not, in other words, entitled to the protection against surprise attack that the law ordinarily afforded. The *Lex Burgundionum* specifies that "he who follows a fugitive, and by chance kills him while resisting, is free from all blame."[81] As late as Boutillier, the author of the fourteenth-century *Somme rurale*, the authorized slayer of a declared outlaw could not be prosecuted for murder.[82] A felon at large was, in effect, at war with the community. He forfeited all property and contractual rights, including *seisin* of his fief as well as previously established ties of homage.[83] According to Bracton, children born to the outlaw after his banishment were ineligible to inherit either from their father or from anyone else. Even when pardoned, the felon reentered society having given up the property and rights acquired prior to his exclusion. He returned divested of civil personality—possessions, privileges, fealty—having suffered what amounted to secular excommunication. While absent, it was the right and duty of the other members of the community to pursue the outlaw, kill him, and seize his belongings where possible. Harboring a proclaimed outlaw was itself a capital offense.[84] The criminal's family, in particular, was prohibited from pro-

---

81. *Burgundian Code*, p. 27.

82. Boutillier, *La Somme rurale* (Bruges: Colard Mansion, 1479), p. 473; The customal or *keure* of Bruges (1190) contains the following provision: "Qui aliquem bannitum occiderit, nullum in hoc facit forisfactum." "Whoever kills a banished man, commits no crime." (Cited P. Dubois, *Les Asseurements au XIIIe siècle* [Paris: Rousseau, 1900], p. 157); the charter of Saint Dizier deals similarly with outlaws: "Qui occiderit aliquem bannitum in hoc nullum faciet foris factum, si ille ex toto fuerit bannitus." "Whoever kills a banished man commits no crime if the victim is truly an outlaw" (cited *idem*).

83. *Chevalerie Ogier*, v. 9042; Pollock and Maitland, *English Law*, 1: 476–478; 2: 449.

84. "Et etiam latrones quisquis sciens receperit, qui dicitur receptator malorum, et eos offerre iudiciis supersederit, supplicio corporali plectetur cum amissione bonorum. Item forisfacit utlagatus omnia quae pacis sunt, quia a tempore quo utlagatus est caput gerit lupinum, ita quod ab omnibus interfici poterit et impune, maxime si se defenderit vel fugerit ita quod difficilis sit eius captio." "And whoever knowingly harbors thieves (one who is called a harborer of wicked men) and does not hand them over to justice shall undergo

[53]

tecting him and from avenging themselves upon his killers once he had been apprehended. If the slayer of an outlaw were brought to court, proof of the dead man's extraordinary legal status sufficed to waive the normal accusation of murder. A manhunt conducted by "hue and cry" was the equivalent of murder with impunity. It points, furthermore, to the weakness of a legal system with no regular method of law enforcement and no efficient police force to arrest known offenders. Nor was the practice of outlawry uncommon. As the last resort of secular justice, it remained, until the thirteenth century, a prime method of criminal prosecution. Ten men were outlawed in the English eyre courts for every one brought to trial.

A second case in which the rules normally governing public prosecution might be suspended involves the entrapment of an offender in the act, especially in the act of adultery.[85] Since the Church maintained some degree of jurisdiction over marriage throughout the Middle Ages, and since canon law is, to a large extent, based on Roman procedure, the sources of medieval marriage law can be traced back to their Roman roots. By the time of the Empire, adultery already belonged to a special category of infraction. Although Imperial law distinguished *stuprum*, sexual relations with a woman who was not a prostitute, from adultery, it dealt most severely with violations of the conjugal rights of husbands. A married woman caught in the act might be condemned to death by a domestic tribunal composed of her husband and her blood relations; or, as Aulus Gellius stipulates in the *Noctes Atticae*, she may be slain with her lover on the spot.[86] Adultery thus fell within the private jurisdiction of the family and, as such, it pertained more specifically to the authority of the *gens* than to the *jus civile* of the state. The first-century B.C. *Lex Julia de adulteriis* represented, in fact, an attempt on the part of Augustus to remove the crime of adultery from the private sphere—*judicium domesticum*—and to bring it within the competence of the public court, the

---

corporal punishment along with a loss of his property. Likewise, the outlaw forfeits everything connected with the peace, and until he is captured bears the wolf's head; thus he can be slain by all with impunity, especially if he defends himself or flees so that his capture is difficult" (Bracton, *De Legibus*, p. 362).

85. Bongert, *Cours d'histoire*, pp. 365–369; Esmein, *Cours élémentaire*, p. 88; Esmein, *Criminal Procedure*, p. 61; Pollock and Maitland, *English Law*, 1: 53.

86. P. Corbett, *The Roman Law of Marriage* (Oxford: The Clarendon Press, 1930), p. 127.

quaestio perpetua. Consequently, even though slaves, family freedmen, or condemned criminals could still be slain if caught in the home, only the father retained the right to kill his daughter and her companion. The husband who slayed his wife and who was then brought to trial received a reduced sentence, not immunity, for having acted in the heat of passion. Justinian provided for trial followed by divorce, or scourging and seclusion in a nunnery for the wife publicly convicted of adultery; according to Novel 117, the cuckold husband retained the right to kill the adulterous couple as long as he had warned his wife's lover beforehand not to frequent her.[87]

According to medieval customary law, if a man captured his wife in a compromising situation with another man, he had the right to slay both wife and lover without risk to himself. "If adulterers are discovered, let the man and woman be killed"—so reads the *Lex Burgundionum.*[88] In contrast to the elaborate procedure governing all other hand-to-hand struggles, the regulations affixed to the slaughter of adulterers in *flagrante delicto* were minimal. Boutillier specified that "no homicide can be claimed when a man finds another sleeping with his wife or daughter."[89] Beaumanoir, like Justinian, permits the offended husband to take justice into his own hands provided that he has warned his rival "before a court or before honest witnesses" not to enter his house "to pursue his shame" (1: 933: 472). Nor is it necessary actually to prove adultery as long as there is a relative lack of doubt regarding the offenders' presence together; the difficulty of spying or of breaking down doors may inhibit entrapment by providing time for them to disengage or to dress; and even if the lovers are not caught in the act of physical union, the mere fact of being "alone in a private place"—*seul à seul en lieu privé*—suffices to establish criminal guilt (Beaumanoir 1: 934: 473).

Once the adultery had been confirmed, the husband might slay the couple without penalty or fear of vengeance on the part of the victim's kin. He need only raise the public cry—*le clameur de haro*—in order that the deed be known.[90] The slaying must take place immediately, however,

---

87. Justinian, *Corpus Iuris Civilis: Novellae*, ed. R. Schoell (Berlin: Weidmann, 1912), p. 557.

88. *Burgundian Code*, p. 68.

89. Boutillier, *Somme rurale*, p. 275.

90. ". . . et s'il i vient seur la defense et li maris le puet trouver ou present forfet de sa fame, si commes s'il gisent ensemble, s'il avient qu'il l'ocie et lieve le cri par quoi la verités puist estre seue, il n'en pert ne vie ne membre par nostre coustume." ". . . and if he (the lover)

[55]

for the man who did not kill his adversary on the spot could later be prosecuted for murder (Beaumanoir 1: 934: 473). The difficulty, under medieval law, of establishing criminal guilt subsequent to the infraction itself accounts for the insistence upon immediate vengeance. Unless the slain bodies can be exhibited as proof of adultery, the crime reverts to an ordinary case of alleged wrongdoing, for which the injured party must follow the prescribed procedure—accusation and battle—in order to obtain redress. The cuckhold husband has, in this instance, relinquished the right to private vengeance and must bring the matter to court if he wishes to pursue it beyond the bedroom. The author of the *Assizes des Bourgeois* goes even further: a man who captures his wife and her lover in *flagrante delicto* is obliged to kill them both at the time of his discovery.[91] Hesitation or separate slayings can lead, again, to indictment for murder.

The public procedure governing homicide in *flagrante delicto* is relatively simple, certainly less complicated than full-scale trial by battle. As long as the original violation has been observed by a number of witnesses, the husband who has raised the cry need only proceed to court in order to declare what has occurred. Acquittal is automatic. In the event that the injured party does not succeed in slaying or chooses not to slay the couple, the procedure of trial is also somewhat abbreviated.[92] The offender is either captured on the spot or pursued, as in the case of outlawry, by "hue and cry." Upon arrest, he is bound and brought before the court which has the power to condemn him upon the oath of those who have witnessed his capture.[93] In some instances the husband may even have the privilege

---

defies the prohibition and the husband can find him in *flagrante delicto* with his wife, as if they are lying together; if it happens that he kills him and raises the cry by which the truth may be known, he will lose neither life nor member according to our custom" (Beaumanoir 2: 1637: 337).

91. *Cour des Bourgeois*, p. 218.

92. A debate over the captured party's right to trial takes place in Béroul's *Roman de Tristan* following the entrapment of Tristan and the queen. The inhabitants of Marc's realm claim that the king should not execute his wife without due process (v. 884). Marc, however, is determined to avenge his shame immediately (v. 888). Dinas de Dinan later tries to convince him that it would not be appropriate to execute the couple without trial (v. 1097), but Marc persists (v. 1126).

93. "Mes il i a bien autre voie que de droit apel, car ains que l'apeaus soit fes, se cil qui veut acuser veut, il puet denoncier au juge que teus mesfès a esté fes a la veue et a la seue de tant de bonnes gens qu'il ne puet estre celés, et seur ce il en doit fere comme bons juges. Adonques li souverains en doit enquerre tout soit ce que la partie ne se vueille couchier en enqueste; et s'il trueve le mesfet notoire et apert, il le puet justicier selonc le mesfet, car male

of serving as the amateur executioner of the man who has seduced his wife, the assumption being that certain violations remain within the sphere of personal vengeance. Despite the appeal to public justice, the court delegates its power of punishment to the private party involved. Even today, killing an adulterous mate, a crime of passion, enjoys a special status analogous to momentary insanity; and in such cases the degree of criminal responsibility is necessarily attenuated.

Both outcomes of entrapment—capture followed by slaying, and capture followed by summary judgment—differ fundamentally from the normal procedure of the judicial duel. In the first place, cases in which the offender was apprehended in the act of transgression could be heard in the lower or *hundret* courts, whose jurisdiction would have otherwise precluded "Pleas of the Sword."[94] Complaints punishable by death or involving bloodshed were ordinarily reserved for the upper courts, whose cognizance covered what today would be considered a felony as opposed to a misdemeanor. Second, the law governing capture in the act encouraged the plaintiff to dispense with the formal rules of accusation, denial, wagers, and combat in order to take justice into his own hands. He retained the right, in this exceptional situation, to settle his quarrel without recourse to any but the most perfunctory public process. The defendant who was seized rather than slain in *flagrante delicto* was deprived of the right to defend himself through the regular procedure of denial and battle. Finally, the judge in cases of capture had the power to make the kind of cognitive decisions which, however limited, were nonetheless foreign to his purely supervisory role within the *judicium Dei*. Relying upon his capacity to make rational distinctions and positive

---

chose seroit, se l'en avoit ocis mon prochien parent en pleine feste ou devant grant plenté de bonne gent, s'il convenoit que je me combatisse pour le vengement pourchacier; et pour ce puet on en teus cas qui sont apert aler avant par voie de denonciacion." "But there is a different way than that of lawful accusation, for before the accusation is made, if he who would accuse wishes, he can denounce to the judge such a crime done in the sight and the knowing of so many good people that it cannot be hidden, and concerning which he should act as a good judge. Then the sovereign should order an inquiry, even though the party may not want to turn his compliant into an inquest; and if the judge finds the crime clear and evident, he can render justice according to the crime; for it would be a bad thing, if someone had killed a close relative of mine in the middle of a festival or in front of a large number of people, if I had to fight him to obtain vengeance; and for this reason in cases which are overt one can proceed by means of denunciation" (Beaumanoir 2: 1710: 375).

94. Bloch, *Feudal Society*, 2: 364.

identifications of fact, he alone determined the accuracy of testimony, assessed relevant evidence—stolen goods in the case of theft, wounds in the case of rape—and condemned the guilty party when warranted, all without the obvious advantages to the accused of the chance to defend himself through trial by battle. The entrapment in *flagrante delicto* remained one of the few cases under feudal law in which the judge, acting upon the claim of a single party, was able to proceed with the hearing and to initiate an inquiry of his own accord, owing, as Beaumanoir is careful to emphasize, to the clear and evident nature of the offense—*mesfet notoire et aperte.*

The extraordinary procedure governing capture in the act is noteworthy in yet another respect. Through it the law formally sanctioned what in any other context was defined as murder. Treacherous killing, slaying without challenge or warning, without open quarrel or equality in the means of confrontation, constituted, under any other circumstance, an unemendable crime punishable by death. In fact, the slaughter of an adulterous couple in bed corresponds both literally and figuratively to Saint Louis' basic prescription for treacherous homicide (see above p. 36): *Murtres si est d'ome ou de fame quant l'en la tue en son lit ou en aucune meniere, por coi ce ne soit en mellée* (*Etablissements* 1: 238). For Louis the *lieu parfait* of willful murder, the bed, automatically implies premeditation on the part of the murderer and therefore excludes the possibility of justifiable manslaughter. Where entrapment is feasible, however, the law does not apply. A man seized in the act of serious offense was considered to be outside of the law at the time of infraction and, like the outlaw, was not entitled to the customary protection against surprise attack. Significantly, both the manhunt by "hue and cry" and the entrapment in *flagrante delicto* circumvent the normal mandatory vendetta carried out by the murder victim's family against the guilty party. It was assumed that the openness of the crime justified its unusual punishment and that resolution of a dispute in this manner was the equivalent of public trial, the point beyond which retribution for harm inflicted was no longer permitted. Through the procedure for entrapment the law not only allowed the ambush of one's enemy, but encouraged it.

If slaying in the act commands a privileged position next to the almost universal interdiction against secret or devious homicide, it is because, in this case, guilt can be established beyond a shadow of doubt. Blame is so apparent that custom deems even the layman capable of judging its presence and of inflicting the appropriate penalty. Trial seems, in contrast, a risky affair. Compared to the *judicium Dei* in which the guilty party enjoys in practice—though not in theory—an equal chance of winning the encounter, entrapment is foolproof; the man caught red-handed is guilty by definition; blame can be attributed to its agent independently of the need for subsequent validation. From the immediate and concrete proof of capture stems a necessary correlation between the sureness of punishment and the certainty of infraction. Possessed of a degree of truthfulness unmatched by the duel, entrapment represents the only category under feudal law in which justice and truth are even remotely allied. At the very least, chance and error have been minimized, because of the unequal confrontation between an unarmed (and sometimes undressed) offender and his well-prepared accuser. Through the *prise de mainour*, custom tips the scales of justice in such a manner that the injured party enjoys an immense physical advantage over the party that injures him. In addition, the attempt to seize a wrongdoer in the course of wrongdoing betrays a feeble, but nonetheless palpable, effort to verify empirically the facts surrounding infraction and to preserve them. The *cri de haro* following every entrapment, successful or not, is aimed at prolonging the act beyond its actual duration in order to affirm publicly its occurrence. The testimony of witnesses which is then delivered to the court is again oriented toward confirmation of the deed itself, its preservation in the memory of those who have seized the culprit and, with him, the truth of the crime.

Within a feudal accusatory system entrapment in *flagrante delicto* represents the chief method of verifying suspected criminal offense: *de prendre toutes manieres de maufeteurs ou de soupeçoneus de cas de crime.*[95] Since the judge cannot accuse on his own and since the plaintiff must wait until an infraction has actually taken place before lodging an *apel*, the attempt to set the stage for and to lure the criminal into purposeful wrongdoing was an important prosecutory mechanism of the feudal court. Its use in *La Mort Artu* constitutes the second judicial test of the Arthurian realm.

When Arthur learns of the secret meetings between Lancelot and the queen following Guinevere's trial, he asks Agravains, his informant, to arrange an entrapment so that vengeance can occur (110). Agravains

95. Of capturing wrongdoers or others suspected of crime (Beaumanoir 2: 1571: 295).

proposes a plan similar to that carried out by the dwarf Frocin in the capture of Tristan and Iseult (Béroul v. 643): Arthur and his court will leave Camelot under the pretense of hunting in a nearby forest. Once the knights have departed, it is assumed that Lancelot will rush to the queen's side where Agravains's men, lying in wait, can seize him.

The trap set for Lancelot succeeds up to a point. As soon as Arthur has left, Lancelot does come to his mistress's bedroom. Unfortunately for Agravains, however, the intended victim also takes the precaution of locking the door behind him; the lovers therefore have time to dress and to prepare for attack when their would-be captors enter the room.[96] Lancelot manages to kill his first assailant, a knight named Tanaguins, then dons the dead man's armour in order to greet the others. Seeing him arrayed for a full-fledged fight, they flee. Lancelot returns to the hostel where he is lodged, consults Hector, then leaves Camelot in order to wait for the queen's condemnation as well as the proper moment for her rescue.

Guinevere has, in the meantime, been taken prisoner and Arthur informed of the couple's guilt. Under his right as judge, but not as husband, he condemns the queen and requests that the barons determine the manner of death. They, in turn, order a shameful execution—*par droit qu'ele en devroit morir a honte*—in anticipation of which Arthur commands a fire to be built outside of the city walls. Gawain is the only dissenter, evoking the image of war without end between Lancelot and the king if Guinevere perishes at her husband's hands. Despite his nephew's protest, renunciation of fealty, and abrupt departure from court, Arthur persists in appointing a force of eighty knights to conduct his wife to the stake. In course of the melee which follows, Lancelot's men kill all but three of the escorts, including Gawain's three brothers, Gaheriet, Guerrehet, and Agravains. Their deaths, ironically, mark the beginning of the war between Lancelot and Gawain that fulfills the latter's prediction of endless conflict between the lineages of Arthur and Ban.

As is evident, the entrapment engineered by Agravains falls short of its primary goal, which is the seizure of the guilty parties and their automatic conviction based on the fact of their presence together in Guinevere's bedroom. By affording Lancelot sufficient time to dress and arm himself, the locked door foils the attempt at surprise. When the door is finally opened, the potential victim defeats his would-be captors, killing one

---

96. The outcome of Agravains's scheme must not have been uncommon, since Beaumanoir provides specifically for "the difficulty of trapping lovers lying together" (1: 934: 473).

and dispersing the rest. What should have been a foolproof method of criminal prosecution thus becomes a dangerous procedure that is also inefficient. Applied to a man of superior force, like Lancelot, entrapment fails ignominiously. Physical struggle is still required; and a powerful lover can sometimes overcome a less potent husband even though the latter stands, theoretically, in the right. The success of the technique depends, moreover, upon unpredictable variables, a quirk of fate like Lancelot's precautionary bolting of the bedroom door. With it, the legalized imbalance between husband and lover ceases to exist. And in spite of the openness of intentional misdeed—for Lancelot chooses to go to the queen despite Boort's warnings—the feudal practice of capture in the act is no more effective than the judicial duel.

The breakdown of entrapment becomes doubly significant through the irony that it engenders. The episode revolves around a paradox of intention and consequence that lends an air of tragic pessimism to what has been, up until this point, melodramatic farce. In framing the lovers, those who try the hardest to prevent any possible mishap resulting from discovery and seizure are the very ones drawn, despite their caution, into personal engagement. Those who resist the project at the outset become its unwilling victims. Once Agravains's plot has been accepted, Gaheriet attempts to avoid trouble by inviting Lancelot to spend the day with him, hoping to keep him from the queen. He all but reveals the nature of the danger (*La Mort* 113). After the abortive trap Gaheriet protests the execution of Guinevere, again expressing personal indifference to the whole affair:

Ore, Agravain, fet Gaheriet, cuidiez vos que g'i soie venuz por moi mesler a Lancelot, se il vouloit la reïne rescorre? Or sachiez bien que ja ne me mellerai a lui; einz voudroie ge mielz qu'il la tenist toz les jorz de sa vie einz que ele moreust issi.

Now, Agravains, said Gaheriet, do you think I have come to fight with Lancelot, if he wants to save the queen? Now understand that I will not fight with him; I would rather he kept her for the rest of his life than that she should die thus.

(*La Mort* 123)

Gaheriet's lack of interest in punishing adultery emphasizes the futility of his death in the melee which follows. Gawain's obligation to avenge a reluctant Gaheriet adds pathos to the irony of his brother's destruction. He too opposes the plan of entrapment, predicts grave consequences if it is carried out, and resists the queen's condemnation before accepting the eventual necessity of retribution. Lancelot's closest ally in the effort to keep the adultery hidden from Arthur thus becomes his most vehement enemy because of the death of a man who, by his own admission, could not care less about the issue at stake. Willing to lie to uncle and lord in order to protect his friend, Gawain finds himself unsuspectingly pulled by forces beyond his control into the blood-feud which he has, with full consciousness, tried to avoid.

Gaheriet's and Gawain's fear of confrontation between Lancelot and Arthur is surpassed by the conflict between Lancelot and Gawain, an encounter originating in the attempted capture in *flagrante delicto*. Jean Frappier has attributed Gawain's unavoidable entrance into the closed cycle of vendetta to "deaf Fate": *la marche sourde du Destin qui mène tout un lot de victimes prises dans l'engrenage des passions et des événements.*[97] One might well ask, however, if Gawain's role in avenging his brothers is the product of personal nemesis, as Frappier suggests, or if fate does not, more likely, work at the level of institutions. Ultimately, it is the fate of feudal justice and of the feudal world that depends upon the abortive *prise de mainour*. The war between families is not a result of fated passion or the discovery of adultery, but the direct consequence of an outmoded procedure of entrapment, summary trial, and execution. Irony, and not destiny, stands between Gawain's desire for clemency and the events that overtake him. The dramatic tension that it produces reveals a crisis, again grounded in the epistemology of feudal justice, which seals the fate of Arthur's realm. For while the knights of Logres are capable of discovering the truth of adultery, capable even of proving suspected guilt, the legal system at their disposal has no means of assimilating the notion of judicial truth or of enforcing the prescribed penalty for infraction. Under the trial by combat the rapport between justice and truth is haphazard; sometimes the outcome of trail is allied with the facts, as in Guinevere's acquittal; elsewhere, as in Lancelot's victory over Gawain, they bear no necessary relation. With entrapment, the alliance of justice and truth, though theoretically possible, becomes meaningless because of the ineffectiveness and danger of prosecution. Those charged with the implementation of justice—Lancelot's captors and Guinevere's executioners—continue to risk as much as the guilty party caught in the act or the prisoner sentenced by the court to die. Justice still represents a physical contest not wholly divorced from the ordeal of battle in which might, rather than truth, as often as not makes right.

97. Frappier, *Etude*, p. 246; see also p. 277.

CHAPTER II

Warfare in the Feudal Epic Cycle

The judicial duel represented the means by which a plaintiff might bring his claim to court, settling it according to prescribed procedure before the community as a whole. Entrapment, on the other hand, constituted a semipublic method of prosecution in which the court, under special circumstances, delegated the power of proof and punishment to private individuals. While the husband who had been wronged might decide where right lay, he still had to observe the precepts governing capture in order to escape subsequent indictment for murder. He was obliged either to declare the deed to the judge as a matter of routine or to deliver the guilty party to the appropriate tribunal.

Neither public trial by combat nor semipublic condemnation by capture was aimed at justice as we conceive of it today. They were not directed toward the preservation of regularized social order through the punishment of infringements of the law or infractions against the commonweal. The justice of the duel functioned laterally between men of roughly equal social status and power—warrior aristocrats, potential enemies—in order to prevent more extended military encounter. Where war was inevitable the duel served to contain prolonged campaigns of vengeance between rival family clans.[1] Implicity, the *judicium Dei* fostered the physical survival of the community by providing an alternative to the blood feud. As an antidote to unlimited violence, trial by battle

---

1. Y. Bongert, *Recherches sur les cours laïques du Xe au XIIIe siècle* (Paris: Picard, 1948), pp. 211–213; R. Girard, *La Violence et le sacré* (Paris: Grasset, 1972), chapt. 1.

contributed only indirectly, however, to the maintenance of any broader notion of public polity. Under an immanent mode of proof the judicial process does not represent a contest by which the state affirms its sovereignty. On the contrary, combat was most frequently used to resolve conflicts between nobles—that is to say, in cases where sovereignty was either nonexistent or contested. The procedure was rarely employed in disputes between *vilains* or between vassal and lord, in cases where sovereignty was taken for granted. Yet it is precisely in the latter situation that infractions against public order were most effectively punished. The lord's *voyer* or provost was both chief administrative representative and police officer within the seigneurial city or domain. Charged with the repression of crime among its inhabitants, he could accuse of his own accord, force conciliation between parties, or judge unilaterally those under his jurisdiction.[2] Trial and capture served, on the other hand, to limit and regularize the vendettas of those who had the power to make war. They were based upon the idea of retribution for injury inflicted rather than penal correction. In his claim against Lancelot, Mador does not insist upon the danger to society of unpunished criminal behavior or the need for rehabilitation of known offenders, but upon the necessity of retaliation (*La Mort* 84). For Arthur the desire to punish Lancelot is in no way linked to the repression of illicit love affairs. The king seeks, simply, to avenge his honor, besmirched by public knowledge of the couple's sin; and he is willing to risk death to achieve it: *mielz vieut il mourir que sa honte ne soit vengiee devant lui.*[3]

Wars, Large and Small

A persistent fact of life in the Middle Ages, vengeance carried out independently by private individuals did not necessarily involve either public or semipublic legal process. An injured party had, at least in theory, the choice of bringing his grievance to court, with the result of a

---

2. L. Halphen, "Les Institutions judiciaires en France au XIe siècle: région angevine," *Revue Historique* 77 (1901): 279–307.

3. He would rather die than that his shame not be avenged before him (*La Mort* 111); Béroul's King Marc finds himself in an analogous situation before the sleeping lovers of Morrois Forest, and he expresses the necessity of vengeance in similar terms:

De la cité s'en est issuz	He left the city
Et dist mex veut estre penduz	Saying that he would rather be hanged
Qu'il ne prenge de ceus vengance	Than not to take vengeance
Que li ont fait tel avilance.	Upon those who had so wronged him.

(Béroul v. 1953)

judicial duel, or of settling the matter himself through vendetta and private war. Recourse to arms was, in the absence of any more reliable means of prosecution, the most efficient means of obtaining redress. The difficulties of trial were, up until the thirteenth century, often insurmountable.[4] When conflicting parties had agreed to seek an accord, they had to agree upon a mediator acceptable to both. The problem of choice was further compounded by the extreme complexity of conflicting jurisdictions and by the lack of fixed tribunals to hear ordinary pleas. In essence, a new court had to be constituted in terms of membership, location, and assignation for each individual case. Because of the added delays of adjournment and verification where witnesses were to be called and evidence examined, the feudal court functioned slowly; and the alternative to trial often appeared crudely efficacious. Even where no problem of jurisdiction arose, the lord who exercised justice within any given territory might be reluctant or powerless to take on a particular cause. The high incidence of *dénis de justice*, refusals to hear a plea, attests to the precariousness of seigneurial justice throughout the feudal period. Asked by the monks of Saint Florent to prosecute their legitimate claim against a certain Aubry, Foulque le Réchin replied that the culprit was "now old and decrepit, that he had served him in the past and that he (Foulque) did not want to disturb him."[5] When the nuns of Ronceray tried to prosecute Hugue de Juvardeil for having attacked the abbey and killing one of the Bishop of Anger's men, they were told to take their complaint to the defendant's own tribunal![6] Once the feudal judge —ecclesiastical or secular—had consented to hear a given case there still remained the task of forcing the accused to appear on the day set for trial. Once trial had begun there was the problem of encouraging witnesses to testify, since testimony was strictly voluntary in secular courts as late as Beaumanoir's time.[7] Finally, once a verdict had been rendered, there was the problem of forcing the condemned party to comply with the ruling. Threat of excommunication and moral suasion were often the only arms by which the feudal court could enforce its decision.

4. Bongert, *Recherches*, pp. 38, 57; G. Duby, *La Société aux XIe et XIIe siècles dans la region mâconnaise* (Paris: Armand-Colin, 1953), p. 202.

5. Cited Halphen, "Institutions judiciares," p. 298.

6. *Idem*.

7. "Nus n'est tenus a tesmoignier pour autrui en cas ou il puet avoir apel, ne n'en doit estre contrains par nule justice, s'il ne li plest." "No one is obliged to testify for another in cases that can lead to judgment, nor should he be forced to do so if it does not please him" (Beaumanoir 2: 1766: 395).

The lack of effective judicial control over those who preferred vengeance to justice was, from the tenth to the twelfth centuries, almost universal. For the feudal warrior aristocracy private war constituted a standard method of resolving disputes when no more peaceful accord could be reached. In addition to its economic importance, military venture represented a legitimate means of preserving right.[8] Whereas recourse to legal process gradually became a learned response with the waning of the feudal age, vengeance remained an instinct.[9] In the period between Charlemagne's efforts to curb private military campaigns and their suppression in the twelfth through the fourteenth centuries, war could, theoretically, be declared any time with or without warning or reason. The king himself engaged in a number of private quarrels, the excuse of military intervention serving in many regions as the first indication of renascent monarchic presence. Louis VII and Philippe-Auguste's three expeditions into Burgundy in the second half of the twelfth century show a growing willingness, despite opposition to any but royal war, to become involved in essentially private fights, to become a party to disputes originally affecting monarchy only indirectly. Beaumanoir acknowledges the legitimacy of private war for those of noble birth. While ordinary men were obliged to submit their quarrels to public judgment "according to the crime," noblemen alone retained the right to settle their differences by force (Beaumanoir 2: 1671: 356). Provided that war had been openly declared, that both parties were willing to fight, and that they had agreed to wait forty days in order to notify members of the family not present at the formal declaration of hostilities, armed conflict was as legal as trial.

As a response to the dissolution of the Carolingian Empire and the disappearance of what must have seemed, in retrospect, an efficient machine of state, war represented the principal cause and the sustaining goal of feudal organization. With the collapse of a centralized political systems capable of providing protection against outside attack, the retreat into smaller local political groups oriented almost exclusively around the problem of defense represented the only means of resisting invasion

8. For a discussion of the economic importance of war during the feudal period see G. Duby, *Guerriers et paysans au moyen âge* (Paris: Gallimard, 1973).

9. "Au XIe siècle lorsqu'un chevalier subit un dommage, son premier geste est de tirer vengeance (*vindicta*) de son agresseur; contre lui il conduit la faide jusqu'à ce que le préjudice soit réparé" (Duby, *Société mâconnaise*, p. 201).

during the period following Charlemagne's death.[10] Although the effort to repel the second wave of invasions—Hungarians from the East, Arabs from the South, and Scandinavians from the North—was not always successful, the attempt to establish an effective bulwark against destruction constituted the chief *raison d'être* of the feudal knight-warrior caste.

Large personal armies at the command of private individuals offered at least a temporary safeguard against annihilation from without. Problems arose, however, with respect to the limits of self-defense: as a deterrent to attack, the power to make war was frequently directed not against a foreign invader, but against a neighboring or rival chief. The limits of political sovereignty coincided with the limits of combative strength; statehood was predicated along lines of military might, a factor of great importance to the legal organization of the post-Carolingian state. With the dismemberment of Empire the centralized court system developed under Charlemagne perished as well. In the absence of any operative civil judiciary, the control of armed force was tantamount to judicial control. Only the man who was strong enough to purchase and maintain arms possessed the wherewithal to govern. The regular army at his disposal represented a potent means of resolving disputes with his peers. Alongside the regularized jurisdiction of the Arthurian-feudal court, where the king's vassals could seek redress by battle or composition according to custom, there stood the personal justice of Arthur's army, subject almost entirely to the will of its commander.

Unlike the ideological wars—the crusades—that both accompanied and affirmed the resurgence of the national state, the feudal vendetta was a pragmatic undertaking. Its sole justification was a prior injury or offense. Sanctioned in Roman Gaul in cases of murder, rape, adultery, or theft, the blood vengeance implied a solidarity of family lineage rivaled only by the lord-vassal tie. The Germanic *faida* functioned under the assumption that harm done to any member of the immediate kin group or the extended family, the *maisnie*, represented an affront to the group as a whole. As such, it required a collective effort at retribution. Both maternal and paternal lines were obliged to participate in the vendetta that became a sacred right, "a duty to be pursued beyond the grave."[11] The author of the Old French *Gui de Bourgogne* equates a son's vengeance with pious

10. M. Bloch, *Feudal Society* (Chicago: University of Chicago Press, 1966), 2: 356–357.
11. *Ibid.*, 1: 125; F. Lot and R. Fawtier, *Les Institutions françaises du moyen âge* (Paris: Presses Universitaires de France, 1958), 2: 422.

donation; together they insure the salvation of the dead man's soul.[12] In *Raoul de Cambrai*, Bernier's whole lineage is responsible for Raoul's death; Guerri vows to reject all offers of peace until he has vindicated his nephew.[13] Kriemhild waits for seventeen years to avenge her husband's slaying in the *Nibelungenlied*. The Old French epic bears witness to the solidarity of family allegiance—sons of Aymon, Girart de Roussillon's clan, Cambresis, Vermandois, Lorrains, and Burgundians—which, as late as the fourteenth century, caused Philip the Fair to complain to Clement V of the "insidious custom of the realm by which noblemen can make war, drawing both relatives and friends into the fray."[14] A similar loyalty to the extended clan is evident in the historical blood feuds of which we have some written record: those, for example, between the Giroy and Talvas families of Normandy, between the counts of Foix and Armagnac, and amongst the eleventh-century Burgundian aristocracy.

As a deterrent to infraction, the *faida* relied upon the *a priori* fear of reprisal rather than the *a posteriori* punishment of wrongdoing for the repression of offense. Through it each knight became party to a limited but stringent mutual defense pact. The medieval blood feud, like the *lex talionis* of Old Testament justice, implied absolute reciprocity of retribution: each act of violence necessitated an equal and opposite response. It did not so much serve to end a dispute as to insure the process of retaliation. The knight who avenged the death of a "friend by blood," however distant the paternity, was himself insured of vengeance should the same fate befall him.[15] Nor, according to custom, was it always necessary to kill the perpetrator of the original deed. Guilt, like ven-

---

12. *Gui de Bourgogne*, ed. F. Guessard and H. Michelant (Paris: P. Jannet, 1859), p. 2.
13. "Biax niés dist il, "por vos grant dolor ai.

"Qi vos a mort jamais ne l'amerai,
"Pais ne acorde ne trives n'en prendra
"Desq'a cele eure qe toz morz les arai:
"Pendus a forches toz les essillerai.

"Good nephew," he said, "for you I feel great pain.
I will never love those who killed you,
A truce or accord I will not accept
Until that hour when I will have killed them:
Hanged on the forks, they will be vanquished.

(*Raoul* v. 3168)

14. Cited G. Ducoudray, *Origines du parlement de Paris et la justice au XIIIᵉ et XIVᵉ siècles* (Paris: Hachette, 1902), p. 342.

15. It is not until the thirteenth century that jurists began to talk of restricting the degrees of paternity of those obligated by vendetta; (see below p. 113).

geance, functioned collectively. The clan or *comitatus* was responsible for the infractions of its own members as well as for avenging wrong inflicted upon it from without.[16] Pecuniary reparation or composition was paid by the whole group when one of their number was at fault; and it was divided appropriately when they had been wronged.[17] Ganelon's thirty relatives rise to his defense at the end of *Roland* and are condemned as a unit after his conviction. More than a century after the poem's composition, the Senechal of Normandy felt compelled to prohibit his agents from executing a criminal's kin along with the felon.[18] Even after the duke's court had decided to pardon a murderer, it first had to obtain the permission of the victim's family: *Li dus ne puet fere pes d'omecide envers celui qui l'a fet, se il n'est avant reconciliez as amis a celi qu'il ocist.*[19] Pressure brought to bear by relatives and friends was, in many instances, the only way of forcing a guilty party to court and of guaranteeing the court's decision. Conversely, an accord between warring individuals often specifically promised compliance of the entire family group. Even where peace was contracted by the head of the clan, the lineage as a whole assured its maintenance. When the Dame de Brancion agreed, in the early thirteenth century, to terminate her quarrel with the church and bourgeois of Cluny, she pledged peace in her own name—*in propria persona juravit*—as well as that of all her relatives.[20] At a time at which it was impossible to distinguish national wars from regional conflicts setting counties, duchies, baronies, and even monasteries against each other, the appeal of arms remained a local clannish affair in which vengeance was considered a right, and combat the law of the land.

One such cycle of vengeance and private war shapes the second half of

16. Bloch, *Feudal Society*, 1: 125; Lot and Fawtier, *Institutions*, 2: 426–431.

17. The *Lex Salica* contains the following entry under *De compositione homicidii*: "Si alicujus pater occissus fuerit, medietatem compositionis filii colligant, et aliam medietatem parentes qui proximiores fueriat, tam de paterna quam de materna generatione dividant." "If someone's father has been killed, the sons collect half the composition, and the other half is collected by close relatives, divided equally between maternal and paternal lines" (cited P. Dubois, *Les Asseurements au XIIIᵉ siècle* [Paris: Rousseau, 1900], p. 18).

18. "Li bailli le duc souloient prandre les paranz a aucun quant il avoit fet aucun mesfet. ... De ce dit li senechaus que nus n'em doit estre mis en painne fors li malfeteurs ou cil qui est par(c)eniers du mesfet." "The duke's bailiff used to arrest the relatives of the man who committed a crime. . . . But the Senechal says that no man should be held except the wrongdoer or his accomplice" (*TAC* 49).

19. The duke cannot make peace with a murderer until he has been reconciled with the relatives of the man he has killed (*TAC* 27).

20. Cited Dubois, *Asseurements*, p. 185; see also Bongert, *Recherches*, p. 54.

La Mort le roi Artu. Gawain, faced with the knowledge of his brothers' death, and Arthur, faced with proof of adultery, join in common retaliatory purpose against Lancelot. Two and a half months of siege and intermittent fighting before the castle of *La Joyeuse Garde* are ended by papal intervention. According to the peace worked out by the Archbishop of Rochester, Guinevere will return to Arthur in exchange for Lancelot's safe passage home and what he assumes to be peace. Gawain, however, understands the agreement differently. Obsessed by the necessity of retribution—*Biaus frere. . . . je sui cil qui plus ne quier vivre, fors tant sanz plus que ge vos aie vengié,* he insists upon pursuit of his brothers' slayer.[21] With Mordret in command at home, the Briton army embarks for France where another two months of siege produces frustration and defeat. On the way back to Logres Arthur learns of Mordret's usurpation of throne and queen; and it is in the attempt to avenge this betrayal that father and son slay each other. Lancelot, hearing in the meantime of the king's misfortune, returns to Logres for the final vendetta of the Arthurian age, that against the sons of Mordret who have seized the realm upon their father's death. At the conclusion of the carnage on Salisbury Plain, where a hundred thousand knights perish in a single day, little remains. Arthur's kingdom has been destroyed and the ranks of the Round Table decimated by an accelerated series of vendettas whose precise origin remains obscure.[22]

Epic Warfare

The world produced by Lancelot's slaying of Gawain's brothers and Gawain's obsession with revenge is a world at war with itself, a universe out of joint, in which those capable of preventing annihilation lack the will to do so and those who most seek peace find themselves overwhelmed by circumstance. In essence, the disunity of the Round Table, the alienation of its most esteemed members, and the *coup d'état* of Arthur's last few days point to a single source: feudalism turned upon itself in slavish obedience to its own most cherished ideals. In stepping back from the

21. Dear brother. . . . I am he who no longer wants to live, except that I may avenge you (*La Mort* 131).

22. Despite the obvious *terminus a quo* in Lancelot's attempt to rescue the queen, the origin of the hostility between Agravains and Lancelot, that which led to entrapment in the first place, is never really explained. For a discussion of the vendettas of *La Mort Artu* see my article entitled "The Death of King Arthur and the Waning of the Feudal Age," *Orbis Litterarum* 29 (1974): 291–305.

golden heritage of twelfth-century romance, the author of *La Mort* explores the inherent pitfalls of feudal institutions pushed to their natural limits: trial by battle in which an innocent plaintiff stands defeated, capture in *flagrante delicto* in which the captured overwhelms his opponents, and, most importantly, vendetta and war that cross the bounds of personal affinity and family loyalty to submerge an entire kingdom. The fate that hangs inexorably over the Arthurian world is that of violence itself. Once the closed circuit of reciprocal vendetta has been engaged, once the irreversible cycle of family wars has gained mastery over those who have the power of peace and war, catastrophe becomes inevitable. In fulfilment of Gawain's prophecy of everlasting war—*la guerre qui ja ne prendra fin*—vengeance within the Arthurian state is postulated at the level of all-out civil conflict. In this respect *La Mort Artu* belongs less to the tradition of courtly romance than to that of the feudal epic, where the internecine quarrels of rival barons or baronage against monarchy have replaced the moral imperative of foreign crusade. Its particular mixture of realistic and tragic elements—hubris, madness, the necessity of impossible choices between conflicting loyalties, betrayal, and anarchy—resemble more than superficially the chaotic universe of *Raoul de Cambrai*, *Les Quatre Filz Aymon*, *Girart de Roussillon*, or *La Chevalerie Ogier*.

Among the vernacular forms of the twelfth century, the epic best captures and expresses the military aspirations of the feudal warrior aristocracy. As its name suggests, the *chanson de geste*, a song of both deeds and of lineage, is designed to encourage feats of prowess, adherence to a well-defined code of knightly honor, and strict loyalty to the global warrior group. Within the universe of the Old French epic, heroic action is rewarded with riches, while treachery and cowardliness are punished with disgrace, exile, or death. Even its language, whose vocabulary, metrical forms, texture, and themes are superbly suited to the experience of war, serves to crystallize the ideals of the chivalric nobility. And yet the *chanson de geste* is, paradoxically, also the genre of war's decline, a chronicle of its decreasing effectiveness as a tool for the resolution of human conflict. The epic appeared in France at a time of crisis within the feudal aristocracy—at the very moment at which its power and prestige were threatened from above by the growing strength of monarchy and from below by the increased role of a bourgeoisie in the economic activity of northern urban centers. Within the earliest heroic poems—*Roland*, *La*

Chanson de Guillaume, Gormond et Isembard—the critical situation of the *de facto* nobility, whose ability to govern was indistinguishable from its right to rule by military force, manifests itself in terms of an emergent weariness of war along with an intensified awareness that military might, however great, can no longer guarantee victory. Even where victory occurs, it seems, often, pyrrhic: Charlemagne stands, at the end of *Roland*, in proud isolation, triumphant but separated by war and death from those whom he most loved. Guillaume d'Orange, in the oldest work of the cycle bearing his name, suffers a number of severe military setbacks and is only able to conquer the Saracen foe because of the cleverness and steadfastness of his wife Guiborc. Isembard, the renegade hero of France's earliest epic of revolt, recognizes the folly of war, pardons his slayers, and returns to the Christian fold before death.

It is within the late twelfth- and thirteenth-century epic cycle of the rebellious barons that the failure of war is most acutely felt and its horror most fully exploited. Within fifty years of the first *chanson de geste*, the military ethos of which it was the ideal literary expression yields tragedy and renewed violence in the place of victory and peace. Across the panoramic spectrum of the feudal epic, the personal dilemmas of those who fight, the inefficiency of the conventional means of terminating conflict, and the degraded character and dimensions of battle itself are the obvious symptoms of profound uneasiness at the center of the knightly ideal.

The degree of irony and paradox that war engenders far outweighs its physical risk. Time after time, pursuit of an external foe turns, in the long run, upon oneself; and the price of violence in every case exceeds the rewards of triumph. The cycle of the rebellious barons marks the rebirth in medieval Europe of a literary tradition in which the glorification of martial values is accompanied by a progressive intrusion of human realities upon the immediate and unreflective military response.[23] Compared to the universe of *La Chanson de Roland*, that of the late epic is one of agonizing psychological drama, a world of alienation closer in spirit to the *Odyssey* than to the *Iliad*. The theme of alienation is reflected in a growing discrepancy between the hero's consciousness and being, between his awareness of his own condition and that condition itself; through it, the epic poet like the author of *La Mort*, explores the paradoxical limits of the late feudal world. The Bernier of *Raoul de Cambrai* finds himself caught

23. W. C. Calin, *The Old French Epic of Revolt* (Geneva: Droz, 1961), p. 137.

between loyalty to his friend and lord, Raoul, and loyalty to his family. Raoul's murder of his mother causes him first to seek refuge at his father's side and then to commit the ultimate crime under feudal law: the slaying of one's seigneur. Despite his essential righteousness, his attempt to prevent confrontation, and his strict observance of judicial procedure, once combat becomes unavoidable, Bernier is forced to choose between irreconcilable courses of action. Neither, except under the most extreme circumstances, would have seemed acceptable.

The Turpin of *La Chevalerie Ogier* finds himself in the untenable position of having captured his own cousin and Charles's enemy, Ogier. He is obliged to decide between yielding a blood relative to what he assumes to be certain death and defying his lord's command. Nor is Charlemagne himself immune from the dilemmas which plague his vassals. When the pagan King Braihier invades and ravages his lands, the only knight capable of stopping the devastation is Ogier, whom the emperor has condemned to prison; and Ogier demands, as a prerequisite for fighting, the death of Charles's son Charlot (*Chevalerie Ogier* v. 10,367). Charles Martel discovers, in *Girart de Roussillon*, that he must alienate his vassal Girart's fief, cede it to him as an allod, in order to marry a woman, Elissent, who not only loves Girart, but has been promised to him in marriage. The attempt to resolve the dilemma of sexual and political inclination becomes the motivating force of prolonged conflict. Girart, in turn, becomes hopelessly enmeshed in the archetypal courtly situation of loving the wife of his lord.

Les Quatre Filz Aymon abounds in the tragic irony of impossible choices. Aymon himself must decide between true and fictive paternity, blood relation and homage, in the struggle of his sons against Charles (*Quatre Filz* v. 2967). Ironically, Aymon elects to fight his sons only to have Charles turn against him. Caught in the tragic position of starving them at the siege of Montauban, a wizened and broken father utilizes the siege machines to catapult supplies to his hungry sons. For Aymon the price of war is madness. Both Yon and Ogier are torn between fidelity to lord and sovereign, on the one hand, and parentage on the other: Renaud is Yon's brother-in-law and liege vassal, Ogier his cousin. Having saved Renaud's life, Ogier finds himself trapped between his subsequent rejection and Charles's accusation of treason. The cousins eventually meet in single combat. Renaud's own dilemma resembles that of Lancelot in *La Mort le roi Artu*. Like the knight from France, he has played a major role in the consolidation of his lord's power before becoming his foe. And like

Lancelot, he remains capable of victory but refuses it. Renaud pardons his enemy in the attempt to restore peace, to return to an ideal sense of order prior to the outbreak of hostilities. Aware of the preeminence of a transcendent notion of state sovereignty as opposed to the more limited sovereignty of lineage, he is quick to offer magnanimous compromise. Renaud to Roland:

> Ja sui de vo geste et de vo parenté
> Se le volies dire de povre bacheler.
> Je devendrai vos hom et plevis et jurés
> Et Aallars mes freres et Guichars autretel,
> Et Richars tous li mendres, se vos le comendes.
> Montauban vos donrai environ et en lés
> Et Baiart mon cheval que j'ai ci amené,
> Si nos faites au roi paier et acorder.

> I will always be of your family and your kin,
> If you choose to say it of a poor young knight,
> I will become your man, pledged and sworn
> And Aallars my brother and Guichars as well
> And Richard at the least, if you command it,
> I will give you Montauban and the lands around it
> And my horse Baiart which I have brought here,
> If you reconcile us and make peace with the king.
> *(Quatre Filz* v. 8934)

A good example of collective judicial resolution, Renaud's offer of peace, and of his and his three brothers' homage, is aimed at cutting short the cycle of mandatory vendetta. He clearly shows himself willing to place the common social good above both personal and clannish interest.

Renaud's proposal and Roland's refusal emphasize the difficulty of terminating a war of vengeance once it has begun. The question of how to stop a fight was of great concern not only to those involved in historical struggles, but to the poet as well. One of the central themes of the rebel barons cycle is, in fact, the ineffectiveness of the conventional means—duel, expiatory pilgrimage, and homage—of ending a dispute already in progress.

The Means to Peace

Among epic authors a predeliction for the combat of enemy chiefs—Charlemagne and Baligant, Louis and Gormont—is surpassed only by the obsession with formal judicial combat, the method of clôture, *par excel-*

lence. Unable to persuade Roland to renounce war, Renaud urges battle. He hopes, as a last resort, to substitute the confrontation of two individuals for the clash of entire armies and thus to avoid "the death of so many armed knights and the destruction of so much rich land" (*Quatre Filz* v. 8969). Similarly, Gautier proposes to end the blood feud between the relatives of Herman de Vermandois and those of Raoul de Cambrai by fighting Bernier (*Raoul* v. 4259). Charlemagne agrees, at the beginning of *La Chevalerie Ogier*, to conclude the campaign against the Saracens according to the outcome of Ogier's struggle against Karaeus. Routed by Charles Martel at Roussillon, Girart offers judgment by battle at Vaubeton. And Charles, having lost this first encounter, later threatens to seize Girart's fief unless he will meet him in single combat.

Significantly, the duels of the feudal epic cycle are even less conclusive than those of *La Mort Artu*. The symbolic confrontation of individuals fails to achieve what war cannot guarantee: victory and, ultimately, peace. Further violence—skirmishes, ambush, siege, and pitched battles —follow Renaud's meeting with Roland. The witnesses, whose presence on the sidelines was intended to assure the fairness of Gautier's quarrel with Bernier, themselves enter the fray: Guerri kills Aliaumes in a less formal match. A second battle between the original opponents becomes so fierce that King Louis intervenes; and while recuperating in adjoining beds, the wounded opponents again come to blows. Violence erupts between the two messengers whose duty it is to arrange Charles Martel's meeting with Girart. Furious at his vassal's counter-challenge, the king assembles his armies and attacks at Mont-Amele. He flatly rejects a subsequent offer of battle, pursuing Girart at Civaux. In the five years of war which follow neither leader encounters his enemy head-on. Ogier's duel with Karaeus not only fails to prevent full-scale combat, but leads, through Charlot's offer to fight in Ogier's place and the Dane's derisive rejection, to Baldwin's death and thirty years of hostility between French and Danish forces.

According to Frankish custom, harm inflicted upon another could be rectified by an act of homage as well as monetary compensation. With the consent of his enemy a convicted felon might, like Renaud, submit both himself and his family to the victim or his kin. When the steward of the monastery of Saint Denis ended a disagreement with the Lord of Montmorency in 1208, twenty-nine of his kinsmen pledged fealty along with the guilty party. In 1134 two hundred and forty relatives, accomplices, and vassals of the murderer of the sub-dean of Orléans offered themselves to the family of the dead man.[24] The *Livre Roisin* contains the following formula for homage contracted subsequent to the conclusion of a peace:

> Chou sont les parolles que on doit dire a faire les hommages quant on fait les pais; chi devenes-vous hom a chest hom qui chi est. . . . que vous foit et loialté le porteres desore en avant.

> These are the words which one must speak in order to contract homage when one makes peace; that you become the man of this man who is here. . . . that you promise him faith and loyalty from this time forth.[25]

Expiatory crusade, pilgrimage, and other acts of piety represented increasingly common means of averting or containing blood feuds in the postfeudal era. Ratification of a peace treaty was often accompanied by gestures of contrition as well as composition. Historically, the expiatory pilgrimage can be traced to the Roman penalty of banishment, the *aquae et ignis interdictio* or perpetual exile outside of Italy.[26] Its popularity during the Middle Ages is, however, more likely a function of the importance of pilgrimage in canonical procedure. Ecclesiastical courts traditionally used exile or banishment for the punishment of moral offense. In 1059 Peter Damiani, acting as papal legate, imposed pilgrimages to Rome and Tours upon the simoniacal priests of Milan. An 1186 edict of Frederick Barbarossa left the choice of specific penitential sites to the discretion of the bishop. Expiatory pilgrimage was a standard penalty for heresy at the time of the southern Inquisition. The Synod of Narbonne, for instance, prescribed voyages within the *limina sanctorum* instead of to more distant shrines for heretics who "tell the truth about themselves and others."[27]

In the communal law of northern France, Flanders, and Belgium pilgrimages represented both a means of reparation—to the town and to the victim—and a method of concluding truces. A successor to the indeterminate banishment of outlawry, it was applied to a wide range of religious, civil, and criminal offenses: sorcery, blasphemy, and heresy, infractions of the public peace, counterfeiting and vagrancy, homicide, adultery, rape, and theft. Under the supervision of the local *échevins* and

---

24. Bloch, *Feudal Society*, 1: 130.

25. Cited Dubois, *Asseurements*, p. 222.

26. *Ibid.*, pp. 211–213; S. Lear, *Treason and Related Offenses in Roman and Germanic Law* (Houston: Rice Institute, 1955), p. 28.

27. E. Van Cauwenbergh, *Les Pèlerinages expiatoires et juridiques dans le droit communal de la Belgique au moyen âge* (Louvain: University of Louvain, 1922), pp. 9, 15.

a special tribunal of peacemakers (*paiseurs*), the pilgrim, unarmed except for letters of safe-conduct, departed for a prescribed duration; he was not allowed to return until he had reached his destination and could verify this fact with letters obtained from the Hospital or Temple.[28]

The *Très Ancien Coutumier* prescribes a lifetime of religious service for the nobleman who slays and is then willing to withdraw from secular life (*TAC* 28). The practice of reparation through pious offering—building of monasteries or chapels, donations of land, money, or work—was popular under the late Capetians, particularly during the reign of Saint Louis. Even before the general prohibition of private war, Louis tried to prevent extended vendettas through the imposition of a royal *paix à parties*. Having been convicted under due process, a guilty party could, more often than not, obtain remission upon completion of a reverent journey or other devout undertaking.[29]

Within the feudal epic cycle promises of pilgrimage or homage are no more expedient means of ending war than the judicial duel. More often than not the offer to perform them is rejected. Roland, intent upon battle, declines Renaud's proposal of homage, exile, and pilgrimage (*Quatre Filz* v. 8945).[30] Geurri summarily dismisses Bernier's unilateral bid for repentance following Raoul's death (*Raoul* v. 3427). Bernier's subsequent willingness to become Gautier's commended man—*Vostre hom serai, de vos tenrai mes fiés*—does not prevent their armed encounter; nor does its repetition as both men lie wounded—*Quite te claim ma terre e mon païs*—elicit a more favorable reply.[31] Charlot's offer of pilgrimage and homage to atone for the death of Ogier's son Baldwin is three times proffered and three times rebuffed (*Chevalier Ogier* vv. 8684, 8748, 10,415).

Where the expiatory remission is agreed upon as an alternative to war, it is often ineffective. The peace concluded between Charlemagne and Beuves d'Aigremont, who submits to homage and exile in the case of Lohier's death, is broken when Foulque de Morillon, the man responsible

28. Y. Bongert, *Cours d'histoire du droit pénal: le droit pénal français de la seconde moitié du XIIIᵉ siècle à 1493* (Paris: Cours de Droit, 1970), p. 260; Van Cauwenbergh, *Pèlerinages*, p. 13.

29. C. Petit-Dutaillis, *La Monarchie féodale en France et en Angleterre* (Paris: Albin-Michel, 1971), p. 301.

30. Charlemagne will later reject two identical offers, vv. 12,487, 12,808.

31. I will be your man and hold my fiefs from you. . . . I abandon to you without restriction my lands and my country (*Raoul* vv. 4008, 5187).

for arranging the truce in the first place, convinces the Emperor to renew hostilities (*Quatre Filz* v. 1447). The war against Aymon's lineage passes into a second phase with the ambush and murder of Beuves and the prolonged engagement against Beuves's brothers. Renaud's final defeat and departure for the Holy Land after the siege of Trémoigne restore peace as long as he remains absent. Dormant rivalries are rekindled, however, when the sons of Foulque meet at Charles's court those of Renaud, the slayer of their father at Vaucouleurs. A reconciled Bernier and Guerri set out for Jerusalem together. On the way home they stop at Origni, site of Raoul's death, where Guerri, reminded of his uncle's loss, slays his old enemy, pilgrimage partner, and brother-in-law. The shame connected to the death of a kinsman is—even after thirty years of war, peace, and expiation—still sufficiently strong to warrant further fighting between the sons of Bernier and Guerri (who are, incidentally, grandsons and grandfather). Thierry's return to France from five years of exile after the battle of Vaubeton marks the renewal of hostilities between Charles Martel and Girart de Roussillon. Boson and Seguin, Girart's cousins, murder the repentant pilgrim in order to avenge their father and uncle. At least one late epic, nominally part of the feudal cycle, is based entirely upon the theme of expiatory pilgrimage: *Huon de Bordeaux*. An unjustly accused Huon finds himself bound to a comically exaggerated quest imposed by Charles for the slaying of the emperor's son Charlot. His journey, adventures while abroad, and eventual return to fight his own brother again underscore the precariousness of the institution itself. Appropriately, the author of *Le Roman de Renart* combines a healthy dose of cynicism with comic relief when, in Branch I, Renart's cousin Grimbert convinces King Noble's court to allow Renart to "take the cross" in lieu of execution; the unrepentant fox departs, staff in hand, only to repeat the crime for which he was originally tried (v. 1446).

Ineffective mechanisms for terminating war, the judicial duel, expiatory pilgrimage, and homage tend to mark transitory pauses between consecutive phases of lengthy campaigns, lulls between battles. They do not, as was their historical purpose, provide a more enduring peace. On the contrary, all three serve to emphasize the inherent dangers of fighting. Without effective remedy, war remains virtually uncontrollable; to fight at all means to accept the prospect of limitless war. Because every temporary triumph requires an identical response by the opposite side, the vengeance of the *faida* risks perpetuating itself *ad infinitum.*[32] As the author of *Girart de Roussillon* observes, deep enmities are inherited: *Se gerre orent li paire, rauront le fils.* The reciprocity of the blood feud tends to insure its prolongation. Hypothetically, the end product of the vendetta cycle is the destruction of both sides. In the absence of any practical antidote, retaliation spreads unchecked and reaches catastrophic proportions. Its symmetry, once established, signals the triumph of violence itself. The enemy clans of the feudal epic are, in effect, potential partners in a mutual suicide pact. Uncontrolled, the *faida* consumes all.[33]

A general evolution in both the character and dimensions of epic warfare is the most apparent symptom of its increasing threat to the community as a whole. The limits of struggle are displaced from the foreign campaigns against a well-defined foe in the cycle of the king (*Roland, Aspremont, Le Pèlerinage de Charlemagne*), to local skirmishes against an invading enemy in the cycle of Guillaume d'Orange (*La Chanson de Guillaume, Le Couronnement de Louis, Le Charroi de Nîmes, La Prise d'Orange*), to internecine conflicts between rival families or between high nobility and the king in the rebel barons cycle. Significantly, an expansion of the chronological perimeters of the epic accompanies this shift in the locus of violence toward its geopolitical center.[34] The several days of decisive battle in *Roland*, two and a half weeks of *Guillaume*, and the two days of *Gormond et Isembard* have been stretched into a period of years or decades. The blood feud between the family of Herbert de Vermandois and that of Raoul de Cambrai covers two full generations, a total of twenty-five to thirty years. That between Charlemagne and the sons of Aymon lasts thirty to thirty-five. Ogier takes between fifteen and twenty years to avenge the death of his son Baldwin. The series of wars

---

32. Girard, *La Violence*, p. 46.

33. Herein lies the profoundest, and the simplest, explanation for the frequency in works of the twelfth and thirteenth centuries of the theme of the wasteland, *la terre gaste*. The eventual price of uncontrolled *faida* is the destruction of economic and agricultural order, the fate of Pelles, the Fisher-King. For Chrétien, war and desolation are inextricably linked (see *Le Roman de Perceval*, ed. W. Roach [Geneva: Droz, 1959], vv. 434, 1749, 1999, 2013). Conversely, the restoration of peace signals the revival of prosperity (see *Perceval*, vv. 2524, 2585). The author of *La Mort le roi Artu* understood the direct relationship of war and economic activity (232), as did the authors of the feudal epic; see *Chevalerie Ogier* vv. 97, 186, 402, 419, 427, 10,336; *Girart* vv. 1790, 3432, 8942, 9937; *Raoul* vv. 1823, 7664; *Quatre Filz* vv. 474, 3220.

34. Calin, *Epic of Revolt*, pp. 181–189.

between Girart de Roussillon and Charles Martel go on for thirty-five years before peace is finally achieved. Unlike Roland's ebulliently swift life and death by the sword, war has become a tedious endeavor, an endless process of attrition. In the epic of the late twelfth and thirteenth centuries, the futility of fighting can be seen in the extreme difficulty of achieving lasting victory, in the failure to conclude.

With the prolongation of war's duration comes an increase in its intensity. Battlefield encounters are depicted with growing realism and detail.[35] The idealized struggles of *Roland*, in which 20,000 French withstand 400,000 pagans the first day and 100,000 vanquish 1,500,000 the second, are reduced to more reasonable proportions. In *Gormond et Isembard* the ratio is four to one. In *Raoul de Cambrai* 10,000 Cambresis face 11,000 Vermandois. And in *Girart de Roussillon* Charles Martel's twelve battalions meet Girart's ten at Vaubeton; each battalion comprises 20,000 men. Casualties remain high. On the first day alone 100,000 die at Vaubeton. Of the 3,000 knights who attack Renaud and his brothers at Vaucouleurs only four survive. Richard returns to camp with bowels, liver, and lungs hanging upon his mantle. The author's insistence upon the sordid aspects of fighting again emphasizes the horror of war in human terms.

The confrontations of *Roland*, their neat rows of opposing armies and successive single combats, do not reflect an historically accurate image of twelfth-century battlefield tactics.[36] They do, nonetheless, set the standard of literary idealization by which subsequent engagements can be judged. The battles of the feudal cycle seem chaotic by comparison. Foulque's clash with Girart before the walls of Roussillon is no orderly ideal fight, but a general melee. In the absence of preestablished ranks, whose formation represents a necessary prelude to the battles of *Roland*, everyone fends for himself.

> Onques n'i ot d'escale plait ne conrei,
> Ne de renger bataille, foi que vos dei,
> Mais li caus abanz pot poin a destrei.

> There was never a full batallion or corps,
> Nor ranks of battle, on my faith,
> But whoever could do so first spurred on vigorously.
> (*Girart* v. 1305)

35. *Ibid.*, pp. 195–202.
36. For a discussion of twelfth-century battlefield tactics see G. Duby, *Le Dimanche de Bouvines* (Paris: Gallimard, 1973), p. 118.

The defeat of Braihier and the Saracen army at the end of *La Chevalerie Ogier* offers an extreme example of tactical disorder. With no fixed locus of confrontation and no apparent boundaries to freewheeling struggle Ogier chases the foe across fields and through woods and rocky crevices before singlehandedly forcing them to flee. In some cases, the disorder of ambush replaces that of battle. Aymon's four sons are treacherously attacked at Vaucouleurs; Beuves, on the Plaine de Floride; Renaud and Allard, before the city of Montaudan. King Louis lies in wait for Bernier on his way home from his own wedding, and Charles Martel approves an abortive ambush attempt against Girart. Elsewhere, the relatively clear-cut strategy of open encounter degenerates into pillage. Raoul burns the abbey of Origny, Girart that of Vaucouleurs. Bernard and Gautier together burn and plunder Paris.

The Siege

Alongside the general evolution from foreign to domestic foe, from swift triumph against unrealistic odds to extended struggle against an obdurate enemy, there occurs a significant shift away from open engagement with discernible outcome towards protracted siege without issue. The geography of military strategy carries the epic poet from the expansive apocalyptic settings of Roland at Roncevaux, Charles at Ebro, and from the less dramatic backdrops of William at Archamp and Isembard at Cayeux, to the fixed locus of the tactics of the château-fort. The checked siege becomes as much a part of the tactics of the late *chanson de geste* as the pitched battles of which it is the antithesis. Where the overt confrontation of the battlefield produces only increased violence and horror, the siege demonstrates the increasing difficulty of engaging the foe. The former embodies the negative consequences of war, the latter its impossibility.

The motif of the checked siege is as old as the genre itself. Charlemagne before the walls of Saragossa faces for the first time his own incapacity to carry the beleaguerment of a foreign city to rapid conclusion. The triumphant Spanish campaign, seven years during which the emperor has "pushed as far as the sea" and conquered every castle in sight, comes to a sudden halt before the impenetrable mountain city:

> N'i ad castel ki devant lui remaigne;
> Mur ne citet n'i est remés a fraindre,
> Fors Sarraguce, ki est en une muntaigne.

> No castle remains before him;
> No wall or city remains to be broken,
> Except Saragossa, which is on a hill.

+ resolve

(Roland v. 4)

If the failure of force to prevail represents a unique event in the military history of Charles's reign, it foreshadows a pattern of repeated strategic setback. The Charlemagne of *Les Quatre Filz Aymon* spends seven years locating Renaud and his brothers in the adulterine castle—*chastel bastart*—of Montessor. Having found the fortress, he remains unable to take it. Montessor resists for five years, withstands betrayal from within, and falls in the end only because of reduced provisions (v. 2625). A subsequent attempt to starve the rebellious barons into submission in the castle of Montauban turns out to be equally inconclusive. Despite encirclement, general famine, common burial without ceremony, and the slaughter of horses for sustenance, the siege is unsuccessful. Charles cannot capture the stronghold; Renaud remains unable to repel the royal army. After a year of active beleaguerment Aymon's four sons escape Montauban through a secret tunnel (v. 13,741). It is only with the failure of the third and final siege, that of Trémoigne, that stalemate forces both sides to recognize the folly of war and to accept at least a temporary truce: *Finée est la grans guerre, nus n'i a mais esgarde.*[37] Diplomacy has succeeded where war has failed.

Charles Martel's first assault upon Roussillon lasts an entire summer without appreciable damage to the city's defenses. Roussillon is taken only because of the defection of an apprehensive gatekeeper. Girart, like the Aymon brothers, escapes to Avignon through a small trap door (*Girart* v. 975). The second siege of Roussillon is hardly more propitious. Again forced to flee because of treachery within his own ranks, Girart maneuvers Charles into the beleaguered city, as the besieged attacks his original besieger (v. 6238).

The siege of *La Chevalerie Ogier* is the most exaggerated of the cycle of the rebellious barons. Banished by Charlemagne, Ogier takes refuge at the court of King Desïer of Pavia. Together they reinforce the Chastel Fort from which Ogier resists the emperor for a total of seven years (*Chevalerie Ogier* v. 3475). Charles employs virtually every method of medieval siegecraft—bridges across the moat, attempts at drainage,

---

37. The great war is over, no one considers it any more (*Quatre Filz*, v. 15,208).

ladders, mangonels, encirclement, and Greek fire—to little avail. After five years and the reduction of the garrison to a force of ten, Naimes acknowledges the futility of assault:

> Fors est la ville ou il sont enserré;
> Ja per asalt nul jor ne les prendrés.

> Strong is the city in which they are shut;
> You will never take them by assault.

> (*Chevalerie Ogier* v. 7556)

Treachery further diminishes their ranks until Ogier, alone except for his horse, fastens wooden dummies to the ramparts of Chastel Fort to give the illusion of numbers. Inside, he grinds his own grain, kneads and bakes his own bread, fetches his own water and wine, and cooks his own meals. His food stocks depleted, Ogier fasts for seven days before emerging, attacking Charles's son, and escaping into the night. Seven years and an attack force of 100,000 men have not proved sufficient to capture a single fortress and its single determined defender.

Within the cycle of Guillaume d'Orange the proportions of the checked siege are modulated somewhat. Rather than full-scale resistance from an entire castle, the more limited tower vigil tends to dominate. Here the elaborate stone fortifications of Montessor, Roussillon, and Chastel Fort have been reduced to their most basic element: the donjon. Having been recognized and denounced to the enemy King Arragon, the William of *La Prise d'Orange* escapes to one such keep with only two companions; there he manages to survive until the Turks penetrate its walls by means of a secret tunnel.[38] After the city of Narbonne falls by treason in *La Mort Aymeri de Narbonne*, the hero's wife Hermengard retreats to an inner tower with fifteen handmaidens. Corsolt, the Saracen chief, camps at its base but cannot capture the citadel.[39] Hermengard resists her attackers until Aymeri arrives to rescue her along with three survivors. Similarly, the hero of *Les Enfances Vivien* succeeds in fending off 100,000 enemy troops surrounding the city of Luiserne until the emperor, after some hesitation, decides to save him from certain death.

The *topos* of impossible siege is no less common in genres other than epic. Benoît de Sainte-Maure adapts the classical theme of prolonged

---

38. *La Prise d'Orange*, ed. B. Katz (New York: King's Crown Press, 1947), v. 824.
39. *La Mort Aymeri de Narbonne*, ed. J. Du Parc (Paris: Firmin Didot, 1884), v. 1700.

beleaguerment broken by ruse to the tastes of his twelfth-century audience. The author of *Le Roman de Troie* dwells at some length upon Priam's rebuilding of Troy after its initial destruction.[40] He is careful to point out that the weakest house of the newly fortified city "would not yield to the King of France and all his empire."[41] The Achilles of *Le Roman de Thèbes* tries to discourage Polynice from attacking the castle of Monflor by reminding him that the stronghold "has sufficient provisions to last fourteen months."[42] Assault does eventually fail in spite of Polynice's utilization of a complete line of offensive siege weaponry: arrows, ladders, bores, mines, Greek fire, and *trébuchier*.

While less well-developed and less exaggerated than elsewhere, Chrétien's treatment of the difficulty of siege tends to support its counterparts in the epic and the *roman d'antiquité*. In *Cligés* Arthur's recapture of Windsor castle takes three months (*Cligés* v. 1626).[43] The fortress finally falls because of ruse: disguised as one of the foe, Alexandre enters and slays its defenders. The Marc of Béroul's *Tristan* is constantly plagued by the barons' threat to withdraw to their strongholds. Conscious of their power to resist militarily once they are within their fortified walls, he finds himself at their mercy

40. The description of the reconstruction of Troy parallels the renovation of many archaic twelfth-century structures:

> Mout la trouverent deguastee,
> Mais cent tanz mieuz l'ont restoree;
> Mout la refirent bele et gente.
> Mout i mist Prianz grante entente:
> Mout la fist close de bons murs
> De marbre hauz, espèz et durs;
> Mout en erent haut li terrier.
> Al meins le trait a un archier,
> Aveit granz tors tot environ,

> Though they found it all destroyed,
> They restored it a hundred times better than before;
> They rebuilt it beautifully.
> Priam expended a great deal of energy:
> He made it safe with strong high walls
> Of marble, thick and hard;
> The site was on high land.
> There were all around
> Towers as high as a bow's shot

(Benoît de Sainte-Maure, *Le Roman de Troie*, ed. L. Constans [Paris: Firmin Didot, 1904], v. 3001).

41. *Ibid.*, v. 3015.

42. *Le Roman de Thèbes*, ed. L. Constans (Paris: Firmin Didot, 1890), v. 2855.

43. See also *Yvain*, v. 3766.

A la cort avoit trois barons,
Ainz ne veïstes plus felons;
Par soirement s'estoient pris
Que, se li rois de son païs
N'en faisot son nevo partir,
Il nu voudroient mais soufrir,
A lor chasteaus sus s'en trairoient
Et au roi Marc gerre feroient.

At court there were three barons,
You have never seen greater felons;
They swore an oath
That if the king did not expel
His nephew from the country
They would suffer him no longer,
But would withdraw to their castles
And make war on King Marc.

(Béroul v. 581)

Finally, in a comic rendition of the rebellious baron motif, Renart emphasizes his deadly serious ability to withstand attack. Summoned to Noble's court for judgment, he reminds his family of the alternatives to trial (*Renart* v. 1137). Noble's encirclement of Malpertuis again demonstrates the futility of siege:

Or puet avoir paor Renarz,
Mes par asaut n'iert ja conquis
ne ne sera a force pris
se traïz n'est ou afamez,
ja ne sera par aus grevez.
* * *
Onques ne laissierent nul jor
que n'assaillisent a la tor,
mes ne la porent enpirer
dont el vausist mains un denier.

Now may Renart be afraid,
But he will not be conquered by assault
Nor will he be taken by force
If he is not betrayed or starved out,
He will not be harmed by them.
* * *
They never let pass a day
Without assaulting the tower,
But they could not damage it
Or diminish its worth by one penny.

(*Renart* vv. 1700, 1826)

Renart—like Aymon's sons, Girart, Ogier, William, his nephew Vivien and daughter-in-law Hermengard, the inhabitants of Troy, Monflor, and Tintagel—is able to resist almost indefinitely and against overwhelming odds the attempt to take his castle by armed force.

The checked siege motif of the epic, the *roman d'antiquité*, romance, and satirical literature reflects an essentially accurate image of late twelfth- and thirteenth-century military strategy. The long encampments without issue correspond to an historical evolution in the locus and nature of medieval warfare—the displacement of combat from battlefield to castle and from open engagement to protracted siege.[44] The capacity to resist for an apparently unlimited period is indicative of a gradual shift in the balance of military power from the offensive to the defensive side. As the art of fortification became increasingly refined in the postfeudal era, clear-cut triumphs like Hastings, Taillebourg, or Bouvines came to be more the exception than the rule. Beginning in the twelfth century, campaigns tended to resemble Charles's beleaguerment of Montessor, Trémoigne, or Chastel Fort more than William's crossing of the Channel, Louis's surprise of Henry III, or Philippe-Auguste's defeat of John's coalition from the north—all three the product of superior maneuvering followed by a single day of battle.

The transformation of medieval warfare in the period following the First Crusade was the result of an immense progress in the science of defensive fortification, accompanied by relatively slight progress in siegecraft from the Conquest to the introduction of gunpowder and artillery three centuries later. Despite the survival of a learned art of siegecraft in the Eastern Empire, where the Byzantines withstood Barbarian and Asian incursions, little innovation occurred in the West from the time of Alexander to the thirteenth century.[45] Progress had been slow after the Germanic invasions. Feudalism, itself the beneficiary of Arabic fighting technology, added little to Europe's knowledge of offensive strategy.

Medieval siegecraft was essentially Roman; the Germans possessed only limited experience of stationary assault tactics before settling in France. It called initially for the storming of a garrison and its capture, where possible, by direct strike. Moats and ditches were filled in with

44. J. Beeler, *Warfare in Feudal Europe 730–1200* (Ithaca: Cornell University Press, 1971), pp. 44–45; C. Oman, *A History of the Art of War* (London: Methuen, 1898), p. 551.

45. J.-F. Finó, *Forteresses de la France médiévale* (Paris: Picard, 1970), p. 91; A. Norman and D. Pottinger, *Warrior to Soldier 449–1660* (London: Weidenfeld and Nicolson, 1964), p. 52; Oman, *Art of War*, p. 356; J. Patrick, *Artillery and Warfare during the Thirteenth and Fourteenth Centuries* (Utah: Utah State University Press, 1961), pp. 22–55.

dirt; ladders were lowered upon the walls.[46] When time permitted, large wooden towers or belfries (*beffrois*) were constructured nearby and rolled into place against the ramparts. These could hold a moderate force, twelve to twenty men, who, protected by mantlets or light shields made from animal skins, attempted to clear the upper parapet of its defenders. Behind them, archers provided covering fire while a ground force attacked the walls themselves. The great offensive weapons of the early Middle Ages were the ram and bore, instruments designed to weaken the structural foundation. Also protected by mantlets from falling objects—rocks, arrows, or hot oil—teams of sappers armed with tools resembling the modern crowbar and pick tried to dislodge the stones at the castle's base.[47] Even the strongest defense might be caused to crumble with persistence and luck. More advanced assaults included a wooden penthouse in addition to the tower. Much like a New England covered bridge draped with skins, the penthouse permitted those inside to batter the masonry with a ram suspended from its ceiling. The ram, manipulated back and forth with sufficient force, could, in concert with the bore, open a breach in the walls. Otherwise, the shelter that it afforded raised the possibility of mining an already weakened foundation. Soil removed by excavation at the base of a wall or at the corner between two walls was replaced by wooden timbers which held the structure in place temporarily. Once enough dirt had been dislodged, the timbers were ignited, causing the ramparts to collapse along a well-defined fault. When, at the siege of Nicaea (1097) the defenders managed to repair by night the damage inflicted by rams and bores during the preceding day, the assailants brought a penthouse up to the ramparts for the purpose of mining.[48] Only after the timberworks had been set on fire and a fissure opened in the main tower did the city surrender.

Scaling, battering, and mining operations directed against the lower masonry afforded ample time for the building of projectile weapons to be used against the upper stories.[49] Here again, medieval military technology showed little advance over that of Rome. The siege engines de-

---

46. L. Montross, *War through the Ages* (New York: Harper and Row, 1960), pp. 160–164; Oman, *Art of War*, p. 131; S. Toy, *Castles: A Short History of Fortifications from 1600 B.C. to A.D. 1600* (London: Heinemann, 1939), pp. 141–143; see also *Chevalerie Ogier* vv. 6092, 6098, 8094 and *Le Roman de Thèbes* v. 3051.

47. *Chevalerie Ogier* v. 6115; *Le Roman de Thèbes* v. 2963.

48. Toy, *Castles*, p. 144; *Le Roman de Thèbes* v. 8140.

49. *Chevalerie Ogier* vv. 6143, 6661, 6701; *Quatre Filz* vv. 13,250, 14,217; *Le Roman de Thèbes* v. 2905.

scribed by Vegetius, Procopius, and Ammianus are essentially the same as those employed almost a thousand years later in Western Europe.[50] Of these, two types dominated offensive siegecraft until the thirteenth century. The machines that work by tension—spring devices or *balista*—were nothing more than giant crossbows. Men standing on either side drew back a thick cord with the assistance of small winches; they then released either an arrow or a metal bolt in the direction of the foe. According to Procopius, missiles launched from the *balista* were capable of "breaking stones and piercing trees." Abbot Ebolus maintains that a single shaft from a defensive spring device impaled several Danes at the siege of Paris in 885.[51]

A second class of projectile weapons included those which function by torsion. In the firing of the mangonel or catapult, a rope attached to a giant fulcrum was twisted between two posts causing a great deal of potential energy to be generated along its length. Rocks, lead bolts, or stone balls were placed in the fulcrum's spoon-shaped tip before it was released. The mangonel represented an especially effective weapon of bombardment since it could send a moderately heavy load high into the air. It was not until the late twelfth century, however, that heavy projectile weaponry was developed in what constituted the only true innovation in siegecraft since the Empire. The large petrary known as the *trébuchet* could launch immense stones through application of the principle of counterpoise.[52] Cumbersome weights attached to one end of a rotating lever were raised in order to permit the loading of a lighter missile at the opposite end. When freed, gravity forced the raised portion to the ground, thrusting its load upward. At the siege of Acre (1189–90) Richard the Lionhearted supposedly possessed a *trébuchet* that killed twelve men in a single shot. Blanche de Castille is reported to have employed a similar device against the rebellious Pierre Mauclerc at the siege of Bellême (1230).

Alongside the heavy rocks projected by the larger *petrariae* and the metal bolts and shafts launched by smaller machines, medieval armies were also familiar with both offensive and defensive incendiary arms. Torches and burning pitch were hurled by either side to ignite wooden castle towers or to counteract the effect of an attacking belfry or pent-

---

50. Finó, *Forteresses*, pp. 141–151; Montross, *War through the Ages*, p. 160; Oman, *Art of War*, pp. 136–140; Toy, *Castles*, p. 143.

51. Oman, *Art of War*, pp. 137–138.

52. Finó, *Forteresses*, p. 216; Toy, *Castles*, p. 143.

house. Greek fire, the medieval equivalent of napalm, came to Europe via the Middle East where it played an important role—as early as the seventh century—in Byzantine sieges and naval battles. Used against both the Arabs and Russians, *le fou grezeis* represented a viscous substance that exploded upon impact, spreading a deadly mass of flame.[53] Its exact chemical formula remained a closely guarded "state secret" throughout the Middle Ages; nonetheless, experts generally agree it consisted of grease, oil, sulfur, naptha, and saltpeter, the last of which was available in its natural state in the arid climate of the Middle East. When mixed in the right proportions, Greek fire could either be squirted through a long tube from the prow of a ship or loaded into thin clay pots that were projected across long distances by mechanical means.

The attempt to storm a garrison, to take it by force, was usually combined with a less direct attack upon the morale of its inhabitants. One highly respected military historian maintains that diseased corpses were sometimes hurled over the walls in order to spread an epidemic, to pollute the water supply or, simply, to provoke fear within the garrison.[54] Such practices were, however, quite rare. Economic embargo—devastation of the countryside surrounding a fortress, its encirclement and blockade— was much more common.[55] During the initial stages of the siege of Acre the crusaders assembled a fleet of floating tower-barges to prevent access from the sea. They then proceeded to entrench themselves upon land in order to close the stronghold entirely. Before advancing siege machines upon the formidable Château Gaillard (1203), Philippe-Auguste first ordered a row of trenches around the town and a series of fortified guard towers along the newly created defensive line. The fortress was so tightly sealed from the outside world that hundreds of townsmen trapped between its walls and the encamped royal troops died of hunger. The castle of Rochester was starved into submission by John Lackland in 1215.[56]

Blockade and starvation required a great deal of patience on the part of an offensive army, which sometimes had to wait as long as two or three years for the surrender of a well-provisioned fort. Short of starvation,

53. Finó, *Forteresses*, p. 155; Oman, *Art of War*, p. 550; Toy, *Castles*, p. 143; *Chevalerie Ogier* v. 6717; *La Prise d'Orange* v. 824; *Le Roman de Thèbes* v. 3037.

54. Finó, *Forteresses*, p. 155.

55. *Chevalerie Ogier* vv. 6178, 6188; *Quatre Filz* vv. 2185, 2447, 5493, 13,055, 13,146.

56. Toy, *Castles*, pp. 145–150.

every effort was made to encourage individual acts of treachery or general mutiny within its walls. A number of literary defenders—Hermangard, Girart, and Ogier—are betrayed by their own gatekeepers and watchmen. Historically, the city of Antioch was captured (1098) after a long and effective defense because of the betrayal of its leader's brother, the Emir Feir. Six months of beleaguerment of the Château Gaillard were ended when two French soldiers crawled through a latrine drain connecting the fort to the Seine. By lifting their comrades through the window of an adjoining chapel, they duped the defenders into thinking that a large enemy detachment had penetrated the citadel. A lukewarm effort at defense culminated in the capitulation of the central gate, as the drawbridge was lowered and the middle bailey of France's strongest castle was taken.

The Castle

While there was little essential change in the methods of siegecraft from the Gothic storming of Rome in 537 to the ninth-century Viking siege of Paris and the crusader campaigns of a subsequent era, there was some increase in the power and range of the weaponry employed. This remained a purely quantitative advance, however. Even though later siege machines were capable of projecting heavier missiles than their Roman counterparts, their destructive potential was neutralized at almost every step by corresponding developments in defensive armament. The same mangonels, *balista*, and Greek fire used to attack a well-equipped stronghold could also be used in its defense. Furthermore, the immense progress in castle construction from the late eleventh through the thirteenth century tended to counteract even the most startling progress in offensive tactics. Siegecraft was rapidly becoming a retrogressive art.

It is only from the third century onward that the Romans in Gaul developed an effective military architecture. Fortification in the late Empire and up until the end of the feudal age was, to a large degree, a matter of continuation and reparation of existing Roman walls.[57] In some areas, post-Carolingian France for example, Gallo-Roman defenses were abandoned altogether. At the time of the Norman incursion into the region of the Seine, Charles the Bald found himself obliged to issue several decrees for the construction of city walls (862 and 864). None-

57. Finó, *Forteresses*, p. 52; Oman, *Art of War*, p. 517; Toy, *Castles*, p. 145.

theless, when the Danes arrived in Paris some twenty-one years later, the two bridgeheads and stone towers originally ordered had only been partially completed. The city's defenders were forced to pile hastily laid beams and planks upon stones that had been cast into the river in order to provide a minimum bulwark against attack.

Castles constructed entirely of stone were rare before the late eleventh century. Even where Roman *enceintes* had been repaired or replaced, mud and wood were usually substituted for the standing masonry structure. Most castles north of the Loire were of the motte-and-bailey or earth and "ring-works" type. Like the English *burh* or shell-keep, they consisted of a bank and ditch palisaded around the residence of a private landholder.[58] Towers, donjons, and walls were made exclusively of wood, which, for a long time, had offered a number of advantages. Timber was available in abundant quantities throughout the feudal period. Its preparation and utilization required no special skill beyond the ken of the simplest peasant forester or carpenter. In addition, wood permitted rapid construction at almost any given site. Lambert d'Ardes reports that in repairing the damage inflicted by Arnoul de Guines, Henri de Bourbourg raised a completely new edifice at Audruicq in the space of a single night.[59] The chateau of Puiset was destroyed by Louis VI and rebuilt by its lord three times in seven years. William I utilized motte-and-bailey construction to great advantage in controlling Norman England after the Conquest. Literally hundreds of mud and wood "ring-works" appeared almost overnight throughout the English countryside.

As the population of Western Europe increased towards the end of the feudal era, wood construction presented a number of difficulties which, like the contemporary crisis in natural resources, had not been foreseen. The multiplication of castles over a period of centuries had contributed to the depletion of the forests of Northern France. Even by moderate estimates it took two hundred years for a tree to grow to a size suitable for cutting, and it is doubtful that any of the motte-and-bailey forts lasted that long. Furthermore, building with wood took a lot of trees. The Danish castle of Trelleborg (ca. 1000), for instance, consumed eight thousand large trees covering two hundred acres of forestland. Abbot Suger complained that the castle building which accompanied the wars

58. Beeler, *Warfare*, p. 28; Finó, *Forteresses*, pp. 46, 105; Toy, *Castles*, pp. 53–57.
59. Finó, *Forteresses*, p. 77.

among Milon de Chevreuse, the French king, and Amaury de Montfort had so reduced the forests around Saint Denis that carpenters had to travel as far as Auxerre to find trees large enough for the cathedral beams.[60] More important, castles of wood and mud were considerably more vulnerable to the weapons of conventional siegecraft than were the stone fortresses of a later age. Even the highest earthworks could be mined successfully; wooden walls and towers could be ignited with relative ease.

Beginning in the late eleventh century stone gradually replaced wood as the dominant building material. With the razing of vast areas of French timberland in preceding centuries, it represented a logical substitute despite the obvious difficulties of quarrying and transportation. Where possible, the castle builders of the twelfth century, like the Gallo-Romans, used pre-cut stones belonging to existent structures. A popular dictum attests to the popularity of the technique: *chastel abatuz est demi refez*.[61] According to the chronicler Flodoard, Foulques de Reims ordered the Church of Saint Denis to be destroyed in order to reinforce the city walls. Otherwise, a number of technical advances facilitated the cutting, handling, and emplacement of the great stone blocks that comprised the fortresses of the late Middle Ages. As early as the mid-twelfth century a special hammer with teeth, the *brette* or *bretture*, along with a perfected stone-saw, rendered the cutting process less difficult than before. Large rocks were usually trimmed to a usable size directly after mining in order to avoid excessive transportation costs. Geography permitting, water routes furnished the cheapest means of transporting cut stones from quarry to building site. The orginal keeps of Canterbury and the Tower of London were constructed with materials floated in barges across the Channel from Caen. Overland, a pair of oxen could carry a load of up to 3,500 lbs. a day across a distance of ten miles. Development of a cylindric furnance sometime before the middle of the twelfth century gave added impetus to the use of quicklime for the caulking of castle walls.[62] The mortar dating from that period onward seems to show a marked improvement over that of the preceding era. In fact, the medieval construction site probably did not vary a great deal from that of today.

60. *Ibid.*, pp. 80, 119.
61. The demolished castle is half rebuilt (Cited Finó, *Forteresses*, p. 121); see note 40, p. 84.
62. Finó, *Forteresses*, pp. 120–122.

Scaffolding and ladders surrounded large edifices, while heavy baskets of stone and mortar were raised by an elaborate pulley system. According to architectural drawings and church murals, the scaffold and pulley technique was known by the time of the First Crusade.[63]

The stone fortresses predating the golden era of Norman and Angevine construction—Brionne, Langeais, Loches, Canterbury, and Colchester, to mention just a few—were patterned around massive rectangular keeps two to four stories in height.[64] Their entrances, usually on the second storey, were protected by forebuildings connected to the main bailey by a stairway along the side of the keep. Strengthened by buttresses, their walls tended to be extremely thick. At Loches they measure nine feet; at Rochester, twelve feet; and at Dover they vary between seventeen and twenty-one feet. The White Tower of London is perhaps the most distinctive of the early square stone castles. Begun by William I shortly after the Conquest (1070), its four stories rise to a height of ninety feet. It quadrangular keep measures 107 by 118 feet, excluding the turrets at the corner of each parapet. The walls are fifteen feet thick on the ground floor, thirteen feet on the second. Neither contains windows to be penetrated or woodwork to be set on fire. A limited area in front of the Tower combined with its narrow single entrance left little room for an offensive army to exit and even less room for open engagement should such a sally occur. The fortress to which Guinevere retreats at the end of *La Mort Artu* represents a purely defensive stronghold from which even a small garrison could withstand a long siege. In fact, the Tower of London, like most of its counterparts, was provisioned for an entire year.

European castle building underwent a virtual renaissance in the period following the First Crusade, a renaissance due in large part to crusader contact with the fortresses of the Middle East: Nicaea, Antioch, Jerusalem, Constantinople, Krak des Chevaliers, etc.[65] Because of the lack of forestland and the persistence of major wars, the art of stone fortification had progressed much more rapidly in the Eastern Empire than in the West. In any case, assimilation on the Continent of the architectural lessons learned abroad did not lag far behind. As early as the 1120s many

---

63. *Ibid.*, pp. 123–216.

64. *Ibid.*, pp. 156–179; Oman, *Art of War*, pp. 522–523; Toy, *Castles*, pp. 66, 70.

65. Montross, *War through the Ages*, p. 161; Oman, *Art of War*, p. 331; Toy, *Castles*, p. 30. The renaissance in stone castle building beginning in the 1120s was accompanied by an increased interest in urban fortification as well.

of the old timber structures of the motte-and-bailey type were converted into the more sophisticated stone shell-keeps.

While the ease with which mud and wood castles could be raised had led to a certain arbitrariness in their location, the choice of building site gained increasing importance from the time of Philip the First on. An effort was made to situate the stone citadel atop a steep hill with the inner bailey, a refuge of last resort, against the cliff. The outer defenses, consisting of two or three lines of supplementary fortification, were thus concentrated in the direction of approach. At the same time, greater attention was paid to the geological stratum upon which the entire structure rested. Stone fortresses built upon natural rock foundations became more and more common, since rock thwarted even the most persevering attempts at mining. A gradual evolution in the shape of the castle itself accompanied the shift in location, as the archaic square donjons of the eleventh century were replaced by rounded or multi-angular towers and keeps.[66] These tended to be much sounder structurally, more resistant both to mining at corners and to the use of rams along the surface of the walls. Rounded towers permitted a greater defensive range. Those firing from windows enjoyed an extended field of vision, which meant that an assailant armed with ladders or pick might easily find himself caught in between the crossfire from adjacent posts situated along the same wall. The introduction of multiple towers set in tandem on all sides of an elliptic curtain functioned both to reinforce the outer ramparts and to lure attackers into a position in which crossfire would be possible.

A system of vaulted construction made the castles of the twelfth century lighter and less vulnerable to mining, battering, and fire. When applied to all levels, it transformed the military fort into a series of stacked conical layers higher and more resilient as a whole than its quadrilateral predecessors. Ramparts and ceilings supported from within no longer sustained their own weight plus that of the floors above. Concomitantly, the château-fort expanded horizontally. Concentric curtains of defense began to supplant the single-walled keep. In some instances two or three baileys were added to existing fortification. At Carcassonne, for example, Roman and Visigothic curtains and towers were strengthened over a period of forty years by the addition of several parallel walls.[67] Henry III annexed a system of concentric defense to the Tower of London. Castles

66. Finó, *Forteresses*, p. 174; Toy, *Castles*, pp. 90, 116.
67. Finó, *Forteresses*, pp. 175, 217; Oman, *Art of War*, p. 542; Toy, *Castles*, p. 139.

erected subsequent to the middle of the twelfth century featured, almost without exception, coaxial outerwards and foreworks connected by communicating corridors. Both served to shield the inner keep where, in peacetime, its inhabitants conducted their daily affairs. When necessary, the protective walls of graduated heights permitted those inside to defend themselves in stages, since the enemy that penetrated a single ward did not automatically gain control of the entire stronghold. He had to win a series of battles fought along successive buffer zones, risking, at each step along the way, entrapment by crossfire from the bridges perpendicular to the walls. Once Philippe-Auguste had taken the outer bailey of the Château Gaillard he still faced the formidable task of capturing its inner ramparts. The stone fortress of the late Middle Ages was, in reality, a castle within another castle which was itself encased in a third.[68]

The military architecture of the twelfth century culminated in the Château Gaillard (1196–98) begun by Richard the Lionhearted upon his return from the Holy Land.[69] In this citadel overlooking the city of Rouen Richard set out to apply all the principles of Byzantine construc-

68. Included in the overall transformation of the wooden shell-keep and tower of the ninth century to the massive citadel of the thirteenth were a number of minor architectural refinements affecting the fine points of defense. Whereas the early stone fortress had few windows in the lower stories and wide vulnerable openings above, hollow towers perforated at every level by narrow arrow-slits or *meutrières* became more and more common. These apertures, which afforded the defender both greater protection and increased firing range, were themselves eventually replaced by the perfected *archères*, long vertical windows sometimes reaching a height of five feet and offering an even wider perspective. Nonetheless, once an enemy had lodged himself at the base of the walls, no window, however long, permitted counterattack at an angle of ninety degrees. For this purpose the early castle builders had introduced a series of wooden balconies or *hourds* complete with roof and walls and situated strategically over doors and towers (Finó, *Forteresses*, pp. 162, 164, 218). The floors of this loggia-type structure contained holes through which oil could be poured or arrows fired vertically upon the enemy below. Often the *hourd* was combined with a graded wall or plinth (*talus*) at the foot of the ramparts. In addition to strengthening them and making them more difficult to scale, the plinth deflected arrows shot from above, causing them to ricochet horizontally towards the foe before he could manage to entrench himself. Later, stone machicolation over doors and along the length of the parapet served the same purpose and was also less susceptible to heavy missile fire. With the perfection of the upper defenses, the entrance itself, always the weakest point of early fortification, grew exceedingly complex (Finó, *Forteresses*, p. 167; Toy, *Castles*, p. 117). Mobile drawbridges replaced permanent stairways, making the entire structure less accessible. Towers constructed on either side were designed to trap an assailant about to enter the door in a cross fire from behind. Eventually, the installation of protected gates and barbicanes in front of the approach transformed the main entrance into an independent mini-fortress which had to be reckoned with before the door could be taken.

69. G. Hindley, *Medieval Warfare* (New York: Putnam, 1971), p. 38; Toy, *Castles*, p. 116.

tion learned while abroad. With cliffs on three sides, the Château Gaillard comprises a system of two concentric baileys around a donjon, both protected by an outer bailey which is itself separated from the surrounding area by a circular moat. An extension of the exterior waterway runs between the foreworks and middle bailey, which are connected only by a bridge. Another moat within the central keep isolates the inner bailey and donjon from the rest of the fortifications. The walls vary in thickness between nine and twelve feet. Stone machicolation protects the single entrance to the innermost refuge. In all, three independent curtains of defense strengthened by four round towers on the outer bailey and three on the middle bailey create the impression of a coordinated defense unit vastly more complex than the Tower of London. Its capture was, in fact, the result of subterfuge rather than storm. Despite Philippe-Auguste's blockade, mining, and combined assault with large siege engines and high towers, the Château Gaillard resisted for a period of six months.[70]

The difficulty of capturing a single fortress like the Château Gaillard emphasizes the increasing ineffectiveness of offensive tactics against an advanced system of fortification. Sophisticated siege weapons were, furthermore, hard to transport. Joinville and Froissart both allude to the great effort required to move heavy equipment from one location to another.[71] Construction on the spot required the assistance of a corps of trained engineers as well as a plentiful supply of available timber. Once assembled, even the most powerful *trébuchet* had little effect upon walls that were fifteen feet thick. Mining, boring, and battering posed less and less of a threat to rounded fortifications set upon a bedrock foundation. Incendiary devices were next to useless against structures made entirely of stone. If famine, epidemic, treachery, or plain war-weariness did not force the capitulation of a well-ensconced garrison, it could, in theory, hold out almost indefinitely.[72] William the Conqueror beleaguered the Vicomte de Beaumont for a period of three years before finally having to

70. Oman, *Art of War*, p. 552; Toy, *Castles*, p. 148.

71. Froissart, *Chroniques*, ed. G. Raynaud (Paris: Renouard, 1894), 9: 7; Joinville, *Histoire de Saint Louis*, ed. N. de Wailly (Paris: Firmin-Didot, 1874), p. 164.

72. Finó, *Forteresses*, p. 153; see also *Chevalerie Ogier* vv. 6615, 7556; *Girart* v. 975; *Mort Aymeri* v. 969; *Quatre Filz* vv. 5486, 5500, 5537, 13,064; *Le Roman de Troie* v. 3001. The advantage of defense over offense becomes even more significant in light of the disproportionate size of offensive forces. At Montessor the four Aymon brothers aided by 600 men fend off all the knights that Charles can muster; the brothers fight unassisted at Montauban. Girart's force of 400 repels Charles Martel's whole army at Roussillon. The most exaggerated case is, of course, Ogier's defense of Chastel Fort. A single knight from an original garrison of 300 manages to hold off 100,000 assault troops.

abandon the endeavor. The siege of Acre lasted for two years beyond the Turks' initial surrender and unsuccessful negotiation of terms. All of which meant that a district guarded by three or four strongholds each requiring several months of siege might take years to conquer. A coordinated line of castle defense such as that established by the crusaders against the Mameluke Sultans, the line of forts along the English Pale in Ireland, or the Epte line—Gisors, Bangu, Neaufles, Châteauneuf—ordered by William Rufus to protect the Vexin against Philip the First, was virtually impossible to master.[73]

The technological dominance of fortification over siegecraft accounts for the futility of so many twelfth- and thirteenth-century campaigns. Organized military adventures tended, often, to degenerate into either plundering raids or protracted assaults against a single fortress. What this means, once again, is that the theme of the checked siege so characteristic of the rebellious barons cycle is the literary expression of this shift of tactical advantage in favor of defense. As the open field engagement became less and less frequent during the period under consideration, the epic portrayal of battlefield disorder or non-engagement before the walls of an impregnable stronghold becomes an increasingly important symptom of military crisis.

Demographic Implications

The spread of stone fortification from the late eleventh century onward was a contributing factor in the demographic evolution of postfeudal France. It led in two directions. On the one hand, the construction of

---

73. This crisis was also complicated by a similar evolution in defensive armor. As early as the tenth century the simple mail shirt had been reinforced by the addition of a coif or hood of mail covering the neck and face. Coif and shirt were eventually joined in a single garment topped by an improved crestless conical helmet. At approximately the same time the warrior's lance seems to have grown in length, thus becoming more useful as a shock weapon than as an arm of attack. The sword, too, underwent modification. Its dimensions and weight increased; its pointed tip was supplanted by a rounded stubbed end. Both indicate a weapon too unwieldly for throwing—one that is, in other words, no longer employed as a vigorous offensive tool. By the twelfth century the mail shirt had been extended to the knees; gloves of mail accompanied the panoply. Returning crusaders introduced the gambeson (O.F. *hauqueton*), a short cassock with layers of quilted rags sewn to leather and covered with linen, to be worn under armor. Finally, the appearance of the conical "pot-helm" or casque along with the first plate armor transformed the mounted warrior into a mobile human fortress. Like the castle in which he lived and whose image he reflected, the knight of the thirteenth century had become a military monolith whose size and capacity for self-defense changed not only the scope of Western warfare, but the political shape of Europe as well (Duby, *Bouvines*, p. 60; Finó, *Forteresses*, pp. 129–139; Montross, *War through the Ages*, p. 163).

impregnable strongholds at royal or communal expense and under royal supervision served to bolster the impetus towards centralization on the part of an already strengthened monarchy. Some landholders—both ecclesiastical and lay—were willing to grant castles to the king in order to place their holdings under protection.[74] He, in turn, dispatched permanent administrative agents, began to regularize taxation, and raised additional strongholds. The renovation of structures such as Carcassonne or Provins was often directly connected to the suppression of local rebellions with the ultimate aim of controlling the territory involved. As the protector of ecclesiastical interests in the region of Mâcon, for example, royalty forced the lay aristocracy to give up many of its gains made in the tenth and eleventh centuries at Church expense. The three rapid campaigns into Burgundy in 1166, 1171, and 1180 enabled the French king both to restore royal rights over existing castles and to establish a chain of forts along the Burgundain frontier: Tornus, Montbellet, Verizet, La-Salle, Mâcon, Vinzelles and Crêches. The construction of new fortifications at other strategic military points—Dourdan, Yèvre-le-Chatel, Aigues-Morte, Najac, Gisors, Loches—furthered the drive toward domination of newly annexed territories and essential frontiers. The royal officers in charge of guarding their walls were pledged both to protect the individual fort under their superintendence and, that failing, to sound the alarm for assistance from their counterparts elsewhere. They belonged, at least in theory, to a network of independent castles each part of a mutual defense league.

Replacement of the motte-and-bailey or wooden shell-keep by the stone fortress contributed, on the other hand, to a corresponding shift in population towards larger demographic centers. While the rise of towns and communes under royal franchise generally favored the expansion of royal authority, a parallel centripetal movement within the large feudal states worked against the interests of monarchy. Here again, the improvement of military fortification played an important role both as consequence and cause. Marc Bloch has observed that in the period following the first feudal age an overall rise in population necessitated the clearance of vast areas of forestland for agricultural purposes.[75] Combined with the persistent use of great quantities of timber for construction

---

74. Duby, *Société mâconnaise*, p. 546; Finó, *Forteresses*, p. 182.
75. Bloch, *Feudal Society*, 2: 421.

during preceding centuries, this sudden increase in the extent of land clearance had a profound effect upon the ability of small landholders to survive independently of the more powerful magnates from whom they held land in fief. With the razing of the forests of northern France, armies became increasingly mobile, able to cover greater distances in a single day. As a result, those who possessed large forces, the high nobility in particular, found themsevles better equipped to maintain large areas of the countryside under their control. The scarcity of wood for the construction of second-rate defensive forts together with their growing ineffectiveness against attack further weakened the position of the lower nobility, the *hobereaux* or squireen, who were forced to seek the fortified protection of a more affluent benefactor. The defense of wooden castles demanded a proportionately high number of men, more than most petty vassals could afford.[76] Only the rich had the wherewithal to build in stone in an age in which only stone provided adequate protection; hence the schism, beginning in the twelfth century, within the knight-warrior class. Great landholders who could afford it used the penury of the lower aristocracy to enlarge their own domains, to act, in other words, like the king himself. By offering an impoverished *châtelain* the equivalent of several years of revenue from a particular *allod*, the wealthy lord might permanently alienate it to himself. He acquired, through the transaction, the sole basis for control of the surrounding area: the castle. Thus, the evolution in defensive warfare signaled the advent of a progressively well-defined hierarchy between the large landholder, possessed of the means of defense and support, and the petty landholder, who not only depended upon his lord economically, but who lived in ever greater numbers within the confines of his estate. The great feudal magnates of the twelfth and thirteenth centuries augmented the number of their direct vassals while extending their legal jurisdiction and sovereignty. Through the elimination of the independence of less powerful *châtelains* and an increase in the autonomy of the already powerful high nobility, the feudal hierarchy of the postfeudal era was, on the whole, simplified.

As the stone citadel came to represent more and more of a strategic necessity, it became an increasingly independent administrative, judicial, and military center. Supported from below by the influx of dispossessed lower nobles and sure of his own security against easy attack, the great

---

76. *Ibid.*, 2: 301.

feudal potentate was capable of resisting incursions upon his domain with greater efficiency than ever. The king remained powerless, throughout most of the Middle Ages, to prevent the erection of new fortresses or to protect against the claims of an ambitious *châtelain* those he himself had built.[77] The prevalence of adulterine castles in Normandy, Languedoc, Aquitaine, Toulouse, and Poitou testifies to the tenacity of the powerful feudatory princes. Because of their enhanced power of physical resistance, the independence of a Hughes de Lusignan, Alphonse de Poitiers, Thibaut de Champagne, Pierre Mauclerc, Philippe Hurepel, the Dukes of Normandy, Burgundy, and Brittany was great indeed. They paid no taxes beyond the exceptional cases. They often refused to send levies to the king's army or sent minimum contingents. Even when reprimanded, they managed, as often as not, to exclude the agents of the Crown from their jurisdiction. Within their territories they retained the rights to exercise high justice, mint money, accord charters, make laws and, most importantly, make war. The system of *faida* and private war contributed, along with the rise of stone fortifications, to the long survival of small independent states among greedy neighbors and particularly among a greedy monarchy with an expanding domain.

Critical Perspectives

Literary critics have been anxious to stress the tension between monarchy and high nobility as it is reflected in the feudal epic cycle. Viewing the theme of war from the perspective of the combatants themselves, they have tended to emphasize, almost without exception, either the general conflict of interest between royalty and aristocracy or a more specific quarrel involving family lines. The blood feuds of the Cambresis and Vermandois, of the Lorrains and Burgundians, are incidences of clannish rivalry due to conflicting claims to the same fief. Those between Louis and Gormond, Charlemagne and Renaud or Ogier, Charles Martel and Girart may or may not have been sparked to an actual offense. They reflect, nonetheless, an inherent tension between the interests of monarchy and feudal aristocracy. In the first case, the causes of war become irrelevant once the reciprocity of the vendetta has come into play. In the second, it is always an injustice on the part of the king—a dispossession, unlawful slaying, cruel punishment, violation of promise, refusal

77. *Ibid.*, 2: 431.

of justice—that sets an often weak and incompetent sovereign against his victimized vassal.[78] Right lies on the side of an oppressed aristocracy which, through the means of self-help and resistance at its disposal, upholds the principle of justice against the more restrictive monarchic principle of order. In effect, the rebellious baron takes the law into his own hands for the sake of that which he knows to be right, and which is right according to the most fundamental feudal practice. The king, in contrast, rejects any claim to right other than his own for the sake of what he perceives to be the *sine qua non* of his own authority and hence the order of the realm. The universal victory of royalty over nobility represents, then, a triumph of might over right. A swan song of declining aristocracy, the epic of the late twelfth and thirteenth centuries is, in effect, France's first literature of protest.

According to William C. Calin, who has written a comprehensive study of the feudal cycle, these poems of rebellion are the product of aristocratic reaction to monarchy's growing interference in baronial affairs, especially in the matter of succession.[79] Combining archaic Carolingian legends of revolt with a heavy dose of daydreaming about the ineffectual kings of bygone days, they constitute a "positive answer to a keenly felt danger." The epics of revolt embody a collective fantasy of power on the part of a weakened chivalry. If the barons lose in the end, it is because the "ultimate lesson of the *chanson de geste* is one of order and harmony," of necessary submission to authority. Reto Bezzola argues, on the other hand, that the feudal epic represents a response not to the king's growing power, but to his inability to provide adequate political control.[80] According to Bezzola, when a society no longer succeeds in imposing its law upon individuals, they rebel by expropriating the power of central government to themselves. As a gauntlet tossed in the face of Capetian rule, a challenge to govern forcefully, the late *chanson de geste* is a reaction against the anarchy of the late eleventh and twelfth centuries.

From a slightly different perspective, Alfred Adler concurs with Calin: the epic manifests an element of daydreaming about an age in which great feudal magnates were as strong as, if not stronger than, the king; an age,

---

78. Actually, this is just as true for *Raoul de Cambrai* as for the other works mentioned.
79. Calin, *Epic of Revolt.*
80. R. Bezzola, "De *Roland* à *Raoul de Cambrai*," in *Mélanges Hoepffner* (Paris: Les Belles Lettres, 1949), pp. 195–213; "A propos de la valeur littéraire des chansons féodales," in *La Technique littéraire des chansons de geste* (Paris: Les Belles Lettres, 1959), pp. 183–195.

too, in which the necessity of hierarchy, the interdependence of vassal and king, was taken for granted.[81] A monarch must be powerful enough to provide protection for the members of his *mesnie*. The vassal, in turn, must be strong enough to furnish effective aid to his sovereign when his assistance is needed. And yet, as Adler insists, the necessity of adequate power on the part of both lord and vassal leads to a double paradox: the king's strength allows him to restrain his subjects unilaterally, while the baron's strength affords him a certain measure of independence with regard to his lord's control. In order to offer the king what he requires, a baron must assert sovereignty in his own right; in order to provide what his vassals seek, monarchy creates the conditions to dominate them. For Adler, the late epic represents a forum in which the tension built into feudalism itself is worked out, the stage upon which a delicate balance of monarchic and aristocratic power is achieved.[82] Finally, Karl-Heinz Bender maintains that the epic in general, and the epic of revolt in particular, reflect an essentially accurate image of contemporary social reality.[83] Concern with issues of right, duty, limits and responsibilities of sovereignty follows, from *Roland* to romance, the pattern of royalty's historical relation to baronage. *Roland* projects an idealized picture of monarchy. The *Couronnement de Louis* offers a more realistic portrayal of a weak king surrounded by valorous vassals. The epic of revolt reflects the steady increase in the power of royalty under Philippe-Auguste.

All four recent perspectives upon the feudal cycle are plagued by internal difficulties. If, as Calin contends, the "ultimate lesson of the *chanson de geste* is one of order and harmony," why does the epic author sympathize so strongly with a victimized aristocracy? And why does he so consistently portray the chief agent of central authority, the king, as a pitifully weak and bumbling figure? If, as Bezzola asserts, the epic is symptomatic of nobility's all-pervasive yearning for peace, why does this desire take the form of revolt? How do the barons seek to overcome anarchy by promoting it? Assuming that the author secretly sides with

81. A. Adler, *Rückzug in epischer Parade* (Frankfurt: Klosterman, 1963).

82. See also P. Matarasso, *Recherches historiques et littéraires sur "Raoul de Cambrai"* (Paris: Nizet, 1962). Mme. Matarasso believes the rebel barons cycle reflects nobility's reaction against the encroaching power of royalty. Like Calin, she views these poems as a combination of daydreaming about a violent past and an expression of contemporary historical crisis. But like Bezzola, she also sees them as appeals for stronger central control.

83. K.-H. Bender, *König und Vassal. Untersuchungen zur Chanson de geste des XII. Jahrhunderts* (Heidelberg: Carl Winter, 1967).

the principle of strong central organization, what then justifies the favorable portrait of nobility as the persecuted partisans of right against the triumphant principle of royal injustice? If, as Adler argues, the feudal cycle aspires to ideal political balance, why does monarchy inevitably succeed in vanquishing—exiling, killing, or converting—vassalage? And if, as Bender suggests, the epic mirrors historical reality, how does one reconcile *Roland*'s place as ideal with its early composition? How does one account for roughly contemporaneous works such as *La Chanson de Guillaume* and *Gormond et Isembard* in which the image of monarchy could not be further from ideal? What explains the important differences between the kings of the late epic, between the inept Louis of *Raoul de Cambrai* and the powerful Charlemagne of *Les Quatre Filz*, for example?

The relationship of monarchy to baronage is, as the theories of Calin, Bezzola, Adler, and Bender suggest, subject to the most contradictory interpretation. It is, we suspect, more problematic than they are willing to admit. Indeed, there may be no logical ground upon which the author's moral alliance with the underdog and his material alliance with the winner can be reconciled. Calin has argued skillfully that it is this very unresolved quality of the poems of revolt that places them within the mode of "high mimetic tragedy." And yet, a step outside of the traditional perspective of royalty versus nobility reveals much that is common to both. Ultimately, the fundamental identity of king and vassal with respect to the question of war itself far outweighs the differences that divide them with respect to any particular dispute. In reality, the paradox of the feudal epic implies the preeminence of neither monarchy nor aristocracy *per se*. It points, rather, to the more general failure of war, like the duel, to provide adequate responses to the problems of the postfeudal age. Both royalty and nobility remain unable to achieve lasting and meaningful military victory. Their triumphs are either temporary—like those of Charlemagne over Renaud and Ogier and that of Charles Martel over Girart—or futile. The former accounts for the theme of war's prolongation and exceeding difficulty, the latter for the theme of the hero's violent death, withdrawal from the world, or awareness of his own folly at the conclusion of fighting. The central issue in the late epic is not who wins, but the price of victory. Its key concern is the continued effectiveness of military might for the maintenance of political sovereignty. This concern, which is implicit to the checked siege motif, becomes explicit in the theme of the epic debate.

Epic Debate

The motif of the checked siege is symptomatic of a progressively less efficient fighting strategy within twelfth-century literature generally and within the feudal epic cycle in particular. It would not serve as such a potent symbol of crisis, however, if it were not for an equally frequent and related *topos*: the debate. In the course of almost every battle the pros and cons of war are discussed at the highest levels of chivalry. At the end of almost every prolonged siege stands the epic council, the equivalent of the feudal *concilium* or *parlement*. Tactical stalemate before the walls of Saragossa develops into discussion between Roland and Ganelon. Only then does the choice between relentless pursuit and compromise become an issue of contention. Like his predecessor, the Charlemagne of *Les Quatre Filz* has almost succeeded in conquering all lands within his purview. His inability to subdue a single baron, like Charles's failure to take the last Saracen city, gives rise to the dispute with Naimes whether to proceed militarily or to wait (v. 101). Their quarrel continues after the initial campaign against Beuves d'Aigremont: while Naimes and Galerant urge Charles to accept an offer of peace, the emperor resists (v. 1390). The dispute is revived just prior to the siege of Montauban and again after Renaud's theft of the imperial crown (vv. 4488, 5173, 5702). Debate among the Aymon brothers follows Charles's own capture. Richard favors execution and vengeance; Renaud and Allard sue for clemency and peace. Through discussion they reach an accord:

> Molt parlerent li frere cel jor diversement:
> Li uns li dist issi et li autre [autrement],
> Mais à la fin se tienent tuit à l'acordement.

> That day the brothers spoke much and diversely:
> Some spoke one way and the others spoke otherwise,
> But in the end they all came to an agreement.
> > (*Quatre Filz* v. 12,653)

Old issues are rekindled in the French camp before the battle of Trémoigne. When Naimes fails to convince Charles of the wisdom of peace, Renaud himself presents his case to the king (v. 14,032). During the siege, Naimes repeats his original recommendation; but despite Roland's concurrence, Charles persists (v. 14,740). In the council that meets to consider Renaud's and Richard of Normandy's joint proposal for ending hostilities, Roland, Naimes, Ogier, and Turpin urge acceptance. The obdurate emperor again rejects the advice of his barons (v. 14,947).

The debates of *Raoul de Cambrai* focus no less intently upon the issue of peace and war. Before proceeding against the sons of Herbert de Vermandois, Raoul discusses the imminence of conflict with his mother. Aalais tries to dissuade her son and thereby prevent fighting:

> "Biax fix Raoul," dist la dame au vis afier,
> A si grant tort guere ne commencier.
> Li fil Herbert sont molt bon chevalier,
> Riche d'avoir, si ont maint ami chier.

> "Dear son Raoul," said the lady of proud countenance,
> Don't begin a war which is so ill-advised,
> The sons of Herbert are very good knights,
> Rich in goods, and have many close friends.
>
> (*Raoul* v. 1030)

Raoul's refusal to heed his mother's warning is but the initial phase of a multi-phased debate within his own council. Immediately after the destruction of Origny his enemies offer compromise: if Raoul will vacate their lands, Herbert's sons will pardon the death of Bernier's mother, rebuild the charred monastery, and aid him to recapture his hereditary fief at Cambrai (v. 2101). Guerri recommends compliance, while his nephew resists all attempts at peace. Bernier, like Renaud, repeats the offer in person, and it is again debated within the Cambresian army. This time, however, Raoul mockingly urges acceptance—*Fai le, biaus oncles, por amor Dieu te pri, Acordons nos, si soions bon ami*; and Guerri, shamed in the previous encounter, reverses his position—*Li fil H. sont tuit mi anemi; Ne lor faut guerre, de ma part les desfi!*[84]

After the recapture of Roussillon, Girart's council debates whether or not to pursue the war against Charles Martel (*Girart* v. 1458). Foulque and Don Amadieu counsel caution: a messenger should be dispatched to assess the king's intentions. Girart, on the other hand, would rather fight first and talk afterward. Only after some discussion is he persuaded to send an offer of judgment along with a threat of war if it is rejected. Debate ensues among the French whether or not to accept (v. 1724). Thierri d'Ascance reproaches Charles for having made war initially.

---

84. Do it, dear uncle, for God's love I pray you; Bring us to accord, we will be good friends. . . . The sons of Herbert are all my enemies; They will not lack war, for my part I challenge them (*Raoul* vv. 2297, 2304).

Isembart de Riom blames Girart. Don Enguerrant speaks in favor of trial, but the king, furious at the prospect of facing his enemy on an equal footing, closes discussion and orders attack. Foulque reopens debate with a generous proposal for compromise (v. 1935). And despite the menace of Evroïn de Cambrai, Enguerran, Thierri, and Pons de Claris to abandon his service if he does not accept, Charles persists. The two armies will meet upon Vaubeton Plain, where, on the morning of the second day of battle, the dispute whether or not to continue fighting is again rekindled (v. 2903). This time the barons prove more successful in forcing a truce. As long as the peace lasts, the question of war's feasibility remains dormant. With Thierri's return from pilgrimage and his murder, however, the dialogue continues (v. 3578). Don Esmoïs warns Charles against attacking Roussillon before Girart can be judged. Arman de Beaumoncel advises him to crush the enemy before pressing for peace. The Vicomte de Saint-Martial pleads for acceptance of payment for Thierri's death. Gace de Dreux proposes judging Girart, and, with the consent of his full council, Charles agrees. Girart's own council debates whether to submit to judgment and thus prevent war or to attack (v. 4104). The messenger dispatched to announce the rebel barons' eagerness for trial finds himself in a heated argument with the king (v. 5515). Finally, when all efforts at peace have failed and Girart has maneuvered Charles within the walls of Roussillon, debate erupts within the ranks of the besieging army. Boson and Gilbert speak in favor of all-out war, while Girart acknowledges the futility of fighting—
Seiner, non puis mais gerre far ne sofrir.[85]

Girart's recognition, along with the general failure of war to produce quick, decisive victory or defeat, calls into question the most basic assumptions of any warrior society, namely the limits of armed force. If, on the one hand, the checked siege is the outward sign of a crisis of feudal tactics, the debate, on the other hand, represents an attempt at resolution. It serves, above all, as a forum for the discussion of possible alternatives to war: compromise, trial, expiation, surrender. Unlike the siege, which cannot escape its roots in a strategy of the past, the *topos* of debate looks forward, beyond the limits of fighting. Through it, the epic, a genre based

---

85. Lords, I can no longer make war nor suffer it (*Girart* v. 6869). One final debate follows Girart's recognition: Charles Martel resists his enemy's offer of peace, while the bishop and queen favor it (v. 8942).

upon the implicit preeminence of force, manages to question its own *raison d'être*. For what is at stake in every instance is both a particular military situation—individual personalities, defensive and offensive tactics, battlefield losses versus damage inflicted upon the foe—and the endeavor of war itself. The control of private war and the duel, along with their replacement by a more learned system of inquest, is the subject of our next chapter.

CHAPTER III

The Inquest

The Peace Movement

Suppression of nobility's long-standing right to private war in an age in which tradition constituted law was at best a difficult undertaking. Nonetheless, formal attempts to regulate the potentially limitless violence of the *faida* occurred as early as the tenth century. The first peace movements orginated in clerical reaction to the expropriation of church property during the feudal era. At the Council of Trosly (909) the concept of sacrilege was broadened to include assault upon all goods belonging to the Universal Church. Regardless of whether a particular object or piece of land had been officially consecrated, its unauthorized confiscation automatically incurred excommunication.[1] The anathema of Trosly was renewed five times between its inception and the Council of Padua in 955. Direct opposition to the blood feud began to make itself felt in southern France toward the end of the century. Combining ideology with expediency, the horror of blood with a desire for clerical immunity from attack, the Council of Charroux (989) ratified a special treaty of protection.[2] Under God's Peace, or the *paix de Dieu*, acts of violence

---

1. E. Amman and A. Dumas, *L'Histoire de L'Eglise* (Paris: Blond et Gay, 1940), 7: 491; G. Duby, *Le Dimanche de Bouvines* (Paris: Gallimard, 1973), pp. 80–81.
2. M. Bloch, *Feudal Society* (Chicago: University of Chicago Press, 1966), 2: 413; Y. Bongert, *Recherches sur les cours laïques du Xe au XIIIe siècle* (Paris: Picard, 1948), p. 98; A. Esmein, *Cours élémentaire du droit français* (Paris: Sirey, 1930), p. 251; F. Lot and R. Fawtier, *Les Institutions françaises du moyen âge* (Paris: Presses Universitaires de France, 1958), 2: 423; F. Pollock and F. Maitland, *The History of English Law* (Cambridge: Cambridge University Press, 1923), 1: 75. See also *La Paix* (Brussels: Société Jean Bodin, 1961).

against church property, laborers, peasants, their livestock, and clerics were forbidden under pain of official sanction. The Peace of Charroux took the form of voluntary submission rather than true prohibition and was sponsored by local prelates with the cooperation of the local nobility. It must have been at least partially successful, for similar accords were adopted by the Council of Narbonne in 990 and that of Anse in 994. An agreement concluded at the Synod of Puy (990) extended the protection of God's Peace to merchants, mills, vineyards, and men on their way to or home from church. Pacts of "justice and peace" were signed in 997 by the Bishop of Limoges, the Abbot of Saint-Martial, and the Bishop and Duke of Aquitaine. It was decided at the Council of Poitiers in 1000 that all infractions pertaining to *res invasae* would henceforth be settled by trial rather than war.[3]

Monarchy favored the ecclesiastical peace movement. It appears likely, even, that Robert the Pious attempted to promulgate a declared peace at Orléans in 1010, although he remained unable to enforce it. By the third decade of the eleventh century the spirit of the southern pacts had spread to Burgundy and the North. At the Council of Verdun-le-Doubs (1016) the lay aristocracy of the region promised, in the presence of the archbishops of Lyon and Besancon: (1) not to violate the peace of sanctuaries; (2) not to enter forcefully the *atrium* of any church except to apprehend violators of the peace; (3) not to attack unarmed clerics, monks, or their men; (4) not to appropriate their goods except to compensate for legitimate wrong inflicted.[4] The Council of Soissons adopted an identical formula in 1023, as did the Councils of Anse in 1025, Poitiers in 1026, Charroux in 1028, and Limoges in 1031. Elsewhere, the bishops elicited individual promises of nonviolence from members of a particular diocese. At the request of the Abbot of Cluny and in the presence of the archbishop and the high clergy of the region of Mâcon, numerous Burgundian nobles swore in 1153 to refrain from attacking church property, to resist those who did, and to besiege the castles to which they withdrew if necessary.

A variation of the *paix de Dieu* was concluded by the bishops of Soissons and Beauvais. The *pactum sive treuga*, or *trêve de Dieu*, forbade violence not according to the object of attack, but according to its time, season or day. Wars of vengeance were initially prohibited during the

---

3. Amman and Dumas, *L'Eglise*, 7: 495.
4. G. Duby, *La Société aux XIe et XIIe siècles dans la région mâconnaise* (Paris: Armand-Colin, 1953), p. 199.

seasons of Easter, Toussaint, and Ascension. In addition to their oath governing sacred property and clerics, the subscribers of the Council of Verdun-le-Doubs swore: (1) not to participate during certain periods of the year in any military expedition other than that of the king, local prelate, or count; (2) to abstain for the duration of authorized wars from pillaging and violating the peace of churches; (3) not to attack unarmed knights during Lent.[5] The Council of Toulouse added certain saints' feast days to the list of proscribed dates; the bishops of Vienne and Besançon included Christmas and the Lenten season. Carolingian interdiction of the blood feud on Sundays was revived by the Synod of Roussillon in 1027.[6] From Sunday it was gradually extended to include almost the entire week: first from Friday at vespers to Monday morning and then from Wednesday sundown to Monday. Pope Nicholas declared a general *paix de Dieu* at the Lateran Council of 1059, preparing the way for Urban II's Peace of Clermont in anticipation of the First Crusade. In general, the domestic peace movement gained momentum because of the Crusades. Innocent IV's effort to curb internal anarchy inspired, in 1245, a letter granting settlements to all private parties who requested them. Along with Louis's instruction to his *prévôts* and *baillis* before departing for the Holy Land, the interdiction of war joined papacy with monarchy for the purpose of directing toward a mutual foreign foe the crusader spirit that might have otherwise been wasted upon petty civil strife.

Municipal opposition to private war accompanied the communal movements of the eleventh and twelfth centuries. Though theoretically excluded from participating in the blood feud and protected by local peace pacts, the merchants living in northern and eastern France were nonetheless subject to the ravages of vendetta. An abundance of evidence indicates a willingness on the part of some municipal residents to settle their differences independently of civil procedure.[7] Most, however, sought more regular means of settlement. When it came to handling arms, the merchant, like the cleric, found himself at a distinct disadvantage. The commune was, in essence, a peace league, a specially designated civil space whose inhabitants were guaranteed the right to trial

5. *Ibid.*, p. 200.

6. Amman and Dumas, *L'Eglise*, 7: 499; Bloch, *Feudal Society*, 2: 414.

7. Bloch, *Feudal Society*, 2: 417; P. Dubois, *Les Asseurements au XIIIe siècle* (Paris: Rousseau, 1900), pp. 45, 102–114; C. Petit-Dutaillis, *La Monarchie féodale en France et en Angleterre* (Paris: Albin-Michel, 1971), p. 280; C. Petit-Dutaillis, *Documents nouveaux sur les moeurs populaires et la vengeance* (Paris: Champion, 1908).

without combat. Among the founding principles of the municipality of LeMans (1070) were the repression of vendettas among the members of the urban "friendship" and mutual protection against external attack. The charter of Laon (1128) was entitled *institutio pacis*; that of Tornai, *forma pacis et compositionis*.[8] The pact of Verdun-le-Doubs was, in effect, an earlier version of the twelfth-century *convenance de la paix*, a protective agreement organized by artisan and trade guilds. In 1182 a carpenter from Le Puy founded a brotherhood of merchants and manufacturers devoted to the suppression of violence. Not only were feuds prohibited within the group, but when a murder did occur, the family of the victim was expected to seek reconciliation with the guilty party by inviting him to its house.[9] The peace league of Le Puy had spread throughout Languedoc, Auxerre, and Berry before seigneurial uneasiness with institutional restraints upon the right to private war led to its own suppression. In spite of constant and often violent opposition, similar *confréries de paix* appeared in Champagne, Burgundy, and Picardie under Philip the Fair and his sons.

The seigneurial peace movement in the large northern feudatory states, themselves large enough to be governed as small kingdoms, prefigured any sustained monarchic attempt to control private war. An accord ratified in Flanders at the Council of Thérouanne (1042–3) regulated the right of the Flemish aristocracy to bear arms; the count alone could make war during periods of prescribed abstinence.[10] Angevine Normandy, inspired by the Flemish example, was sufficiently advanced administratively and judicially to serve as a model for Philippe-Auguste after royal annexation of the duchy in the early thirteenth century. The *trêve de Dieu* signed at Caen in 1047 had validated the principle of ducal regulation of private campaigns. According to an inquest conducted in 1091 by Robert Curthose and William Rufus, William I had enacted, as early as 1075, a *paix de Duc* limiting blood feuds and placing numerous restrictions upon the conduct of any but his own expeditions.[11] The *Consuetudines et Iusticie* of the Conqueror prohibited seeking one's enemy with hauberk, standard, and sounding horn; it forbade the taking of captives and the expro-

8. Dubois, *Asseurements*, p. 92.

9. Bloch, *Feudal Society*, 2: 416; Duby, *Bouvines*, p. 87.

10. Duby, *Bouvines*, p. 89. A similar peace had been concluded in 1030 between Badouin de Flandre and the Bishop of Noyon-Tornai. Another was ratified in 1082 by the bishop and the barons of the diocese of Liège.

11. C. H. Haskins, *Norman Institutions* (Cambridge: Harvard University Press, 1918), pp. 38, 60, 277.

priation of arms, horses, or property in the course of a feud. Burning, plunder, and wasting of fields were forbidden in disputes involving the right of seisin. Assault and ambush were outlawed in the duke's forest; and, except for the capture of an offender in *flagrante delicto*, no one was to be condemned to loss of life or limb without due process in a ducal court. William's law thus reflects a double current in the control of wars of vendetta. On the one hand, it limits the methods of private campaigns without prohibiting them altogether. On the other, it reserves jurisdiction over certain cases of serious infraction for the duke's own court, thus bypassing the local seigneurial judge who would ordinarily have enjoyed exclusive cognizance over the crimes committed within his fief.

The effects of William's original effort to control private war and to extend ducal prerogative through a special peace and reserved jurisdiction are evident in the earliest French customal. The *Très Ancien Coutumier de Normandie* prohibits military response to offenses normally requiring vendetta; instead, it enjoins the offender to trial:

Nus homs n'ost fere guerre envers autre; mes qui leur fera tort, si se plaignent al duc e a sa justice, e se ce est cause citeaine, il fera amander le mesfet par chatel; se elle est criminnal, il le fera amander par les membres.

No man dares make war against another; if someone does him wrong, let him complain to the duke and his justiciar, and if the matter is civil, he [the justiciar] will cause the wronged party to be recompensed in chattel; and if it is criminal, he will cause recompense to be made in limbs.

(TAC 24)

The *Grand Coutumier* specifically marked a number of crimes—homicide, theft, rape, arson, assault at home or on the duke's highway, counterfeiting—for the duke's justice. In addition, the duke alone was responsible for maintaining the Norman Truce of God; any infractions of his peace reverted automatically to his court. Under Henry I a fixed fine of nine pounds accompanied all such convictions. The revenue went directly to the bishop; ducal officers were charged with its collection. The rest of the guilty party's personal belongings escheated to the duke for whom the exercise of high justice represented a lucrative source of income.[12]

Monarchic opposition to private war followed the Norman pattern of limitation and, eventually, prohibition. As early as Louis VII's reign, Suger considered it the duty of kings to repress, "with their powerful

12. *Ibid.*, p. 36; *GC* 64–65.

hands and through the rights of their office," any but royal wars. Although unable to control the *faida* with any certainty until well into the thirteenth century, the Crown did support a number of measures restricting the right to war. According to Beaumanoir, only noblemen can legally settle a dispute through recourse to arms; a conflict between a nobleman and a bourgeois or a peasant was to be resolved in public court (2: 1702: 372). Brothers and even stepbrothers were prohibited from fighting each other (2: 1667: 354). Furthermore, the Bailiff of Clermont carefully defines the limits of family obligation in pursuit of blood feuds. Duty to one's kin-group had formerly extended to the seventh degree. Beaumanoir maintains that since the Church had set impediments to marriage only at the fourth degree, kinsmen of more remote paternity were not obligated to come to the aid of distant relatives (2: 1686: 362). Thus, while the collective responsibility of the feudal *comitatus* had not been eliminated entirely, it was curtailed somewhat.

The rules pertaining to initiation and cessation of hostilities were a crucial factor in the limitation of vendetta. As Beaumanoir specifies, fighting may begin either by face-to-face challenge or by messenger. In both cases the declaration must be made clearly and openly; war without public defiance is the equivalent of murder without warning, or treason:

Qui autrui veut metre en guerre par paroles, il ne les doit pas dire doubles ne couvertes, mes si cleres et si apertes que cil a qui les paroles sont dites ou envoïes sache qu'il convient qu'il se gart; et qui autrement le feroit, ce seroit traïsons.

He who wishes to initiate war against another by declaration, must not do so ambiguously or covertly, but so clearly and so openly that he to whom the declaration is spoken or sent may know that he should be on his guard; and he who proceeds otherwise, commits treason.

(Beaumanoir 2: 1675: 358)

Once war had been declared, the parties had to wait forty days before actually coming to blows in order to alert those not present at the original declaration (2: 1702: 372). This waiting period or *quarantaine le roi*, which was attributed to Philippe-Auguste and renewed by Saint Louis, again emphasizes the distinction between open and secretive homicide; it broadens the criminal concept to cover the domain of general warfare. Surprise attack upon an enemy clan prior to the end of the forty day injunction constituted an act of treason as opposed to legitimate vengeance (Beaumanoir 2: 1704: 372). For Beaumanoir the precepts governing peace were designed to encourage and facilitate the cessation of hostilities. In the event that both parties agreed to stop fighting, they need only declare a cease-fire according to the same procedure that they had originally used to declare war. Peace was symbolically validated by breaking bread together (Beaumanoir 2: 1680: 360). When both parties agreed to renounce open warfare without disclaiming the dispute that led to war in the first place, the matter was to be settled by judicial duel. Or, if either side sought to bring the quarrel to court instead of fighting, his opponent was obliged to comply. Finally, in the absence of a demand for peace from either or both sides, the suzerain retained the power to impose a settlement whenever he felt it in the interest of the common good (2: 1681–2: 361). Regardless of the route followed to public arbitration rather than war, pursuit of the vendetta became illegal once a judgment in court had occurred.

The goal of Beaumanoir's prescriptions was the establishment of either a *trêve*, a ceasefire of limited duration, or an *asseurement*, which was a more permanent truce. Both consisted of solemn promises by the two principle adversaries along with their families not to engage in violence for a prescribed term. Breaking the peace was considered a capital offense warranting the automatic intervention of higher judicial authority.

The early history of such armistices or *paix à parties* reveals a preponderance of voluntary submission to royal jurisdiction.[13] As monarchy grew progressively stronger, settlements imposed from above, with or without the consent of the parties involved, became increasingly frequent. By the thirteenth century the Crown maintained, at least in theory, the right to intercede whenever war seemed imminent. Potential enemies were, in such instances, summoned to appear before a royal court. Refusal to comply could result in seizure of the reluctant baron's personal possessions as well as his lands (Beaumanoir 2: 1669, 1708: 355, 374). Regularization of the obligatory *paix à parties* was given great impetus by Louis IX's general peace prior to departure for the Middle East. Louis VII, in conjunction with the Archbishop of Reims, the Duke of Burgundy, and the counts of Champagne and Flanders, had declared a ten year *trêve* almost a century earlier (1155). Following his great-grandfather's example, Saint Louis ordered his representatives to conclude five year settlements between warring parties whether or not they

---

13. L. Buisson, *König Ludwig IX, der Heilige, und das Recht* (Freidburg: Herder, 1954), p. 191; Dubois, *Asseurements*, pp. 131–145, 174; Esmein, *Cours élémentaire*, p. 253.

had previously requested intervention. Though some maintain that Louis issued at the same time an ordinance prohibiting private war for an identical period, the text of this proclamation has never been found.

The Parlement records of the second half of the thirteenth century contain a large number of *trêves* and *asseurements* concluded in the presence of royal judicial officers. In a typical formula the Count of Saint-Pol, upon the king's order, promised that neither he nor any member of his family would attack his enemy Jean Bailleul: *Dominus Johannes non habet gardem de me, nec de meis, nec ipse, nec sui.*[14] Despite the advice of his counsellors, who saw in the reconciliation of bellicose vassals at war with each other a potentially unified threat to monarchy, Louis personally negotiated numerous treaties between the most powerful lords of the realm: between the Count of Chalon and his son, between John of Chalon and Thibaud of Champagne, and between the warring families of Burgundy and Lorraine. According to Joinville, the Saint-King would best be remembered for his persistent effort to curtail internal conflicts among his subjects.[15] Louis, upon his deathbed, is supposed to have exhorted the young Philip to act swiftly to seek peace in the realm whenever war threatened: *Se guerres et contens meuvent entre tes sougis, apaise-les au plus tost que tu pourras.*[16]

The imposition of either a royal injunction, where war seemed unavoidable, or a temporary treaty, once it had already begun, represented a haphazard means of controlling private military campaigns. *Trêves* and *asseurements* were applied on an *ad hoc* basis to individual cases; they provided a makeshift solution to a specific crisis without the binding legitimacy of universal law. Nonetheless, as part of a general monarchic policy of limitation, the *paix à parties* constituted a necessary step toward the statutory prohibition of private warfare that is believed to have

14. Lord John shall not fear me, nor my family, nor I him and his family (cited G. Ducoudray, *Les Origines du Parlement de Paris et la justice au XIIIᵉ et XIVᵉ siècles* [Paris: Hachette, 1902], p. 331); Similarly, Bernard d'Amiens promised not to attack Peter Griffart: "Dominica in Trinitate, Bernardus Ambianis, miles, assecuravit de se et suis Petrum Griffart et suos; et contra idem Petrus de se et suis, dictum Bernardum et suos." "On Trinity Sunday Bernard of Amiens, a knight, assured himself and his family to Peter Griffart and his family; and the same Peter and his family assured Bernard and his family" (cited Dubois, *Asseurements*, p. 179).

15. Joinville, *Histoire de Saint Louis*, ed. N. de Wailly (Paris: Firmin Didot, 1874), p. 375; see also Petit-Dutaillis, *Monarchie féodale*, p. 278.

16. If war and strife arise between your subjects, restore peace between them as soon as you can (Joinville, *Histoire*, p. 404).

occurred between 1254 and 1258. Like the hypothetical earlier ordinance of Pontoise, the exact date and nature of interdiction remains somewhat of a mystery. Nevertheless, the systematic legal suppression of any but the official wars of the Crown was a step of monumental importance for late Capetian monarchy.[17] The progress of royalty against the feudal aristocracy, for whom war represented a right of class indistinguishable from their own sovereignty, can be measured in the precarious history of Louis's law.

The persistence of wars of vengeance following the Saint-King's death is apparent in the large number of *trêves* concluded in the Parlement of Paris during the reign of Philip the Bold.[18] Despite the attempt to continue his father's policy of suppression, Philip remained more capable of terminating conflicts already under way than preventing the outbreak of new wars. Philip the Fair experienced even greater difficulty in controlling the resurgence of independent military ventures among his vassals. Under pressure from the northern municipalities, he tried on four separate occasions—1296, 1304, 1311, and 1314—to renew Louis's original interdiction. Philip's ordinances were less comprehensive, however, than that of his grandfather. For while the king demanded the cessation of private hostilities for the duration of his own campaigns, as soon as the Crown was not at war, nobles had the right to settle their quarrels as they saw fit. Moreover, the disorders of the end of his reign—the conflicts in Flanders and Guyenne, the dispute with Boniface VIII—forced him to grant numerous exceptions in return for taxes and support.

Obliged to seek the aid of nobility for his own struggle in Flanders, Louis X, like Philip IV, granted the right of war on an individual basis. According to a charter of 1315, the king conferred upon the barons of Burgundy "arms and wars in the manner to which they were formerly accustomed."[19] Louis promised to conduct an inquest to determine the status of baronial privilege in Burgundy at the time of Saint Louis and to set local policy accordingly. Just a year later he found it necessary to grant war-making powers to the nobles of Toulouse, Périgeux, Rodez, Beau-

17. R. Cazelles, "La Réglementation de la guerre privée de Saint Louis à Charles V et la précarité des ordonnances," *Revue Historique du Droit Français et Etranger* 38 (1960): 530–548; Dubois, *Asseurements*, pp. 75–79; Lot and Fawtier, *Institutions*, 2:425; J. Tardif, "La Date et le caractère de l'ordonnance de Saint Louis sur le duel judiciaire," *Revue Historique du Droit Français et Etranger* 11 (1887): 163.

18. Buisson, *Ludwig IX*, p. 205; Ducoudray, *Parlement*, p. 335.

19. Cazelles, "Guerre privée," p. 541.

caire, and Lyon. Here, however, the king managed to maintain certain ground-rules reminiscent of earlier controls as well as of the ecclesiastic *paix de Dieu*. Private war was forbidden during royal campaigns. Otherwise, a challenger had to wait eight days after declaring war before launching an attack. In the event that his challenge was refused, the monarch retained the right to impose a six-month armistice. A special clause forbade hostilities against widows and children.

Philip VII of Valois adopted a formula similar to that of Louis X in a charter granted to the barons of Aquitaine, the "Letters patent by which the King permits private wars in the Duchy of Aquitaine."[20] In keeping with well-established custom, Philip agreed to allow those of noble birth to fight each other providing that proper warning had been given and that the challenge had been accepted. All internecine conflicts must cease, however, during times of national war. As far as the general maintenance of arms was concerned, the king promised to make an inquiry into the custom at the time the duchy was held by England in order to determine the present status of the law. In response to a request from the towns of Normandy, John the Good forbade private war despite preexisting statutes of the *Très Ancien* and *Grand Coutumier*. A universal interdiction was proclaimed in 1352, almost a century after Louis's original decree. The privilege of war continued to be exchanged for taxes and military assistance throughout the 1350s and 1360s. A charter obtained from Charles V in 1370 recognized the legality of private hostilities in the regions of Burgundy, Nivernais, and Dauphiné. It was not until 1374 that Charles's general military proclamation, the equivalent of the twelfth-century English *Assizes des Armes*, established the legal basis for the recruitment, administration, and command of a permanent national army.

The precariousness of ordinances dealing with private war reveals much about the fundamental nature of law and kingship in the Middle Ages. First of all, the laws abolishing war represented conditional prescriptions indissolubly linked to the personality of their author. The statutes of a particular king perished with him, and his successors were obliged to renew all previously enacted measures in order to preserve any sense of legal continuity. The strength of custom was, as late as the middle of the fourteenth century, a powerful deterrent to new legislation.

20. *Idem.*

Second, almost all of the statutes of prohibition and the charters granting the right to bear arms were rooted in a specific situation calling for either injunction or sanction. Vendetta might be outlawed for the duration of the king's wars, but with the conclusion of a royal armistice the legitimacy of individual proscriptions also terminated. Conversely, monarchy's need for taxes and support often produced authorizations that were subsequently revoked when the situation or the price permitted. Laws and charters were designed to deal with a particular set of circumstances for a limited amount of time; once a crisis had subsided, the legislation that it had elicited tended to be forgotten as well. Two years of crusade had provoked Louis VII's first general secular peace. The imminence of Louis IX's prolonged absence from France inspired mandatory five-year *trêves* along with what may have been the first permanent interdiction of war. The financial burden of Philip IV's campaign in Flanders led to the issuance of widespread war-making powers elsewhere in the realm. Philip VI's confirmation of the *foras, consuetudines et usus antiquos* of the Aquitanian nobility was intended to relieve Edward III of his remaining holdings in Guyenne.

Finally, the right to engage in private war constituted a commodity to be bought and sold like any other commercial good. Beginning with Philip the Fair, war became the object of a complex cycle of economic exchange between royalty, bourgeoisie, and feudal aristocracy. During periods of relative domestic peace its prohibition was purchased by those most interested in its suppression. The majority of local interdictions were, in fact, paid for by towns or ecclesiastical communities, although an occasional nobleman involved in an unfavorable struggle might prefer to pay rather than fight. In times of great turmoil or financial need on the part of monarchy, the right to bear arms was sold to those who had the most to gain in waging war themselves. Maintenance of personal military contingents was among the most cherished prerogatives of the high nobility, and aristocracy proved willing on more than one occasion to accept the necessity of payment in order to exercise its traditional military rights. Royalty, in turn, showed itself willing to respect the claims of nobility in one region in order to concentrate more effectively its energies in another: Louis X's charter to the Burgundian lords, like that of his father, was accorded in direct response to a costly Flemish expedition. Unable to eliminate private war altogether, monarchy did manage to transform its regulation into a lucrative source of revenue. The income derived from the alternate sale of prohibition and privilege afforded the late Capetian and Valois kings the means to pursue their own military aims.

Suppression of the Duel

Historically, monarchy's attempts to curtail the clannish vendettas so inimical to the growth of transcendent national sovereignty were linked to a similar campaign directed against war's symbolic sister, the judicial duel. Like the *faida*, the *judicium Dei* represented a right of class incumbent upon noble birth. But where the suppression of vendetta led to the regular exchange of the money for the right to war, efforts to eliminate trial by combat produced the verbal, abstract, and learned judicial forms of the late Middle Ages. In the first instance, violence was transformed into value; in the second, it became mediated through the language of the civil trial. Here again, the Church preceded monarchy in opposing both the duel and its sporting equivalent, the tournament. Innocent II had outlawed tournaments in 1130 and again in 1139. Eugene III followed suit in 1148, Alexander III in 1179, Innocent IV in 1250, and Nicholas III in 1279. The Councils of Valence and Limoges had issued condemnations of the duel in 885 and 994. Nicholas I explicitly forbade it in 867, Innocent III in 1203, and Innocent IV in 1245. In a papal bull of July 1252 addressed to the Bishop of Reims, Innocent IV repeated his previous interdiction. His successor addressed a similar proscription to the Bishop of Auxerre in 1258. The Fourth Lateran Council (1215) not only prohibited clerics from participating in all forms of judicial ordeal, but abolished the unilateral ordeals by fire and boiling water.[21]

Monarchic suppression of the judicial duel was rare before the thirteenth century.[22] Carolingian opposition had been vigorous but shortlived. William the Conqueror restricted the practice in England after the

21. Municipal resistance to the duel was no less intense. The guarantee of trial by known judges as an alternative to trial by combat was, in fact, a feature of many communal charters; see C. Petit-Dutaillis, *Les Communes françaises* (Paris: Albin-Michel, 1970), pp. 44–58. Duels were prohibited by the commune of Genoa in 1056, Ypres in 1116, and Saint Omer in 1127. Elsewhere, abuses of accusation, representation, and actual combat were strictly regulated; see above p. 111.

22. Louis VII forbade the duel in certain specific cases. For instance, a charter issued in 1174 made it illegal for the men of the church of Saint Pierre de Juziers to do battle in matters of disputed franchise. The charter was reconfirmed by Philippe-Auguste in 1183. A charter dated 1886 proscribed trial by combat for the commune of Sens (Bongert, *Recherches*, pp. 234–238).

invasion, specifying that when an Englishman accused a Frenchman of murder, theft, or equivalent infraction and then refused battle, the defendant retained the right of exculpation by oath.[23] Again, at the Council of Lillebonne (1080), William prohibited clerical participation in trials by combat. Henry II made decisive inroads against the duel, which, in reality, never enjoyed the popularity in England that it had on the Continent. Be that as it may, the *Grand Assize* of 1179 upheld the right of an illegally dispossessed tenant to refuse battle and to insist upon a jury trial in a royal court. Ordeals were officially abolished in Britain by a letter patent of January 26, 1219.[24]

The most significant prohibition of the *judicium Dei*, and one of the most important single legal documents of the French Middle Ages, is Saint Louis's ordinance of the late 1250s forbidding trial by combat within the royal domain. Although, again, the exact date and text of proclamation remain unknown, two approximations have survived. The first, a copy of Philip the Fair's interdiction of 1306 published in Savaron's *Traicté contre les duels* (1610), is felt to be a reproduction of Louis's original law. The second appeared in the criminal register in use at the court of Robert d'Artois, the *Livre de Saint-Juste*:

De deffandre batailles et d'amener loiaus prueves.
Nous deffandons les batailles par tout notre domoine en toutes quereles, mais nous n'ostons mie les clains, les respons, les contremanz, ne touz autres erremanz qui aient esté accostumé en cort laie en jusques à ores, selonc les usages de divers païs, fors tant que nos en ostons les batailles; et en leu de batailles, nos metons prueves de tesmoinz et de chartres.

Of the interdiction of battles and the adducing of reliable proof.
We forbid battles throughout our domain in all disputes, but we in no way eliminate the complaints, the replies, the countermands, and all other procedures which have hitherto been in use in the lay court, according to the customs of various regions, except that we eliminate battles from them; and in place of battles, we put proof by witness and charter.

(*Etablissements* 2: 8)

The ordinance against duels, like those against private war, became the object of an exceedingly complex exchange between monarchy and aristocracy. Much evidence can be found to show that it was poorly

23. A. Canel, "Le Combat judiciaire en Normandie," in *Mémoires de la Société des Antiquitaires de Normandie* 22 (1927): 578.

24. Petit-Dutaillis, *Monarchie féodale*, p. 138; Pollock and Maitland, *English Law*, 2: 599, 632.

enforced even during the lifetime of its author. Beaumanoir includes battles among the accepted methods of proof. He reports having personally witnessed several combats conducted by the royal court at Paris subsequent to Louis's decree (2: 1770, 1845: 397, 434). Philip the Fair's renewals of the interdiction of duels in 1296 and 1303 testify to their continued popularity in spite of royal opposition. Under pressure from his barons, Philip was obliged, in 1306, to sanction battles under certain circumstances; eight years later he again limited their use for the duration of royal wars. This final proscription had the most enduring effect of any previous ordinance despite the charters of repeal obtained under Louis X (1315) and Philip the Tall (1319). Its success cannot be attributed to Philip, however. Rather, it was due to the progress of an entirely different procedure implying a radically different judicial and political system.

Inquest

Louis's substitution of "proof by witness and charter"—*prueves de tesmoinz et de chartres*—for combat served to legitimize a procedure that was, in reality, much older: the Frankish technique of inquest practiced at Charlemagne's court, at the ducal court of Normandy, and in the canonical courts, where it was perfected before reintroduction, in the twelfth and thirteenth centuries, within the secular sphere. The Carolingian monarchy had utilized an archaic form of inquest known throughout northern France as the *enquête par turbe*, or *inquisitio per turbam*, for litigation affecting royal rights.[25] Where a question of custom arose, the wise men of the district gathered to determine by discussion the prevailing usage. In cases of possession, for instance, they assembled to decide how long a man had enjoyed seisin over a particular piece of property and whether or not the term of occupancy was sufficient proof of ownership. Invoked only in civil suits, the *enquête par turbe* was a possible source of the Norman and, eventually, the English jury. Unlike the jurors of a later age, however, the experienced elders of the region did not listen to witnesses or attempt to judge an individual case according to its distinct merits. Their sole purpose was to ascertain, by collective and unanimous verdict, the practices which, within a local area of jurisdiction, constituted law. The Carolingian jury of inquiry functioned as a mech-

---

25. Bongert, *Recherches*, pp. 262–266; Ducoudray, *Parlement*, p. 754; Esmein, *Cours élémentaire*, p. 689.

anism for the identification of communal custom and not as a forum for juridical debate. In fact, the *inquisitio per turbam* would have had little or no value alongside a learned procedure of written proofs or any system in which existing documentation provided a basis for judgment.

The Carolingian procedure for inquest in criminal cases, the *enquête du pays*, was much closer to our own idea of indictment and jury trial.[26] Traces survive in the customals of the thirteenth century. According to Beaumanoir, a man suspected of serious offense might be asked to submit to an inquiry concerning the deed in question (2: 1236: 139). If the suspect does not comply, the judge has the power to arrest and imprison him for a year and a day "with little to eat," pending the arrival of an accuser (1: 917: 463). In the event that none appears, the judge can still proceed with trial; although without the accused's consent, inquest cannot lead to loss of life or limb.[27] Where the results of inquiry are negative or no accuser responds to the request for public denunciation, the defendant is automatically acquitted. If, however, during the period of imprisonment he agrees to submit to inquest, the *Grand Coutumier* specifies that twenty-four men likely to know about the infraction are to be called individually before the bailiff and four credible knights of the vicinage (172). The accused is given a chance to object to the witnesses summoned; but objections notwithstanding, their statements under oath are put into writing. The bailiff, together with the judge and his assistants, reaches a decision on the basis of recorded testimony.

26. Y. Bongert, *Cours d'histoire du droit pénal: le droit pénal français de la seconde moitié du XIIIᵉ siècle à 1493* (Paris: Cours de Droit, 1970), p. 101; A. Esmein, *A History of Continental Criminal Procedure* (Boston: Little Brown, 1913), p. 63; A. Esmein, "L'Acceptation de l'enquête dans la procédure criminelle au moyen âge," *Revue Générale du Droit* 12 (1888): 13–27.

27. "Comment justice doit procedier de grous meffaiz sans denonciacion de partie.— Quant un grous meffait est fait en un pays, comme de mutres, de arsseiz de mesons et de biens, ou de roberie, ou de peceyer chemins, ou d'iglise, ou de vesseaux sur mer qui vont ou d'autres grous meffaiz, justice est tenue à en faire jurée des gienz du païs, des hommes, fammes et enffanz, et sergeanz qui poair ont de faire serment, et leur demander où ils furent la journée ou la nuytée que le meffait fut fait." "How justice should work in cases of gross wrongdoing without denunciation.—When a serious crime has been committed, like murder, arson of a house or of goods, theft, attack on the highway, in church, or on sailing vessels, or other serious crimes, the judge is justified in questioning under oath the people of the region, men, women, and children; along with the sergeants who have the power to administer oaths, he should ask them where they were on the day or night of the crime" (*La Très Ancienne Coutume de Bretagne*, ed. M. Planiol [Rennes: Plihon and Hervé, 1896], p. 154).

The great weakness of the *enquête du pays* was the necessity of obtaining either an accusation or permission of the accused in order for its results to be binding. For, as Saint Louis prescribes, even the perpetrator of a capital offense could not be executed unless the original investigation was initiated by accusal or unless it was conducted with the defendant's cooperation (*Etablissements* 2: 386). From the thirteenth century onward mention of the *enquête du pays* becomes increasingly rare, while its ecclesiastic counterpart, the *aprise* (Lat. *aprisio*), seems to merge with and replace it. Like the Frankish inquest, the *aprise* constituted a voluntary inquiry. The judge, as Beaumanoir explains, served as plaintiff for the purpose of a preliminary investigation:

Se cil qui est pris pour soupeçon de vilain cas ne veut atendre l'enqueste du fet, adonques i apartient il aprise: c'est a dire que li juges de son office doit aprendre et encherchier du fet ce qu'il en puet savoir et, s'il trueve par l'aprise le fet notoire par grant plenté de gent, il pourroit bien metre l'aprise en jugement; et pourroient li homme veoir le fet si cler par l'aprise que li pris seroit jugiés.

If he who is taken on suspicion of a serious offense does not want to submit to an inquest concerning the deed, then an *aprise* is called for: which is to say that the judge from his tribunal should undertake to look into the deed, and if by the *aprise* he finds from a large number of people that the deed is evident, he can certainly pass judgment in the *aprise*; and the men can see the deed so clearly by the *aprise* that the prisoner will be judged.

(Beaumanoir 2: 1237: 140)

While the *enquête du pays* and the *aprise* appear quite similar, the former is much closer in format to the accusatory mode of the duel. Through it, the defendant plays a much greater role in an inquiry based upon his naming and objecting to the witnesses summoned. Proportionately greater emphasis is placed upon his consent, without which any further investigation becomes perfunctory. The subtlety of Beaumanoir's wording—*ne veut atendre l'enqueste du fet*—leaves little doubt that in the *aprise* the request to proceed must emanate from the suspect himself; he seems, even, to have an interest in the expedition of trial. The *aprise* represented a means of avoiding a lengthy stay in prison on subsistence rations with, in all probability, the application of torture. As the criminal records of the thirteenth and fourteenth centuries show, more than one prisoner was anxious to accept binding arbitration in order to escape the punishment attached to refusal. Once permission was obtained, the judge proceeded entirely on his own in carrying out an investigation which, if successful, led to indictment: *et pourroient li homme veoir le fet si cler par l'aprise que li pris seroit jugiés.* An indictment upheld by the testimony of respectable witnesses thus came to constitute an act of public notoriety equivalent to capture in the act.

The judicial superiority of the dukes of Normandy over the kings of France was nowhere more apparent than in the prevalence of a regular inquisitional procedure in the Norman courts from the twelfth century onward.[28] There the archaic Frankish *inquisitio* had developed into the sworn inquest, a procedure that may have been introduced into England shortly after the Conquest.[29] The sworn inquest functioned much along the same lines as the English Doomsday and fiscal surveys of the eleventh century, both of which resembled the Carolingian *enquête par turbe.* In disputes involving ownership or custom, a defendant had the right to reject a wager of battle, insisting instead upon a jury trial. The elders of the district were then convoked with a mandate to produce a collective ruling on the issue before the court. The first known application of the sworn inquest occurred in 1133 when Henry I assembled the Norman court in order to determine the possessions of the Bishop of Bayeux. Geoffrey Plantagenet regularized the procedure, extending its cognizance to all disputes involving ecclesiastic fiefs. In an effort to recover the lands lost to the Norman bishops, "good men" of the vicinage were, on several occasions, required to confirm under oath the possessions of a particular see. The duke then issued a charter of title on the basis of a written record of their decision transmitted to him by his justiciar. Henry II, upon accession, further extended the sworn inquest by utilizing it to recover the lands and rights lost by Stephen. By the end of the first decade of Henry's reign, its pertinence had grown to include almost every aspect of civil and criminal procedure. An 1159 charter stipulates that no decision is to be pronounced in ducal courts without the "evidence of neighbors."[30] In point of fact, the universal application of the sworn inquest did not preclude trial by battle any more than Louis's prescription of a century later. The two procedures continued to exist side by side in

---

28. Bongert, *Recherches*, p. 253; Haskins, *Norman Institutions*, pp. 228–230.

29. There is, of course, the possibility that the influence was just the opposite, that the inquest was introduced to Normandy from England after the Conquest.

30. "Rex Anglorum Henricus ad Natale Domini fuit apud Falesiam, et leges instituit ut nullus decanus aliquam personam accusaret sine testimonio vicinorum circummanentium qui bone vite fama laudabiles haberentur." "King Henry of England was at Falaise at Christmas, and he established a law such that no man shall be accused without the testimony of reputable neighbors" (cited Haskins, *Norman Institutions*, p. 239).

Normandy, sometimes giving rise to curious mixtures of judicial tradition. For example, both Geoffrey's and Henry's charters for the town of Rouen relieve its citizens of the obligation to wage combat against a hired champion. In order to determine the professional status of one's adversary, however, a sworn inquiry was to be conducted among ten loyal residents of the town.

By far the most sophisticated form of inquest, and the most influential in Louis's decision to abolish trial by combat, was the ecclesiastic *inquisitio* practiced in canonical courts. Originally, the Church recognized only those cases in which accusation preceded indictment. Gradually, beginning in the 800s, it began to acknowledge certain instances of suspected offense—*infamia* or *mala fama*—in which the canonical judge had the power to proceed unilaterally against an *infamatus*, who was forced to prove his innocence either through the oath of co-swearers (*purgatio canonica*) or by ordeal (*purgatio vulgaris*).[31] Notorious infractions were, in this manner, punished by the judge independently of a third party. The absence of an injured plaintiff served, moreover, as an obstacle to immediate acceptance of the technique. Both Yves de Chartres and Gratian argued, as late as the twelfth century, that the *inquisitio* was illegal because judge and accuser were one and the same. Their objections were at least countered, if not overcome, by a series of decretals issued by Innocent III in 1198, 1199, 1206, and 1212.[32] By the first quarter of the thirteenth century the procedure had developed into the full-scale *processus per inquisitionem* as outlined by the Fourth Lateran Council. According to the synod of bishops, once the judge or his agent had established a reasonable suspicion of guilt, he could proceed to produce witnesses whose testimony was recorded by the canonical notary. The accused was then summoned, acquainted with the evidence against him, and allowed to produce his own witnesses. After hearing both sides the judge decided whether or not the accused had sufficiently exculpated himself to warrant acquittal.

The Lateran formula produced two extraordinary applications of inquisitory procedure: the *inquisitio haereticae pravitatis* and the *inquisitio generalis*. Originally intended for the suppression of clerical abuse, the first was adapted to the universal prosecution of heresy in the campaign

31. Bongert, *Recherches*, p. 269; Esmein, *Criminal Procedure*, p. 79.
32. The future Pope Alexander III objected as late as 1150; so did Bernard of Pavia around the end of the century.

against Cathars and Vaudois (1220s).[33] It was the *inquisitio haereticae*, in fact, that eventually grew into the special procedure of inquisition. The *inquisitio generalis*, on the other hand, provided a regular means for the denunciation of suspected heretics. Similar to the Carolingian *juré de dénonciation*, the diocesan synod, or the *visitatio*, the *inquisitio generalis* permitted an inquiry upon the nonengaging complaint of a third party. The bishop, as presiding ecclesiastical judge, convoked the members of a parish or monastery, both clerical and lay, and compelled them under pain of excommunication to reveal notorious offenders from among their midst. The accused party was obliged to prove his innocence through oath or ordeal.

It was not long after the resuscitation of inquest within the courts Christian that canonical jurists in the service of monarchy adapted the technique to the secular sphere. What occurred, in fact, was a merging of Frankish practice, preserved in Normandy until the time of reannexation, with newly perfected Church usage.[34] Elements of both traditions combined to produce the highly sophisticated royal *enquête*. By the end of the thirteenth century an inquest conducted in the Parlement of Paris represented a complicated affair demanding the professional collaboration of numerous trained personnel.[35] First, a written request was submitted to the Chambre des Requêtes. If accepted, a letter of justice was issued, authorizing judicial action and naming a public prosecutor to supervise the case. At this point the court also instructed its *sergents* to verify the original demand and to inform the adverse party of the charge brought against him. The accused had the right to request adjournment according to the rules of postponement and excuses, *essoines*. But upon expiration of this term, both parties were summoned to court where a date was set for hearing. On the day of assignation the plaintiff exposed his case before the Grande Chambre in the presence of the defendant; the latter again had the right to request adjournment in order to seek council, *jours d'avis*. Or, he might demand that the court appoint delegates to visit

---

33. Esmein, *Criminal Procedure*, p. 81.

34. It has been argued that Norman procedure was not assimilated directly by the French monarchy, that it passed first into the practices of the secular courts of Anjou from which it later became known in the north; see Bongert, *Recherches*, pp. 262–265.

35. Bongert, *Cours d'histoire*, p. 94; Ducoudray, *Parlement*, p. 217; Lot and Fawtier, *Institutions*, 2: 388.

the scene of the litigation or crime in order to see for themselves what they would be judging, *jours de vue* or *de montrée*. After this second verification the court required the plaintiff to submit the "appointments," or *litis contestatio*, a written statement of allegation serving to formalize the process of accusation. These were categorized, clarified, and amplified by parliamentary jurists before submission to the defendant for response. Both parties swore an oath of good faith, *serment de calomnie*, before pronouncing the assurances of belief or nonbelief—*credo* or *non credo*—upon the articles of the adversary. The preliminary stage of the *enquête* was thus completed. The judge authorized his officers to proceed with the investigation: *d'aller avant sur les vérités*.

The specially appointed commissioners left Paris, usually in the late spring, with orders to visit the place of infraction and to collect as much relevant information as possible. Witnesses named in the original *litis contestatio* were summoned, made to swear the *serment de crédulité*, and asked either to approve or disapprove the articles established in the preliminary hearings. They, in turn, had the right to produce their own witnesses in order to corroborate their claims. Meanwhile, all testimony was recorded either by a local notary in the service of the royal judiciary or by one of the traveling *greffiers* attached to the Parlement of Paris. Upon conclusion of interrogation, this material was sealed into sacks to be returned to the capital along with the royal agents and the information gathered in similar cases. The sacks were initially deposited in the Grande Chambre where their validity was debated in the general context of inquisitory procedure. If uncontested, the contents were forwarded to the Chambre des Enquêtes where the findings of the commissioners were examined and assessed before transfer back to the Grande Chambre. There, an *arrêt*, or judgment, was pronounced in the name of the king.

Trial by Inquest and Trial by Battle

The differences between trial by inquest and battle are so numerous as to preclude comprehensive discussion within the limits of the present study. Substitution of inquest for combat was, of course, part of a general trend toward centralization of royal power in the postfeudal period, and we will have occasion later to explore the political implications of monarchy's maneuver. For the moment I would like to concentrate upon the individuation, abstraction, and verbalization of the ordeal of battle in order to demonstrate the similarity of an inquisitory judicial model and the vernacular poetic models of twelfth- and thirteenth-century France and Provence.

Individuation of Trial

The advent of an inquisitory mode served, first of all, to change the nature of the judicial encounter from a symbolic struggle between two relatively limited groups—clans, counties, duchies, even monasteries—to a struggle of an individual against the increasingly comprehensive political body of the state. For the potential violence of clannish vendetta—the violence of some against some—royalty attempted to impose a violence of all against one. The feudal trial had depended upon the accusation of an injured party, a member of his immediate family, or of the *comitatus* to which he belonged in order for the court to assume cognizance; that cognizance was, as we have seen, nothing more than a regularized means of substituting single combat for the clash of entire armies (see above p. 75). Trial by inquest, on the other hand, may depend upon the presence of an accuser, as in the *enquête du pays*, upon denunciation, as in the *inquisitio generalis*, or upon the judge's own initiative, as in the *aprise*. To the extent to which this last alternative, the *ex officio* indictment, became more and more common in the thirteenth and fourteenth centuries, it led to the creation of an independent judicial function, the *promotor* or public prosecutor.

The office of prosecutor, though superfluous within a purely accusatory system, has tended historically to accompany the rise of inquisitory procedure: in Rome of the Empire, in Carolingian France, and in the canonical courts whence it was appropriated by monarchy. By the end of the 1200s it had grown into a titular position attached both to the Parlement of Paris and to the royal courts in every *bailliage* and *sénéchausée*. The *procureur général* stationed in the capital, together with his auxiliary agents elsewhere, was responsible for the protection of monarchic interests throughout the realm. He surveyed royal fiefs, communicated judicial writs and letters of grace, supervised the transfer of titles, intervened in appointments, kept an eye on the workings of ecclesiastical justice, and, most importantly, assured the maintenance of the public peace. In criminal matters the *poursuite d'office* permitted indictment without the complaint of a third party whenever the king's peace was threatened. Originally, the prosecutor was summoned only in certain exceptional cases. As the king's presence in Parlement grew rarer and rarer, however, the role of his appointed defender grew proportionately greater. By the time of Philip the Fair the *promovens* functioned on a regular basis in all litigation; he was responsible for the active discovery and denunciation of all infractions to the appropriate judge. In fact, upon Philip's death, one of the demands of the rebellious barons was the suppression of the public accuser, who either alone or in concert with the judge had the power to indict, prosecute, and condemn a man for notorious wrongdoing: *quod fama praecedat.*

The appearance of the public prosecutor among the regular personnel of the *Curia regis* did not represent a simple quantitative addition to an already inflated professional staff; it altered the dynamics of trial. The *judicium Dei* was, at bottom, a contest between two parties, each of whom risked an identical punishment according to the outcome of struggle.[36] He who challenged a man to battle or forced him to submit to ordeal was, as Boutillier notes, liable to "exactly the same penalty"—*toute autelle peine*—as the accused.[37] The feudal trial was an inalienable contract under which one of the partners, representing his clan as a whole, was, of necessity, at fault and suffered, by rights, whatever pain had been agreed upon at the outset. Both plaintiff and defendant were parties to a direct encounter, and they remained inextricably bound by its results. Under an inquisitory procedure, however, the public prosecutor, a permanent plaintiff, escaped the reciprocal risk involved in trial by oath or combat. Unlike the accuser within an accusatory proceeding, the *promotor* was only indirectly party to the litigation which he initiated and carried to completion. As an informant to the judge, he stood on the margin of the judicial process, a *de facto* participant with no real stake in its egress. If a conviction were obtained, the individual defendant (and not the entire clan) suffered the consequences; and if none were forthcoming, the *promovens* escaped the penalty normally attached to defeat in battle. The

36. This is less true from the twelfth century onward. John of Salisbury provides the following qualification: "A 'calumniator' is one who brings a false accusation. . . . By the *lex Remia* calumniators are required to undergo the same punishment as that prescribed for the crime named in the accusation, provided, however, that after the defendant has been acquitted, there must be a determination of the accuser's knowledge and intention, and if he merely fell into a reasonable error, he must be acquitted. But if he is detected in evident malice, he is condemned to the punishment prescribed by law (*Policraticus*, ed. J. Dickinson [New York: Knopf, 1927], p. 139).

37. Boutillier, *La Somme rurale* (Bruges: Colard Mansion, 1479), p. 222.

inquisitory trial no longer represented a contest between two parties representing a larger legal body, parties with an equal share in the resolution of their differences, but a weighted struggle between the accused and the state. The adversary in both civil and criminal causes was not so much the plaintiff as the more abstract notion of commonweal. Henceforth, infraction could be defined neither in terms of necessary injury nor injury necessarily directed toward a particular individual. Rather, offense became synonymous with the abrogation of the common good, a concept which for the Capetians of twelfth- and thirteenth-century France was subsumed in the category of the King's or God's Peace.

As an important element of what has been termed "the Renaissance of the twelfth century," the personalization of criminal responsibility was part of the tendency toward legitimization of the concept of individualism evident across a broad cultural spectrum in: the writings of monastic reformers; the revival of Classical studies; renewed interest in letter writing and autobiography; the personalization of portraiture and sculpture; altered notions of intention, sin, and penance; the popularity of personal (mystical) religious experience; the appearance of the singular heroes of late epic and satirical forms; and, as we shall see, the valorization of the individual within the courtly novel and lyric.[38] Within the judicial sphere the individuation of trial had far-reaching implications for the organization of the postfeudal state. Monarchy's goal in the transformation of trial from an encounter between relatively autonomous social units into a struggle between an individual and the state was the establishment of direct legal ties between the inhabitants of the royal domain and royalty itself. Judgment of the solitary subjects of the Crown in the place of the clan as a whole served to bypass the justice of the local feudal chief and thus to weaken seigneurial judicial power.[39] Henceforth, the clan was

38. For a discussion of individualism in the twelfth century see: C. Morris, *The Discovery of the Individual 1050–1200* (New York: Harper, 1973); W. Ullmann, *The Individual and Society in the Middle Ages* (Baltimore: Johns Hopkins University Press, 1960).

39. "We know all too little of the history of the medieval family. However, it is possible to discern a slow evolution, starting in the early Middle Ages. The kindred, that is to say the group related by blood, was still a powerful factor. But its boundaries were blurred, while the legal obligations binding on its members tended to become mere moral constraints, little more than habit. Prosecution of a vendetta was still expected by public opinion, but there were no precise laws detailing joint responsibility in criminal matters, whether active or passive. There was still plenty of life in the habit of preserving the family holding intact, to be worked in common by fathers and sons, brothers, or even cousins; but it was nothing more than a habit, since individual ownership was fully recognized by law

no longer responsible for each of its members; nor were they beholden to the clan in cases which would formerly have necessitated a collective act of retribution. The individual was responsible only *to* the state and *for* himself, his link to any sovereign body other than the Crown having been attenuated. The substitution of the legal responsibility of individuals for the collective legal responsibility of the clan set the stage for the growth of a nation of self-governing citizens directly accountable to a progressively wider center of power, as opposed to a loose federation of clans accountable only to each other.

Abstraction of Trial

The substitution of trial by inquest for combat served to transform the physical ordeal of battle into an abstract struggle between an increasingly efficient judicial apparatus and the more abstract notion of judicial truth. As we have seen, the rendering of a judgment by battle had little to do with the nature of the crime being judged: the armed confrontation of two opponents permitted God to distinguish innocence from guilt regardless of what actually occurred at the time of offense. No effort was made by the feudal court to interrogate the coherence of the original criminal act. Inquest, on the other hand, represents a sustained attempt to uncover the truth of infraction, to assemble the facts surrounding any given crime and to determine guilt on that basis. Designed to recreate the reality of past events "as they happened," the *enquête* suddenly introduces the notion of rational truth, human rather than divine, into the center of trial. The pivotal position formerly occupied by customary rules of accusation and denial followed by heavenly intervention is filled by an imperative legal verdict independent of any system of higher causality. From the reign of Saint Louis onward civil causes often involved nothing more than a simple reference to existing documentation. In less clear cases a cursory investigation confirmed the admissibility or nonadmissibility of a particular allegation. The defendant in both civil and criminal

---

and custom and the only established right enjoyed by the kindred was the privilege of preemption when a holding came on the market. This loss of definition at the edges and the sapping of its legal force hastened the disintegration of the kindred group. Where communal life had once been broadly based on the vast patriarchal family, there was now an increasing tendency to concentrate on the conjugal family, a narrower community formed from the descendants of a married couple still living" (M. Bloch, *French Rural History* [Berkeley: University of California Press, 1966], p. 162).

causes had the right to demand a preliminary visit to the disputed property or to the site of infraction. Once the formal inquest had begun, the search for the truth of offense took trained investigators back to the scene of contestation to interview those who might shed light upon the obscure points of inquiry. Unlike the feudal co-swearer's oath of good character (*testis de credulitate*), their testimony, as well as that of secondary witnesses, implied a strong basis in material fact (*testis de facto*). Beaumanoir emphasizes the necessity of first-hand knowledge of wrongdoing in order for testimony to be valid:

Cil qui sont baillié auditeur ou enquesteur ou juge, qui puent et doivent oïr tesmoins, doivent mout regarder et entendre comment li tesmoing respondent as demandes qui leur sont fetes: ou par savoir, ou par croire, ou par cuidier. Car se li tesmoins dit: "Je le sai", l'auditeurs doit demander: "Comment le savés vous", et se li tesmoins respont: "Je l'oï dire a celi et a tel autre", cel tesmoignages est de nule valeur, car il est contraires a soi meisme, quant il dit qu'il set de certain ce qu'il ne set fors par oïr dire. Donques qui veut dire: "Je le sai de certain", il ne le puet dire s'il ne dit: "J'i fui presens et le vi." Et ainsi puet on tesmoignier de savoir ce qu'on tesmoigne certainement.

Those who are empowered to hear pleas or make inquests or judge, who can and should hear witnesses, should pay strict attention to the way in which the witnesses reply to the questions put to them: whether from knowledge, or from belief, or from presumption. Thus if the witness says: "I know it," the auditor should ask: "How do you know it," and if the witness replies: "I heard it from this person and that person," the testimony is worthless, because he contradicts himself when he says that he knows certainly that which he knows only from hearsay. Thus he who would say: "I know it certainly," cannot say it unless he says: "I was present and I saw it." And so one testifies certainly in testifying from material knowledge.

(Beaumanoir 2: 1234: 138)

The information collected by the king's *enquêteurs* was, first and foremost, a truthful account of infraction.

Significantly, the use of criminal expertise becomes increasingly frequent in the trial records of the late thirteenth and fourteenth centuries. Within the canonical courts scribal expertise—proficiency in the examination of documentary evidence—had long been a part of standard procedure.[40] Secular specialists in the assessment of charters, depositions,

---

40. Bongert, *Recherches*, p. 187; L. Halphen, "Les Institutions judiciaires en France au XIᵉ siècle: région angevine," *Revue Historique* 77 (1901): 287.

and writs appeared in the Parlement of Paris alongside a wide range of experts in various fields. Where a conflict between lay and clerical jurisdiction occurred, the judge might summon a barber to examine a suspicious tonsure.[41] Midwives were often called in to verify pregnancies, jewelers to appraise the value of stolen goods, herbalists to identify noxious substances in cases of poisoning. Or, as was most common, a doctor might be consulted in order to confirm the cause of death.[42] The records also indicate that each court retained a permanent staff of reliable consultants—*barbier juré* or *mire juré*—to be convoked whenever the need arose. The use of expertise, like the collection of material testimony, is symptomatic of a judicial process whose sustaining goal is the ascertainment of the truth of infraction. Capture in *flagrante delicto*, the only case under feudal law in which justice and truth are allied, has thus been transformed into a search for and capture of the facts. The necessity of actually trapping a guilty party in the process of misdeed and slaying him or transferring him to court yields to the transmission of testimony and evidence to the Chambre des Enquêtes. There, a system of proof based upon the opposition of truth and error, an abstract ordeal oriented around the discovery and presentation of a cogent scenario of wrongdoing, functions in lieu of the physical ordeal of battle. Like the canonical struggle between the ecclesiastical inquisitor and the devil upon the battleground of the heretic's soul, secular trial represents a struggle between the *enquêteur* and the abstract notion of judicial truth.

While the objective of the feudal court was the designation of guilt followed by its immediate punishment, the aim of the court of inquest was the constitution of a legal dossier—a written account of infraction. From the initial indictment or accusal and drafting of articles to the gathering of testimony and evidence on the spot, their return to the capital and organization into the medieval equivalent of legal brief, every effort of the royal *enquêteur* was directed toward the transcription of the memory of misdeed into concrete transportable form. According to the information obtained "from those likely to know of the infraction," as the *Ancienne Coutume de Bretagne* prescribes, the circumstances of wrongdoing are assembled into comprehensible analytic sequence. Unlike any aspect of

41. Bongert, *Cours d'histoire*, p. 117.
42. *Ibid.*, p. 118.

the duel, the dossier constitutes a studied gestalt of infraction which, if need be, can be conveyed from any location in the royal domain to the Parlement of Paris. Through the written record of wrongdoing compiled after the fact, justice found the mobile from by which every crime, however distant spatially, becomes recuperable in time.

The interposition of the written word, the dossier, between the act of transgression and that of judgment altered the fundamental nature of the medieval French judicial system. With it, justice relinquished all pretense of direct confrontation between opposing sides; trial having become a nonconfrontational encounter in which a third party, the judge, hears opposing testimony independently, studies claims and counter-claims, assesses the material gathered by his appointed agents, and arrives at a mediated solution based upon the assimilation of all available information. Judgment represents a learned process, literacy the *sine qua non* of legal authority.

The advent of the inquisitory dossier was by no means an isolated phenomenon, but part of an overall trend toward the adoption of learned procedures—regular trial records, archival registry, written legislation, letters of justice—under the late Capetians and Valois.[43] This trend, nurtured by the revival of Roman law (Justinian's *Corpus Juris*) and its study at the universities of northern Italy and France, served to reinforce the rift between monarchy, high nobility, and squireen according to each's ability to adapt to the bureaucratization of trials.[44]

For the relatively modest feudal judge of an age in which even some of the most powerful nobles remained unable to read and write, the advent of a lettered mode of criminal procedure was tantamount to judicial disenfranchisement. The uneducated baron of average intelligence, able up until then to handle the relatively straightforward formulas connected to trial by battle, suddenly found himself unequipped to deal with an increasingly technical jurisprudence based upon charter, recorded depositions, and dossier.[45] His position was further complicated by the fact that these documents were drafted in Latin and not in the language of everyday speech. More important, the expense of adapting to the bu-

43. See Esmein, *Cours élémentaire*, p. 422; Lot and Fawtier, *Institutions*, 2: 291–294.

44. See Esmein, *Cours élémentaire*, pp. 92–105; F. Kern, *Kingship and Law in the Middle Ages* (Oxford: Blackwell, 1956), p. 117; P. Vinogradoff, *Roman Law in Mediaeval Europe* (New York: Harper, 1909), pp. 33ff.

45. See E. Auerbach, *Literary Language and its Public in Late Latin Antiquity and in the Middle Ages* (New York: Pantheon, 1965), p. 263; J. W. Thompson, *The Literacy of the Laity in the Middle Ages* (Berkeley: University of California Press, 1939), pp. 123–141.

reaucratic revolution of the twelfth century was, for the majority of petty landholders, prohibitive. Large numbers of lesser nobles were forced not only to relinquish their holdings and to live within the manorial confines of a more powerful lord (see above p. 99), but to enlist, along with the swelling ranks of France's literate bourgeoisie, in the administrative service of the great feudatory princes or of monarchy itself. In this way even those nobles who acquired sufficient education to run an efficient learned judicial system lost the political autonomy and financial resources to profit from their training.

Whereas the imposition of an inquisitory trial procedure served to alienate the less powerful seigneurial judge from an established discourse of judgment, its effect upon the high feudal princes was attenuated by the fact that they themselves were able to develop the same institutions as the King of France. The progress of some principalities had even surpassed that of the French monarchy, as was the case of Normandy. Exposure to the efficient judicial system developed under Angevine rule provided impetus to the revitalization of Capetian institutions. Elsewhere, the Plantagenets had also created a stable administrative system run by competent and devoted civil servants, experts in the execution of judicial, military, and fiscal functions. The administrative organization of the Angevine Empire was further strengthened as a result of reforms enacted after the rebellion against Henry II (1175). Flanders of the twelfth and thirteenth centuries bears witness to the rise of a hierarchical functionary class with a bailiff, the equivalent of the royal public *promotor*, at its head. The chancellery of Flanders employed notaries and clerks, some of whom had received university training in law. Champagne under Henry the Liberal (1152–1187) possessed a local administrative system modelled upon the royal example, with *prévôts* representing the count in all matters affecting his interests; a series of lesser agents—mayors and *sergents*—assured the maintenance of rural and municipal justice. In short, the feudatory princes, assisted by a staff of able administrators, exercised the regal right to mint money, assemble armies, construct fortresses, collect tolls and taxes, make laws, and conduct inquests throughout the period in question. They had their own councils, chancelleries, exchequers, treasuries, parlements, archives, and courts. A class of bureaucrats and bookkeepers, compared to the increasingly impoverished *hobereaux* who were sometimes employed as *ministeriales* in their service, the most powerful lords of the realm were the titular heads of independent governmental systems rivalled only by that of the king.

The effect of the administrative independence of high nobility was, however, double: if the feudal princes of the postfeudal era were able to compete with their royal counterpart, the existence of an autonomous bureaucracy also permitted the ready substitution of royal administrators—the king's own bailiffs, *prévôts*, and clerks—at the time of annexation. An existing machinery of government contributed to the rapid assimilation of captured territories as in the Norman example. When Toulouse was incorporated into the royal domain upon the death of Alphonse of Poitiers (1271), there accrued to the King of France a regular trial, appeal, and parliamentary system with jurisdiction over Languedoc, Poitou, and Toulouse—an administrative organism ready to be utilized effectively regardless of the personal identity of its head. An analogous situation occurred when Champagne was officially united to the Crown upon the accession of Louis Hutin (1314). Thus, in creating the institutions necessary to their independence, the feudatory princes also facilitated their own absorption.

Monarchy's superiority within the area of judicial administration was, to some degree, quantitative: the king dispatched his own agents throughout the realm, whereas any individual lord made his presence felt only within the limited territory under his direct control. The king's representatives in the *Curia regis* at Paris and in the provincial parliaments elsewhere allowed the King of France to assert his interests, though not always his control, over an area which, beginning in the thirteenth century, surpassed that of any of his vassals, including the English king. And yet the advantage of monarchy within the judicial sphere was only partially quantitative. There was one respect in which the justice of the king was qualitatively different from that of even the most powerful feudal prince; that difference was evident in the creation of a hierarchically dominant system of appeal.

The attempted elimination of trial by combat would have had little effect as a tool of judicial centralization if Saint Louis had not instituted, at the same time, a system of appeal.[46] Together, inquest and appeal signal

---

46. "This appellate jurisdiction of the crown was a source of endless annoyance and expense to the seigneurial judges, whether high or low, since under an old law which was still in force as late as the seventeenth century it was the judge in the court of first instance and not the successful plaintiff who was named by the appellant in his suit; furthermore, the very existence of the appellate jurisdiction represented a loss of power and prestige to the inferior courts" (M. Bloch, *Rural History*, p. 103).

a basic shift in the fundamental assumptions of late medieval justice. Under an immanent method of proof, such as the *judicium Dei*, appeal remains an epistemological impossibility. It is assumed as a matter of course that God judges infallibly once and for all whenever put to the test; there can be no room for errors of divine judgment.[47] Furthermore, the local limits of feudal sovereignty placed proportionate limits upon the jurisdiction of the feudal court; and where power ended, there stood the highest level of appeal. In fact, the only means of contesting the probity of the seigneurial judge was to accuse him of having refused to hear a legitimate claim or of having disregarded the customary rules of procedure. In either case, the dissatisfied party had to challenge him to battle, thus reinitiating the entire process of divine judgment. Once again, the question of human as well as divine misjudgment was relegated to the periphery of trial. By admitting the possibility of regular appeal from one court to another, however, one also admits the possibility of error on the part of the judge, faults of a cognitive nature which discredit the substance of his ruling and which reach beyond the charge of recalcitrance or negligence. A system of appeal takes as its basic assumption the fallibility of human reason and the necessity of checks upon every decision rendered. At each step along the way, the humanized court, unlike its immanent feudal counterpart, recognizes a legal authority superior to itself.

Imperial Rome possessed an elaborate appeal system beginning in provincial courts and terminating in the *Curia* of the emperor, who was the chief magistrate of the republic. The Church adopted an analogous schema within the canonical courts, appeal following the ecclesiastical hierarchy up to the papal *Curia*, a tribunal of last resort. With the exception of Carolingian justice, appeal virtually disappeared from the secular sphere until the author of *Les Etablissements* again starts to speak of overturning the findings of lesser courts by those of higher probity. The plaintiff or defendant who feels that he had been treated unfairly can request an *émende*, the equivalent of the Roman *emendatio*. If the irregularity has occurred in the court of a vassal, the request for retrial reverts to that of the judge's lord. From there it proceeds to the second judge's lord,

---

47. "Le bon chrétien en effet doit s'incliner. Toute bataille est décisive. C'est un jet de lumière qui disperse les ténèbres, dessille les yeux, met un terme à toute hesitation, un arrêt qui tombe, sans appel" (Duby, *Bouvines*, p. 154); see also Halphen, "Institutions judiciaires," p. 293.

and so on, throughout the feudal hierarchy from the holders of land in fief to those from whom it is held.[48] At the highest feudal level a contested case is automatically transferred to the local royal court, where it proceeds from *prévôt* to *baillis* and, if necessary, eventually winds up before the Parlement of Paris. Beaumanoir describes the process succinctly:

. . . . car il convient apeler de degré en degré, c'est a dire, selonc ce que li homage descendent, du plus bas au plus haut prochien seigneur après, si comme du prevost au baillif et du baillif au roi es cours ou prevost et baillif jugent.

For it is proper to appeal step by step, that is, as homage is ordered, from the lowest lord to the next higher after him, as from the provost to bailiff and from bailiff to king in the courts where the provost and bailiff preside.

(Beaumanoir 2: 1774: 399)

The creation of a hierarchic system of appeal altered the legitimacy of the feudal and even the lower royal courts to an extent that should not be underestimated. For while every tribunal within an immanent judicial mode had an equal claim to ultimate authority, the supreme authority from the middle of the thirteenth century onward was the *Curia regis* representing the King of France. In substituting for the archaic mechanism of ordeal a system of civil procedure, Louis substituted for a universe in which each forum and act of judgment is equidistant from the divine judge a universe in which every judgment has an independent claim to authenticity according to a graduated scale of lesser and greater degree. At the pinnacle of this hierarchy the Parlement of Paris enjoyed a legitimacy superior to any other court. *Terminus ad quem* of a judicial system of national proportions, its decisions alone were above appeal and could thus be considered to constitute incontestible legal fact. All other courts—seigneurial and royal—admitted the chance of human error and hence the possibility of appeal. Only the Parlement, sharpened tool of divine monarchy, possessed the divine right of infallibility; its judgments were final and could be emended only by direct petition to the king.

Through the double movement implicit to inquest—the dispatch of agents from Paris to outlying districts of the realm and the potential transmission of all causes to the *Curta regis*—monarchy obtained what heretofore pertained only to God, that is to say, immunity from error. If trial by inquest was, in essence, an attempt the discover the truth of infraction, the ultimate determination of that truth rested in the hands of

48. See Esmein, *Cours élémentaire*, pp. 410–412.

royal agents. The obvious advantage of being at the head of such a hierarchy once vertical movement became possible, an advantage evident in the numerous appeals of the vassals of royal vassals, represented an important factor in the absorption of a multiplicity of petty feudal jurisdictions by the monolithic justice of the king.

Verbalization of Trial

The substitution of an inquisitory procedure for battle transformed the archaic test of martial strength into a test of intellectual strength within the confines of formal debate. If the evidence and testimony assembled by the *enquêteur* supposedly contained a truthful account of wrongdoing, his return to Paris only served to prepare the final stage in the scrutiny of the veracity of offense. Debate concerning the methods used in compiling the dossier took place in the Grande Chambre; a discussion of the truth of its substance ensued in the Chambre des Enquêtes. The courtroom became, in this way, a forum in which the man of greatest wit and verbal dexterity, but not necessarily of physical power, possessed the superior claim to right. More precisely, the inquisitory ordeal is essentially one of persuasion, an attempt on the part of both prosecutor and defendant to create the most credible fiction prior to judgment. Without eliminating the conflictual nature of the judicial encounter, inquest produced a fundamental displacement away from the battlefield and toward the "Parlement," the place where, literally, opponents speak instead of fighting. As a supposedly nonviolent civil space, the inquisitory court worked to disguise the potential violence of physical conflict, once the very essence of trial, behind the verbalized violence of disputation. John of Salisbury maintains, in fact, that the purpose of dialectic and of eloquence in general is the conversion of physical conflict into words:

Since dialectic is carried on between two persons, this book (the *Metalogicon*) teaches the matched contestants, whom it trains and provides with reasons and topics, to handle their (proper) weapons and engage in verbal, rather than physical conflict. It instills into its disciples such astute skill that one may clearly see that it is the principle source of the rules of all eloquence, for which it serves as a sort of primary fountainhead.[49]

The transformation of the physical ordeal of battle into an abstract search for the truth of infraction dependent upon learned and written

49. John of Salisbury, *The Metalogicon*, ed. D. D. McGarry (Berkeley: University of California Press, 1955), p. 190.

procedures served to alienate the petty seigneurial judge from the legal process. Inquest combined with appeal tended, similarly, to weaken the jurisdiction of the more powerful feudatory prince. The shift in the medium of trial toward a verbal struggle affected both upper and lower echelons of aristrocracy in a less obvious but nonetheless fundamental way. The verbalization of trial, like the prohibition of private war, represented a direct attack upon the *raison d'être* of feudal nobility, that is to say, the right to bear arms as an acceptable means of resolving differences among themselves. The ability of a feudal judge to govern was indistinguishable from his right to govern by armed force. Likewise, his ability to judge those under his jurisdiction depended, especially in the case of the petty landholder, upon the relatively pragmatic procedures at his disposal. The dominance of France's feudal aristocracy was, above all, a military dominance; any impingement upon its freely exercised right to private war and war's mimetic equivalent, the judicial combat, implied a necessary loss of prestige and power. As an essential element, perhaps the essential element, of monarchy's attempt to pacify the barons of the realm, the banishment of physical violence from the judicial encounter worked to undermine seigneurial sovereignty. We will have occasion later to return to the ideological implications of the inquisitory trial in assessing the social dimensions of courtly tradition.

The reader may have asked himself long before now why we have dwelled at such length upon the procedural models of medieval trial. After all, there are no examples of inquest in the literary texts of the twelfth and thirteenth centuries; and it is possible to understand the workings of judicial combat through reference to contemporary historical material.

If we have insisted upon the importance of the inquisitory trial, it is, first of all, because of the difficulty of distinguishing between a method of judgment and the broader forms of social organization that such a method implies. The judgment of individuals in the place of groups assumes the existence of direct ties of sovereignty between the state and each of its members. Judgment according to the notion of judicial truth depends upon the formulation of stable criteria independent of the act of judgment itself—and thus the existence of a state which, in contrast to feudal polity, could define itself through its laws as something more than a collection of separate subjective rights. Finally, judgment according to a verbal rather than physical ordeal implies at least a modicum of civil organization, a state capable of enforcing its decisions without necessary recourse to arms. In general, the advent of inquest furthered the cause of political centralization, which emphasizes, once again, the impossibility of separating the evolution of judicial models from the historical struggle between monarchy and feudal aristocracy. Since our ultimate goal is to situate the vernacular literature of the postfeudal period within the context of contemporaneous institutions, and more particularly within the context of this class struggle, any less detailed explanation of inquest and its political ramifications would have ill-prepared our conclusion.

And yet there is still another and more compelling reason why we have focused upon inquest: the distinction between epic and courtly literature shows numerous and important similarities to the development of medieval judicial models. In particular, the poetic types which emerged in southern France in the early 1100s and in the north around the middle of the century demonstrate a tendency to individualize, to render abstract, and to verbalize the struggle which in the *chanson de geste* remains collective and concrete. Students of medieval French literature have long noted the preference within courtly romance for an individualized version of the physical ordeal, that of adventure, combined with the spiritual ordeal of love itself. The two seem, in fact, to stand in symbiotic relation, love inspiring the adventures that make a knight worthy of love. Both serve to isolate the individual from the community to which he belongs. Love reduces the individual's rapport with others to a unitary function, as the relation to one other individual subverts the possibility of relation to all others. Even the terms *ami(e)* and *amors*, which within the semantic universe of the epic extended to all the members of one's warrior group, focus exclusively upon a single object of affection.[50] Love conceived as an obsession with another serves to sever the individual's bond with society either because of his own lack of will (Erec and Enide, Yvain and Laudine after marriage), the necessity of hiding adulterous love (Tristan and Iseult, Lancelot and Guinevere, Cligés and Fénice at court), the expulsion from society (Tristan and Iseult in exile), or a lack of fulfillment (Yvain in the forest, the wandering and wounded Lancelot of *La Mort Artu*).

While love, however alienating, may or may not play itself out within

---

50. See G. S. Burgess, *Contribution à l'étude du vocabulaire pré-courtois* (Geneva: Droz, 1970), p. 142.

the confines of the community as a whole, adventure tends to be a solitary experience occurring outside of any social context. Its privileged *locus*, the forest, represents a moral space in which normal social relations—the contractual basis of life at court—remain permanently suspended. Thus the lack of regularity in human exchange, the requisite quality of chance happening.[51] One of the several meanings of the Old French *aventure* transmits the idea of accident, chance, or surprise.

But the word *aventure* can also stand for risk—*Si s'est en aventure mise, come hardie et courageuse*, and it is that meaning which concerns us here.[52] The knight in search of adventure seeks, no less than the warrior hero of epic, to prove his individual worth through a test of physical strength, to establish his position in the chivalric pecking order. As the author of *Perlesvaus* prescribes, *Damedeu nel voloit mie que li bon chevalier s'oceïssent, ainz voloit que li uns seüst de l'autre conbien il valoit.*[53] Though individualized, the ordeal of adventure is none the less a measure of personal prowess involving the risk of injury or death. Erec's initial opportunity to demonstrate his mettle as a knight originates in the unprovoked and inexplicable wounding of Guinevere's handmaiden and terminates in a formal match against the physically huge but morally recreant Yders.[54] Through this act of vengeance Erec not only redeems the queen's honor but wins Enide as well. The series of adventures which later pits Erec against increasingly powerful opponents—three, then five thieves, the Vain Count, Guivret le Petit, two giants, the Count of Limors, and the giant Maboagrain—and which permits the hero to regain his own lost chivalric honor is, again, a demonstration of military might. The mysterious journey in search of opponents leaves a trail of wounded

51. See Erich Köhler, *Ideal und Wirklichkeit in der höfischen Epik* (Tubingen: Max Niemeyer, 1956), pp. 77–82.

52. She risked herself as one who is hardy and courageous (*Le Roman de Perceval*, ed. W. Roach [Geneva: Droz, 1959], v. 1954). Used adjectively, *aventure* can also mean "dangerous": "Sire, fet li hermites a Monseigneur Gavain, vos ne vos desarmerez pas, car ceste forez est molt aventureuse, e nus preudom ne doit estre desgarniz." "Lord, said the hermit to Sir Gawain, you should not disarm for this forest is very dangerous and no man should be disarmed" (*Perlesvaus*, ed. W. Nitze and T. A. Jenkins [Chicago: University of Chicago Press, 1932], 1: 61); see also p. 103. For recent discussions of the term "aventure" see: Burgess, *Vocabulaire pré-courtois*, pp. 44–45; Köhler, *Ideal*, pp. 77–88; P. Zumthor, *Essai de Poétique médiévale* (Paris: Seuil, 1972), p. 361.

53. God did not want for good knights to kill each other but wanted for them to know how much each is worth (*Perlesvaus*, 1: 197).

54. For a discussion of the themes of love and adventure in *Erec et Enide* see R. Bezzola, *Le Sens de l'aventure et de l'amour* (Paris: La Jeune Parque, 1947).

and dead. Similarly, Lancelot's adventures in pursuit of the queen involve combat against first an ambush party of Méléagant's men, then a series of knights guarding the "Pont de l'Epée" and the "Passage des Pierres," and, finally, three formal contests against the persistent Méléagant. It is Calogrenant's story of defeat in a previous adventure which motivates Yvain's departure from court and successful, though bloody, struggle against Esclados. Yvain's voyage of redemption after a period of passivity, like that of Erec, is intended as a demonstration of his intrinsic but lapsed physical prowess; the hero manages to face in combat the Count of Alier, the giant Harpin de la Montagne, Lunete's three accusers, Gauvain, and the two monstrous guardians of the castle of Pesme-Aventure. The exploits of the knights in search of the dominant adventure of thirteenth-century romance, the quest for the Holy Grail, are, as we will have occasion to observe later in discussing the mediatory function of courtly narrative, no less firmly grounded in the violence of physical encounter (see below, pp. 189–211).

What we are suggesting is obvious and does not need further elaboration: that while the collective violence of epic warfare is displaced in the courtly novel toward the individual ordeal of *aventure*, it remains a test of martial prowess. Nothing of the immediacy of physical conflict is denied the hero of romance, who is simultaneously lover and fighter; only the proportions of struggle have been reduced from the pitched battle involving entire armies to the hand-to-hand combat of single knights. Where a similar displacement is less evident, however, is in the courtly lyric. There, the collective violence of the epic and the individualized violence of romance operate as a latent structuring principle despite the lack of realistic setting. That the specific temporal and spatial coordinates of conflict—the *locus* of battle, its duration and outcome, the identity of opponents—often cannot be situated within the lyric poem does not belie its essentially confrontational nature. On the contrary, because the immediacy of physical struggle remains hidden, because the violence underlying the ordeal of love is rarely articulated as theme, it becomes especially important to an understanding of the implicit social function of the early text. The tendency to picture love in terms of a military encounter was, of course, a vital part of classical tradition. According to Ovid, the most probable source of much of the imagery associated with courtly literature, "every lover is a soldier in the service of Cupid." The importance of the *Amores* for Andreas Capellanus's own formulation, even his phraseology, of the laws governing "recruits in Love's army" cannot be denied. And yet the question of influence concerns us less here than the ways in which the violence which remains overt within the epic becomes simultaneously fragmented and covert within the lyric and, ultimately, the relation of both genres to contemporary judicial models—models which are, after all, the culturally sanctioned means of regulating the violence of interpersonal exchange. Our task in the remainder of this chapter is to establish the patterns of conflict common to the lyric, the epic, and the romance.

Individuation of the Poetic Ordeal

Epic violence predicated at the level of nation, religion, or clan, the potential rivalry of some against some, has shifted within the individually oriented courtly universe to a violence of one against all; this, despite the contemporaneous development of both literary types. The struggle of partisans bound by the mandatory *faida* to defend each other against similar groups in specific situations becomes, in the lyric, a struggle against an unidentifiable enemy who is everywhere at all times. No longer is the source of rivalry definable, or even important, since the courtly lover operates within a world in which everyone is a potential enemy and in which injury can occur at any time from a plethora of possible sources. His is a universe of shifting alliances. At any given moment he may feel intensely threatened by a particular woman or by all women; he may sense himself attacked by a personification of love or by a combination of Love and his lady. His struggle may manifest itself in terms of an internal conflict of the poet against himself. In the lyric the poet's rivals in love, the *lauzengers* (O.F. *losengiers*) or false flatterers, constitute, along with all other poets, a persistent threat.

The Poet against his Lady

The most essential opposition within the courtly tradition—northern or southern—is that which sets the poet-lover against his lady. Bernart de Ventadorn accuses his lady of making war upon him, of destroying him systematically and purposefully:

> C'aissi com lo rams si pleya
> lai o'l vens lo vai menan,
> era vas lei qu'm guerreya,
> aclis per far so coman.

> Per aisso m'afol' e'm destrui,
> don a mal linhatge redui. . . .

For, just as the branch bends in the direction that the wind blows it, I was inclined to obey the commandments of she who makes war on me. Thus she vanquishes and destroys me, acting like one of low birth. . . .

> (Ventadorn (Lazar) 148)

Giraut de Bornelh compares his situation in love to a hopeless siege in which he would gladly surrender:

> Domna, aissi cum us chasteus
> Qu'es assetjatz per fortz senhors,
> Can la peirer'abat las tors,
> E.ls chalabres e.ls manganeus,
> Et es tan greus
> La guerra devas totas partz
> Que no lor te pro genhs ni artz,
> E.l dols e.l critz es aitan fers
> De cels dedins quez an grans gers,
> Sembla.us ni.us par
> Que lor ai'obs merce clamar?
> Aissi.us clam merce umilmens,
> Bona domna, pros e valens.

Lady, as when a castle is besieged by grim barons, when the siege engine topples the towers—and the catapult and the mangonel—and the onslaught is so fierce from every side that neither cunning nor guile avails them, and the suffering and the cries are so terrible of those within who are in great anguish, does it not seem to you that there's need for them to cry mercy? In the same way I humbly cry mercy of you, good lady, noble and worthy.[55]

Peire Vidal accuses his lady of killing him slowly but "courteously" (Vidal 35). He, too, compares her brand of warfare to the beleaguerment of a castle (Vidal 37). Gace Brulé claims to live in a state of perpetual anxiety because of the slow death which he suffers at the hands of his *douce dame enemie* (Gace Brulé 12). According to the medieval formula for murder, Le Châtelain de Coucy accuses his lady of having killed him treacherously—*a loi de traïtor*—because her eyes have attacked him without warning—*sans deffianche*. Like Peire Vidal, he would gladly avenge himself if he could, but remains incapable of reaction (Coucy 61). Thibaut de Champagne maintains that his struggle against the guards who

---

55. A. Press, *Anthology of Troubadour Lyric Poetry* (Austin: University of Texas Press, 1971), p. 136.

attack him in his lady's prison is "fiercer than any battle of Roland or Olivier" (Champagne 114). He too feels wrongfully attacked—*navré sans defiance*:

> La moie joie est tornee a pesance.
> Hé, cors sanz cuer! de vos fet grant venjance
> Cele qui m'a navré sanz defiance,
> Et ne por quant je ne la lerai ja.

> My joy is turned to sorrow.
> Ah, body without a heart! she has greatly avenged herself on you
> Who wounded me without warning,
> And yet I will never leave her.

> (Champagne 80)

Thibaut's pain is itself the result of a preceding act of vengeance: *Hé, cors sanz cuer! de vos fet grant venjance*. But unlike Gace Brulé and Peire Vidal, his failure to respond in kind is not so much the product of helplessness as of complicity: *Et ne por quant je ne la lerai ja*.

The dilemma of Bernart, Giraut, Peire, Le Châtelain de Coucy, Gace Brulé, and Thibaut is the direct result of their choice of a single lady as the sole object of desire. The elimination of all others endows each with a singular power over the lover, who finds himself vulnerable because of her seeming uniqueness. Bernart insists, however, that no matter how fixed the love of a particular lady may seem, a different choice would alter nothing:

> Pois vei c'una pro no m'en te
> Vas leis que-m destrui e-m cofon,
> Totas las dopt'e las mescre,
> Car be sai c'atretals se son.

> I see clearly that no [woman] will help me;
> When one kills and destroys me
> I am wary and fearful of all
> For I know they are all alike.

> (Nelli and Lavaud 2: 74)

Despite the irony of his claim, Bernart recognizes that it is not the love of a specific lady that leads to their confrontation. He would have found himself in the same position regardless of the woman in question: *Car be sai c'atretals se son*. The nature of love itself necessitates struggle. There can be no escape from a generalized pattern of conflict inherent to relations between the sexes. In spite of the necessity of choice, of freely given passion on the part of courtly lovers, there is still no lady to whom the poet can turn in order to avoid confrontation.

The Poet against False Flatterers

The lover's struggle against his lady is complicated by his lack of choice, by the necessity of obstacles to true love, and, above all, by the prospect of winning. It represents an unavoidable sacrifice *en route* to one's beloved, a *sine qua non* of eventual satisfaction. The lover, despite the constant assault by a consistently victorious enemy, remains convinced that love is a mixture of negative and positive perceptions and that suffering is a necessary part of his inherently ambiguous condition. As Andreas Capellanus stipulates, the pain of love—obstacles and suffering —is no less essential to genuine passion than the hope of gratification (*Courtly Love* 28, 29, 185). The lady stands always in a problematic light: she is both the agent of damnation and of possible salvation, the source of suffering as well as delight.

The least ambiguous of the lover's opponents in the universal struggle against other individuals like himself are the *lauzengers*, the perpetual enemies who threaten to expose and disrupt true passion whenever they have the chance.[56] Alternately cloaked in the guise of liar, flatterer, bore, and spy, the *lauzenger* maintains a persistent rivalry for rivalry's sake. Though he pursues his adversary with the doggedness of a vendetta, it is by no means certain that "the declared enemy of all joy" stands to gain anything by the lover's loss beyond the pleasure of winning. A conspirator, he remains a wholly evil figure whose omnipresence serves to generalize courtly conflict even further. Cercamon complains that the *lauzenjador* have separated him from his beloved and that he is, as a result, condemned to die (Cercamon 5). Bernart de Ventadorn considers them responsible for a general decline in courtly values as well as for his own unhappy plight (Ventadorn [Lazar] 79). While Bernart seeks to avenge the harm inflicted upon him, "to combat and conquer those who have made war upon him," Arnaut Daniel feels so intimidated by flatterers that

56. For a discussion of the figure of the *lauzenger* see: R. Dragonetti, *La Technique poétique des trouvères dans la chanson courtoise* (Bruges: De Temple, 1960), p. 272; A. Jeanroy, *La Poésie lyrique des troubadours* (Paris: Didier, 1934), p. 105; M. Lazar, *Amour courtois et "Fin' Amors" dans la littérature du XIIᵉ siècle* (Paris: Klincksieck, 1964), p. 61; Zumthor, *Essai*, p. 229. The sin of the *lauzenger* is one of indiscretion, the transgression of Andreas's precept against consciously striving to "break up a correct love affair that someone else is engaged in" (*Courtly Love* 81).

he would rather flee than fight (Nelli and Lavaud 2: 112). Gui d'Ussel recognizes that the only effective arm against them is his lady's favor (Nelli and Lavaud 2: 120). An alliance between lover and lady would be a victory for all those on the side of right. Conversely, loss of her affection is, as Le Châtelain de Coucy notes, a source of delight for the *losengiers*, who have directed all their energy toward his betrayal (Coucy 38). Gace Brulé, like Cercamon, pretends to hover close to death because of the "tricksters and their false words" (Gace Brule 2). Thibaut de Champagne assures his mistress that the infrequency of his visits does not connote a lack of will, but a fear of the *male gent* (Champagne 32). Conon de Béthune has been slandered by the *gent de male guise*, who have maligned him in his absence:

> L'autrier, un jour après le Saint-Denise
> Fui à Béthune, ou j'ai esté souvent;
> La me sovint de gent de male guise,
> Ki m'ont mis sur menchonge a escïent:
> Ke j'ai canté des dames laidement;
> Mais il n'ont pas me canchon bien aprise:
> Je n'en cantai fors d'une seulement,
> Ki bien forfist ke venjance en fust prise.

> Not long ago, one day after the festival of Saint-Denis
> I was at Béthune, where I have often been;
> I was reminded of men of an evil sort,
> Who knowingly told a lie about me:
> That I had sung insultingly of women;
> But they had not well learned my song:
> I sang of one woman only,
> Who was so false that vengeance was taken on her.
> (Béthune 237)

Conon's complaint acknowledges the universality of the enemy: even where no particular lady is involved, the *losengiers* vilify his reputation as lover. The specific nature of their offense suggests something quite different, however. In accusing the poet of insulting all women—*Ke j'ai canté des dames laidement*—the *losengiers* have misinterpreted his song—*Mais il n'ont pas me canchon bien aprise*. Their lack of respect for the *canchon* as Conon has sung it carries us beyond the lover's struggle with faceless opponents who spy and denounce to the poet's rivalry with other poets.

The Poet against Other Poets

As the original subject of the pastoral, a contest between shepherds for the prize of rustic song, the theme of poetic rivalry is almost as old as Western literature. Even when competition does not occur within a formally competitive framework, the rivalry implicit to Classical debate forms broadens the scope of poetic rivalry to seemingly limitless proportions. The Idylls of Theocritus, Virgil's third and seventh eclogues, Catullus's *Carmen* 50, the musical games of the Capitole, Ovid's elegy of the *Amores* (Book III, Elegy I), or the Carolingian *conflictus* are all, in some extended sense, possible sources of the medieval poetic contest. When considered alongside a rich folk tradition of flytings, riddle contests, jongleur parades, and at least circumstantial evidence for the existence of organized literary disputes, the search for certainty with regard to medieval analogues becomes hopelessly abstruse. Leaving the question of origins aside, we might conclude only that the relation between the song contest and more personal forms of rivalry remains close indeed. Even where there are no explicit ground rules for competition, where two poets are involved in actual conflict, as in the exchange of double *sirventes*, or, more probably, in fictional conflict, as in the formally competitive *tenso* or *joc partit*, a struggle based ostensibly upon artistic merit can easily turn into a match of personal worth. The quest for supremacy in singing skill is never very far from the quest for personal supremacy. Bernart de Ventadorn understood the poet's artistic power to be inseparable from his effectiveness as a lover:

> Non es meravelha s'ieu chan
> melhs de nul autre chantador,
> que plus mi tra.l cors vas amor
> e melhs sui faihz a son coman.

> It is no marvel if I sing
> better than all other singers,
> my heart is more strongly attracted to love,
> and I am more fit to serve him.
>
> (Ventadorn (Appel) 188)

In what may be the first legal test of the concept of literary originality, an anonymous thirteenth-century Provençal *vida* describes the rivalry between Arnaut Daniel and another *jongleur* at the court of Richard the Lionhearted. Under the king's supervision each wagers his horse that he can compose the better song. The *jongleur* sets to work assiduously while in an adjoining room Arnaut is content to memorize his opponent's lines as he overhears them. On the actual day of judgment Arnaut performs, is accused of stealing the poem, and then confesses. Richard is so pleased by the joke that he releases both horses and distributes gifts to all. For his cleverness Arnaut receives the song: *E fo donat lo canta a`N Arnaut Daniel.*[57] Like the amoebeans of Theocritus, Virgil, or Calpurnicus, the *vida* demonstrates the ease with which the poetic encounter can become a test of wit.

More important than Bernart's individual sense of his own worth or Arnaut's deception are the inherently competitive forms of the twelfth and thirteenth centuries: the *tenso* and *joc partit*. Whether these can be traced to Classical tradition, to actual verbal jousts before a live audience, or to a universal tendency toward debate apparent throughout the Middle Ages, they are, by their very nature, poetic contests—alternating contradictory stanzas upon a given single topic.[58] In both the southern *tenso* and *joc partit*, as well as their northern equivalents, the sole object of each opponent, whether competition is real or imaginary, is to win the test of intellectual strength, either to force his interlocutor to admit defeat or to convince a third party—the reader, listener, or appointed arbiter—of the superiority of his argument. Often, a great deal of personal animosity lies buried not too far beneath the surface of polite discussion. For example, the troubadour Uguet (probably Uc de Mataplana) accuses his colleague Reculaire of being as poor as a monk even though his low moral stature would preclude tonsure: *Que vos es fols e jugaire, / Et de putans cortejaire.*[59] Reculaire reminds his assailant that riches will not last forever, that when he dies he will take with him as much as the richest man, and that dissolution, in any case, costs but little. Similarly, Gui de Cavaillon accuses his rival Falco of false speech: *Falco, en dire mal / Vey qu'es trop abrivatz.*[60] Falco lets it be understood that his attacker abuses the

---

57. And the song was given to Arnaut Daniel (*Biographies des troubadours*, ed. J. Boutière and A.-H. Schutz [Paris: Nizet, 1964], p. 62).

58. C. Fauriel maintains that the *tenso* was composed rapidly by two adversaries in each other's presence (*Histoire de la poésie provençale* [Paris: Duprat, 1846]); R. Zenker concurs, supporting the position that they were improvised before a live audience (*Die provenzalische Tenzone* [Leipzig: Vogel, 1888]). A. Jeanroy, while maintaining the spontaneous origin of the genre, believes that *tensos* were not improvised; rather, they were composed at the poet's leisure ("La Tenson provençale," *Annales du Midi* 2 [1899]: 381–404, 444–462).

59. For you are brainless, a gambler, and a lecher (D. Jones, *La Tenson provençale* [Paris: Droz, 1934], p. 89).

60. I see, Falco, that you are too quick to slander (*Ibid.*, p. 83).

hospitality of his benefactor Alphonse, to which Gui responds with vigor. Falco threatens to have Gui hanged for his sins; Gui denounces his opponent's love of drink and dice. The latter finally accuses Gui of cruelty to his parents despite his ability to help them.[61]

The tension that tends to be highly personal within the *tenso* and somewhat more abstract within the *joc partit* combines many of the elements of judicial combat—challenge, reciprocal replies, explicit or implicit judgment—in what amounts to verbal warfare; it is, first and foremost, a linguistic duel. The violence which lurks behind fixed poetic forms is nowhere more evident than in an early thirteenth-century debate between the unknown Faure and Falconet. Feigning pleasure at the sight of his rival "because they have not quarreled in such a long time," Faure proposes a contest based upon conflicting military alliances: each side will propose a team of possible opponents for a mock poetic war.[62] Falconet nominates Gui de Cavaillon; Faure counters with the Lord of Maltortel, his brother Raino, and Lord Albaro. Falconet adds Per Bremon to the list, while Faure advances Forcalquier, the Lord of Courthézon, and his uncle Raimon de Mévouillon. Falconet proposes the Lord of Berre and Alanson, the "most prideful and miscreant" lords of Trip and Toulon, and the ferocious Faure de Bergognon. What begins as a hypothetical encounter between the knights of Provence terminates, finally, in overt confrontation, as the enmity underlying Faure and Falconet's matching of military might serves, once again, to emphasize the closeness of the poetic and personal fight.

Indisputable historical evidence of formal poetic contests cannot be found before the thirteenth century. Marcabru and Peire d'Auvergne considered themselves members of what may have been a poetic broth-

---

61. In a *tenso* which sets Bertran d'Alamanon against a *jongleur* named Granet, the latter claims that his protector has not rewarded him sufficiently for faithful service. He threatens to reveal unpleasant details concerning Bertran's morals. Bertran retorts by threatening to expose the truth about his opponent: "Arloz es plen de put aire." "You are a 'no-good' congenitally filled with vice" (*Le Troubadour Bertran d'Alamanon*, ed. J.-J. Salverda de Grave [Toulouse: Privat, 1902], p. 127). G. claims to have learned his vices from B., who counters by admitting to having made a *jongleur* out of G. when he was a mere *courreur*. G. pretends to have consistently praised B. and now wants some profit from it. B. claims not to care at all about G.'s request. Elsewhere, Rambaut de Vaqueiras insults Albert Malaspina with comparable vigor. A. responds by accusing R. of cowardliness, to which R. counters, ironically, with the observation that neither troubadour can be compared to a Roland or an Olivier: "e s'ieu non vail per armas Olivier, / vos non valetz Rotlan, a ma semblanssa." "And if I am no Olivier when it comes to handling arms, / you are, in my opinion, no Roland" (C. Appel, *Provenzalische Chrestomathie* [Leipzig: Reisland, 1895], p. 128).

62. Jones, *Tenson*, p. 77.

erhood—*gen frairina* or *encas confraire*.[63] Similar *confréries* also may have existed in the North as early as 1120. Many of the important northern urban centers of Normandy, Picardie, Flanders, and Artois could boast, among their growing corporate institutions, of a poetic society or *puy*. Like the early peace leagues and the communal movement itself, the *puy* functioned as a mutual aid and burial society. It also represented a forum for poetic competition on saints' and feast days.[64] Internal evidence suggests that much verse written after 1200 was intended for submission to a jury of literary judges and that something resembling a regular court situation served to insure its composition.[65] Once the jury of the *puy* elected, crowned, and praised a winner, he became eligible to sit among their number in succeeding competitions. In addition to intramural encounters, special tourneys as well as dramatic contests united the members of one *puy* against those of another.

The most famous literary challenge of the Middle Ages and that which left the most enduring trace occurred in the South. On November 8, 1323, the poets of Toulouse invited those of Languedoc to meet on the following May first to compete for a gold laurel. The local circle of amateur poets, members of the Toulousian bourgeoisie, also left a document attesting to their incorporation within a formal literary society: the Consistoire du Gai Savoir. Among their activities the seven original *sociétaires* joined by local officials decided to sponsor periodic contests or Jeux Floraux.[66] The municipal government appropriated 120,000 francs to purchase gold and silver crowns for the winners and runners-up. Institutionally, the Consistoire du Gai Savoir combines elements common to the medieval university as well as courts of law.[67] Competition for the expensive *joyas* (prizes) was organized along academic lines; it included a system of exams, titles, rights, and duties pertaining to the various ranks within the poetic community.

63. See A. Denomy, "*Jovens*: the Notion of Youth among the Troubadours, its Meaning and Source," *Medieval Studies* 11 (1949): 10.

64. Dragonetti, *Technique poétique*, p. 371; E. Faral, *Les Jongleurs en France au moyen âge* (Paris: Champion, 1910), pp. 123–142; H. Guy *Essai sur la vie et les oeuvres du trouvère Adan de le Hale* (Paris: Hachette, 1898), p. xliii.

65. See F. Diez, *Essai sur les cours d'amour* (Paris: Labitte, 1842), p. 68; Guy, *Adan de le Hale*, p. L.

66. See C. Chabaneau, *Origine et établissement de l'Académie des Jeux Floraux de Toulouse* (Toulouse: Privat, 1885); Jeanroy, *Poésie*, pp. 303–307.

67. The original Consistoire became, in fact, the Collège de la Science et Art de Rhétorique de Toulouse.

Sometime after its foundation the officers of the Compagnie des Jeux Floraux commissioned a systematic compilation of its own standards of judgment. As stated in its preamble, the *Leys d'Amors*, like the customal, represents an attempt to codify the practices of the past, "to edit the laws of love according to the good troubadours of the old days" (*Leys* 1: 3). Its authors, Guillem Molinier, a lawyer and man of letters, and Barthélemy Marc, Professor of Civil Law, after obtaining the approval of the Vicaire Général de Toulouse, the Grand Inquisitor, and his staff, submitted the *Leys* for ratification in 1356 and deposited it in the local Archive. There are indications that the seven troubadours of Toulouse also established a system of registry for the poems presented and ordered an anthology of prize entries; if such a collection ever appeared, it has been lost.

The best known literary contests of the late Middle Ages were those held at Blois following Charles d'Orléans's return from England. More revealing for the present discussion, however, is a document drafted in the first few years of the fifteenth century at Paris and Vienne: the Love Court Charter of Charles VI.[68] Like the *puy*, sometimes referred to as the *puy d'amour*, and the Consistoire du Gai Savoir, the organization founded by this charter seems to represent a mixture of love court, literary circle, and tribunal. Its terms, couched in legalistic language, provide for the appointment of twenty-four ministers responsible for holding a session of the court on the first Sunday of each month. Each is required to submit a poem on a given refrain to the scrutiny of the assembly. The Love Court Charter made allowance for a gold wreath to be presented to the winner, whose composition, along with his name and coat of arms, was to be recorded by the court scribe. Failure to comply would result in sanction: the "minister" who refused to bring a poem to each meeting or to notify the others was obliged to host a dinner, or, if consistently negligent, to suffer exclusion.

Abstraction of the Poetic Ordeal

The Poet against Love

The underlying mechanism of reciprocal violence is primary to the courtly love relation and serves to structure it. Regardless of a particular poet's own stance with respect to the more theoretical issues of courtly

68. Ed. C. Potvin, *Bulletin de l'Académie Royale de Belgique* 12 (1886): 191; see also A. Piaget, "La Cour amoureuse dite de Charles VI," *Romania* 20 (1891): 417; D. Poirion, *Le Poète et le prince* (Paris: Presses Universitaires de France, 1965), p. 41.

doctrine as outlined in medieval manuals of love, he operates within the parameters of constant conflict. Whether or not he believes that love can exist in marriage, that the lady should be older or younger, of higher or lower social standing than her lover; whether he maintains the necessity of consummation or chastity, the troubadour or *trouvère* tends to picture love as a state of perpetual warfare against an invincible enemy. In the case of his lady and of the *lauzengers* the foe represents a being of flesh and blood. Elsewhere, the generalization of epic combat, its displacement toward a multiplicity of independent opponents, involves its abstraction as well: the lover finds himself universally threatened by the allegorical figure of Love. Cercamon complains of Love's power over him and of his own inability to resist:

> Quant l'aura doussa s'amarzis
> E'l fuelha chai de sul verjan
> E l'auzelh chanjan lor latis,
> Et ieu de sai sospir e chan
> D'Amor que'm te lassat e pres,
> Qu'ieu anc no l'agui en poder.

When the sweet breeze turns bitter and the leaves fall from the branches, when the birds change their song, here I sigh and sing of Love, who keeps me imprisoned in his nets, while I, never again shall I have him in my power.

(Cercamon 1)

Like Cercamon, Marcabru has been trapped in Love's nets; he considers his captor ignoble because he "slays without a sword" (Marcabru 87). Bernart de Ventadorn admits to having engaged in battle with and having been "conquered by Love."[69] Though he blames defeat upon a poor military situation—*Per Deu, Amors! be'm trobas vensedor: ab paucs d'amies e ses autre senhor*—he is also willing to grant his foe's fundamental superiority.[70] Love is, by definition, "an opponent against whom vengeance with sword or lance" remains impossible (Ventadorn [Lazar] 186). For Guiraut de Calanson, Love's advantage lies in his "superior

---

69. car eu me mor e nul semblan no'n fatz;
   e per Amor sui si apoderatz,
   tot m'a vencut a forsa e a batalha.

I die without letting any sign of it appear; for I have been conquered by Love, who overcame me by force and in battle.

(Ventadorn [Lazar] 140)

70. By God, Love, you find me easy to overcome; having few friends, without other lord (Ventadorn [Lazar] 136).

military skill."[71] Peire Vidal acknowledges the futility of his own and of all similar struggles: *Mas vencutz es cui Amors apodera; Son ben apoderatz per amor e vencutz.*[72] So does Folquet de Marseille: *S'ar no'us vens, vencutz sui Amors; venser no'us puesc mas ab Merce.*[73] Arnaut Daniel shares Bernart's, Guiraut's, Peire's, and Folquet's frustration. Love "bends him more easily than a strong man would a flexible stick" (Nelli and Lavaud 2: 114).

The struggle against an allegorical Love is by no means limited to the southern poets. Le Châtelain de Coucy feels perpetually under attack and unable "to defend himself": *Ke ie n'ai mais pooir de moi defendre* (Coucy 82). Gace Brulé concurs: *D'Amour ne me puis defendre; Face de moi son pleisir!*[74] Conon de Béthune accuses Love of murder, of having slain him "without warning" (Béthune 232). In distinguishing between Love and all other opponents, Thibaut de Champagne laments Love's double attack. The allegorized enemy has obscured his senses from within while assaulting him from without:

> Qui voit venir son anemi corant
> Por trere a lui granz saetes d'acier
> Bien se devroit destorner en fuiant
> Et garantir, s'il pouit, de l'archier;
> Mais, quant Amors vient plus a moi lancier,
> Et mains la fui, c'est merveille trop grant,
> Q'ansic reçoif son coup entre la gent
> Com se g'iere touz seus en un avergier.

> Whoever sees his enemy come running
> To shoot at him great arrows of steel
> Ought well to turn in flight
> And protect himself, if he can, from the archer;
> But, when Love came on to shoot at me,
> Rather than flee, (it is quite a wonder),
> I received his blow thus in the midst of people
> As if I were all alone in a garden.

> (Champagne 10)

71. M. Raynouard, *Choix des poésies originales des troubadours* (Paris: Firmin Didot, 1818), 3: 391.

72. But he who is taken by Love is conquered; I am well subdued and conquered by love (Vidal 18, 43).

73. If I cannot conquer you, Love, I am conquered, and I cannot conquer you except with Mercy (*Le Troubadour Folquet de Marseille*, ed. S. Stronski [Cracow: Académie des Sciences, 1910], p. 40).

74. I cannot defend myself against Love; he does with me as he pleases (Gace Brulé 76).

Even victory cannot guarantee an end to Love's assault, which endures long after a particular attachment has concluded (Champagne 54). Love appears, in fact, "to enjoy his victim's pain": *Plere li fet ses dolors* (Champagne 59). Thibaut's acceptance of the permanence of Love's attack corresponds to Bernart's awareness of the universality of combat against all real women (see above, p. 146). For the courtly poet, love represents a state of perpetual striving for unattainable ideals of purity, spiritual and moral perfection, transcendence, possession of a distant love; it implies a state of relentless warfare between the lover and his abstract courtly *daemon*, Love.

Constant combat against the allegorized warrior-god of Love is evident within the narrative courtly forms. Chrétien de Troyes consistently depicts the onset of desire in terms of Love's attack. Offended by Soredamors's resistance in *Cligés*, Love avenges his honor by waging war upon her (v. 450). Alexandre's defeat follows closely that of Soredamors.[75] He accuses his assailant of having attacked him "treacherously," without breaking the customary stick of challenge (*Cligés* v. 850). Soredamors and Alexandre feel helpless in the face of an invincible foe, whose assaults are seemingly without pause: *Fos est qui devers lui se met / Qu'il vialt toz jorz grever les suens.*[76]

Guillaume de Lorris's neophyte lover undergoes a sustained attack once his desire has focused upon a single rose (*Rose* v. 1679). The strategy of Love's initial pursuit of the lover includes five allegorical arrows—Beauty, Simplicity, Courtesy, Companionship, and Fair Seeming—which render him as helpless as Alexandre or Soredamors. Recognizing the uselessness of resistance, his heart becomes the prisoner of victorious Love; he is, henceforth, Love's commended man (*Rose* v. 1882). Love's victory is but the first in a series of amorous battles: From the initial struggle against an allegorical deity there emerges a generalized psychological conflict, the *psychomachia*, that shapes not only Guillaume's portion of *Le Roman de la rose*, but that of his continuator as well.[77]

75. "Amors les deus amanz travaille / Vers cui il a prise bataille." "Love works over the two lovers / Against whom he engages in battle" (*Cligés* v. 565).

76. He is a fool who places himself against (Love) / For he wants always to torment his vassals (*Cligés* v. 667; see also vv. 520, 925); Lancelot too experiences a relentless series of attacks (see *Lancelot* v. 1336).

77. While both the poet's lady and the God of Love are invincible opponents in their own right, nothing prevents an alliance between the two. Bernart de Ventadorn complains that their treacherous complicity causes him to live in constant pain (Ventadorn [Appel]

The Poet against Himself

For troubadours and *trouvères*, for Chrétien and Guillaume de Lorris, the God of Love is, above all, a military man. He remains capable of betrayal, cruelty, prolonged assault, and expedient alliances; his aim is faultless, his arrows sharp, his strategy without equal. And yet he is also an allegorical figure, a facet of the poet's imagination, unlike the lady who may or may not be real. Moreover, Love's attack represents the necessary prelude to an essentially internal struggle within the poet's psyche. An imaginary external battle portrayed as if it were probable serves as catalyst to an inner struggle against the self. The courtly lover is a divided being whose separate selves are in contention with each other. He maintains a constant dialogue within himself. Marcabru admits to having "two thoughts," good and bad, which alternately "tickle and torture him": *Per la bona cuida m'esjau / E per l'avol sui aburzitz* (Marcabru 89). Often the split personality of the lyric poet manifests itself in terms of an inhibition of speech. The poet would like to declare his love, but feels prohibited by the risk involved. Richart de Berbezilh complains of lapsing into dream when he should be pursuing his passion; a forgetful dream-self stands in the way of its more active and aggressive double (Nelli and Lavaud 2: 98). Giraut de Bornelh engages in conversation with an other "self" concerning the psychological barrier to speech; sight of the beloved excludes further communication:

> —Días per que?
> —Per leis garar!
> —No'n sabras donc ab leis parlar?
> Est aissi del tot esperdutz?
> —Oc, can li sui denan vengutz . . . .
> —T'espertz?
> —Oc eu, que no sui de re certz.
>
> —Why? tell me.
> —I will see her!

---

166). Le Châtelain de Coucy, convinced of the impossibility of vengeance against his lady and the lack of recourse for "he whom love destroys and disinherits," dreams of reversing the situation "for just one day"; with love's assistance he could avenge the wrong his lady has inflicted (41). Thibaut de Champagne develops, in "Ainsi comme unicorne sui," an elaborate alliance between his lady and Love, who together capture the poet's heart: "Et moi ont mort d'autel senblant / Amors et ma dame, por voir." "They have rendered me as good as dead / Love and my lady" (113).

—Can't you then speak to her?
Are you distracted to that point?
—Yes, when I come before her . . . .
—The problem?
—Yes, I am no longer sure of anything.
(Nelli and Lavaud 2: 92)

Giraut's uncertainty at the sight of his lady would not have astonished Le Châtelain de Coucy, whose confusion leads to a similar inhibition (Coucy 80). Conon de Béthune compares his own loss of words to a practiced champion who forgets how to defend himself in the middle of battle:

Encor devis coment je li dirai
Le grant dolour ke j'en trai sans anui,
Ke tant l'aour et desir, cant j'i sui,
Ke ne li os descovrir me raison;
Si vait de moi com fait dou campïon
Ki de lonc tens aprent a escrimer,
Et cant il vient ou camp as cous ferir,
Si ne set rien d'escu ne de baston.

Again I meditate how I will tell her
The great sorrow which I suffer without pain,
That I adore and desire her so much, when I am with her,
That I dare not tell her my thoughts;
Thus it goes with me as with a champion
Who learns to fight with swords for a long time,
And when he comes to the field to strike blows,
He knows nothing of shield or of lance.

(Béthune 222)

Conon has, in the above example, come as close as any lyric poet of the twelfth or thirteenth century to articulating the intimate relationship between the violence of judicial combat and the inner violence of self-doubt. His metaphor suggests, through juxtaposition, the transformation of a real and immediate conflict into a psychological struggle between discrete facets of the mind.

The divided poetic personality, torn between a self which desires and recognizes the necessity of speech and a self which rejects it out of fear, extends elsewhere to the poet's whole being. It reaches beyond vague feelings of depersonalization and frustration to disembodiment of his soul, a split between body and heart. Le Châtelain de Coucy accuses his heart of leading him, against his will, to folly (Coucy 41). Thibaut de Champagne complains that his heart has been sundered from reason, that it remains in his lady's power while his body has been left behind (Champagne 79). The poet remains unable to recover his heart no matter how hard he tries; for, as Thibaut admits, love represents "a struggle from which the lover cannot hope to extricate his soul" (Champagne 94). Nor does awareness of his dilemma aid him in the least:

> Je meismes a moi tence,
>   Car reson
> Me dit que je faz enfance,
>   Quant prison
> Tieng ou ne vaut raençon;
>
> I struggle with myself
>   For reason
> Tells me that I am childish
>   When I stay
> In a prison where ransom is worthless.
>   (Champagne 2)

Despite the knowledge on the part of his reasonable self that his other self acts foolishly, there can be no escape from love's prison, which is, in reality, that of the divided self.

The immediate price of internal strife is loss of reason; its ultimate cost—madness and death. Bernart de Ventadorn prides himself on having recovered his sanity—and his power of speech—after a maddening and destructive passion: *Estat ai com om esperdutz . . . . mas era'm sui reconogutz.*[78] Peire Cardenal perceives a threat to the lover's entire being in the conflict between his lady allied with desire and his better self allied with reason. Success in love necessarily implies a loss of one's innermost self; failure carries the consolation of its recovery:

> Anc non gazanhei tan gran re
> Con quam perdei ma mïa;
> Quar, perden leis, gazanhei me,
> Qu'il gazainhat m'avïa.
> Petit gazainha qui pert se,
> Mas qui pert so que dan li te,
> Ieu cre que gazainhs sïa.
> Qu'ieu m'era donatz, per ma fe,
> A tal que.m destruzïa,
> Non sai per que.

I never won anything so great as when I lost my mistress; for, losing her, I won back myself when she had won me over. He wins little who loses himself, but if

---

78. I was like a madman. . . . But now I've come to my senses (Ventadorn [Lazar] 176).

one loses that which does one harm, then I think it's a gain. For I had given myself, in faith, to one such who was destroying me, I know not why.[79]

Peire compares his near escape from self-destruction to the victory of a warrior in battle; the man who manages to conquer his heart and free it from excessive desire gains more honor than "if he had captured a hundred towns." He who fails to master desire is, on the other hand, not only dishonored, but buried, like a defeated warrior, in the attempt.

Once engaged, the internal discourse of the divided self seems to feed upon itself, to generate further conflict *ad infinitum*. The lyric poet thus maintains a constant dialogue with a part of himself that has, through the experience of love, been severed from the rest of his being. While at an extreme lurks the madness of Bernart or Peire Cardenal, alienation is a persistent face of courtliness within both lyric and courtly modes. Whether the heart, the eyes, good or bad thought, the faculties of speech, reason, or dream, the alienated portion of the lover's psyche serves as a constant reminder that courtly violence is, to a great degree, internal.

What is to be concluded from the above discussion? Above all, that it is impossible to separate the existential situation of the lyric poet-lover from a pattern of persistent conflict against vaguely identifiable, but nonetheless threatening, ladies, sexual and professional rivals, the *daemon* of Love, and, ultimately, himself. Whereas the lyric seems to be devoted entirely to the expression of strong emotions, a genre of poetic passivity from which heroic action remains excluded, its thematic content is closer to that of the epic and courtly narrative than is generally recognized. The dominant theme of the lyric is an undefined—almost paradigmatic—violence that never erupts to the point of actual confrontation but that is still the determining factor of the lover's relation with others.

Three distinct strategies toward the expression of physical violence and the implicit relation between individual and community emerge from the three genres under consideration. In the epic it is assumed that war is the natural condition of man, and, in fact, the organizational principle of human society. A peacetime *chanson de geste* is almost inconceivable;[80] and those epics in which peace is established (*Raoul de Cambrai, Les Quatre Filz Aymon*) are quickly transformed into *romans d'aventure*,

---

79. Press, *Anthology*, p. 282.
80. One notable exception is the *Pèlerinage de Charlemagne* which combines elements of the epic and voyage literature.

novelistic texts in which the hero, detached through exile from the warrior community, meets others like himself. In romance, on the other hand, the peace embodied in Arthur's court, represents the natural state of social man. Only when the individual ventures from Camelot does the violence which has been relegated geographically outside the human community become unavoidable. Romance thus embraces both ideals, that of a peaceful existence at court and that of a mandatory test of physical prowess beyond the bounds of society; the ideal knight passes freely between both worlds. Not surprisingly, the courtly novel in which the violence of the forest is allowed to invade the peaceful order of the court has, like *La Mort Artu*, all the earmarks of epic.

In the lyric, man's natural condition is social in only a limited sense, the scope of his relations having been reduced to his lady, perhaps her husband, the *lauzengers*, a few other poets, and sometimes a friend or confidant. And yet the tenor of his dealings with others is characterized by the universality of conflict within the restricted company in which he moves: the lyric poet-lover is perpetually at war despite his apparent passivity. He differs from the warrior-hero of epic and the chivalric hero of romance chiefly in the weapon which he employs. Where the violence of the *chanson de geste* and courtly novel is primarily physical and the arms of struggle are the sword and shield, the violence of the lyric is primarily verbal; the arms of the lover are his words. Here it is possible to distinguish between conflict as a theme and as a principle of poetic structure. For if the lyric seems to be the least representional of Old French and Provençal genres, the least beholden to any reality outside of itself, this is because its theme—the struggle of the poet-lover against omnipresent, shifting, and vaguely defined enemies—is built into and coterminous with the poem itself. Our next chapter deals with the verbal violence of persuasion in relation to the dialectical forms of courtly lyric and to the verbal judicial model *par excellence*—the inquest.

CHAPTER IV

The Text as Inquest

The substitution of trial by inquest for battle was a gradual and discontinuous process which did not reach completion until well after the period under consideration. That inquest gained as wide a place as it did within the secular sphere was symptomatic of a profound crisis within the ranks of France's feudal aristocracy. Because of the technological and political difficulties attached to war in the centuries following the First Crusade, warfare as a means of maintaining sovereignty proved less and less effective. At the same time judicial combat as a method of terminating the conflict of whole armies grew steadily less appropriate to the legal needs of the postfeudal era. More precisely, trial by battle primarily served the interests of a warrior aristocracy, whose traditional right and ability to rule by armed force were threatened by new possibilities for the organization of human communities—by the revival of a money economy along with the rise of towns and by the consolidation and administrative development of the feudal monarchies, especially that of the King of France. Inquest, on the other hand, stood as a response to the crisis of feudalism in decline, since, as a nonviolent means for the resolution of difference, it furthered the commercial interests of a northern bourgeoisie while satisfying the centralizing claims of monarchy.

The predicament of a warrior aristocracy at the end of an age in which there was little distinction between military and political power is, as we have seen, most poignantly reflected in the Old French epic. There, aristocracy's historic capacity for war and its right to rule in the absence of a strong central government come continually into conflict with the horror and the futility of fighting. And if the *chanson de geste* chronicles in an explicit fashion the most pressing issue of late feudal organization—how to prevent and contain the petty clashes of rival chiefs, it offers very little in the way of solution. For the epic author, the difficulty of resolving the dilemmas attached to war in an age in which recourse to arms was becoming progressively problematic is inherent to his medium.

Courtly literature crystallizes much that remains implicit within the *chanson de geste*. This is not to suggest an etiological rapport between contemporaneous literary types, but to emphasize that it is only when the epic becomes most characteristic, most firmly rooted in a military strategy of the past, that it transcends its own formal limits and points not only toward a fundamental change in the relation of individual, clan, and state, but toward other literary forms as well. These moments of rupture tend to occur, as we have observed, after a period of protracted siege which gives way to discussion concerning the feasibility of further war. The failure of war reflected in the siege motif, and in the inevitable controversy over tactics, produces both an internalization and a verbalization of the violence normally reserved for the battlefield and for one's enemies. When the projection of hostility outside of the warrior community becomes impossible, it is displaced spatially toward the group, split—like the French army before the walls of Saragossa, Montessor, Montauban, and Trémoigne—by indecision. It is, at the same time, displaced formally toward its mimetic equivalent, the debate.

The introduction within the military genre *par excellence* of discussion concerning the feasibility of war amounts to both a literary mode and a society caught in the act of questioning its most cherished assumptions and ideals. More important, the epic debate suggests the possibility of a struggle which is neither actual nor physical but mediated and verbal. Although it may eventually lead to action, its violence is for the moment purely representational, symbolically acted out through language. The importance of such a break—the self-reflective clôture of the epic upon itself—should not be underestimated.

It is within the limits of epic debate—violence which is an imitation of true violence rendered problematic—that courtly literature is born. The courtly text responds, implicitly and unconsciously, to the dilemmas of the epic in much the same way that the inquisitory judicial model answers to the crises of military feudalism. And again, though no causal relation between distinct literary types or between judicial and literary forms can be assumed, the displacement of the epic battle toward verbal conflict and, at an extreme, the tendency for lyric debate to proliferate to the proportions of an entire work and thus to constitute an independent form resemble too closely the transformation from battle to inquest for that resemblance to pass unnoticed. We have seen, in the previous chapter, that the thematic conversion of the collective and physical violence of the epic into more abstract, personal, and general equivalents parallels and even anticipates a corresponding shift in legal institutions. What remains to be shown are the ways in which courtly literature speaks to the unresolved issues of epic and the role which it plays in the displacement of the epic ordeal toward verbal substitutes. Here we must bear in mind that lyric and romance modes fulfill a common mediatory function through essentially different means. The former encourages a subliminal substitution of the verbal violence of disputation for that of battle; the latter exploits the ordeal of narration—a striving of the romance hero to tell his story according to the model of deposition—to similar purpose. In the present chapter we shall explore the relation of literary disputation and deposition—structuring principles of lyric and romance—to essentially analogous procedures within the judicial sphere.

Verbalization of the Poetic Ordeal

It would be wrong to assume that a system of abstract jurisprudence was unknown within canonical courts, that allegorical and didactic debate were not popular among Latin poets, or that learned discussion was not a part of school curriculum throughout the Middle Ages. Nonetheless, it is only from the twelfth century onward that a highly developed system of civil judicial procedure, vernacular debate literature, and philosophical dialectic came to subsume so much that was fundamental to late medieval France. The rise of an inquisitory court system, in which argumentation was practiced in the place of battle, along with the increasingly dialectical patterns of Latin and vernacular poetry, attest to the tremendous importance in all areas of cultural life—legal, intellectual, and literary—of what remains the verbal form of violence *par excellence*: the debate.

The validation of debate as a governing principle of intellectual exchange was first apparent in the northern centers of learning. Abelard's controversies with Guillaume de Champeaux and Anselme de Laon were symptomatic, if not determinative, of a new philosophical departure.

[164]

Beginning in the twelfth century, the rudimentary dialectic based upon Boethius's translation of Aristotle, and practiced until then only outside of the Faculty of Theology, was both perfected and applied to all areas of study. Keystone of the Scholastic method, debate figured prominently in the medieval university curriculum. A Master of Theology was versed, above all, in the arts of *legere, praedicare,* and *disputare.*[1] As a student he had participated in the ordinary *disputatio* as well as the extraordinary *collativae* and *sorbonique,* more informal daily discussions. He was required to act either as *oponens* or as *respondens* in at least one improvised debate, or *quodlibet,* before obtaining the *licence*; thereafter, regular participation in similar scholastic contests was necessary for the maintenance of his academic status.

A debate at the University of Paris was a solemn public event supervised by a master and attended by his *bacheliers* and *cursors* as well as by outsiders from other classes. In the northern schools of the thirteenth century, sponsorship of two or three *questions disputées* per week was not unusual. The exercise itself contained two distinct parts: the *discussio,* or alternation of objections between opponents designated by the master; and the *determinatio,* or conclusion. The *discussio,* based upon a thesis announced beforehand, represented a verbal fight between students; the master presided only to help a faltering interlocutor, to sharpen his logic, and to insure the theological probity of the proceedings. His role in the *determinatio,* however, was central. On the first "readable day," the first day on which he would have ordinarily held class, the master summed up the arguments of the preceding session and presented his own opinion. He submitted his decision to doctrinal scrutiny, responding to possible objections before the determination was published. The end product of the entire process, the *sententia,* stood, first and foremost, as a decisive doctrinal conclusion based upon a thorough examination of the question debated along with the reasoning advanced by both *oponens* and *respon-*

1. For a discussion of medieval university debate see: P. Glorieux, "L'Enseignement au moyen âge: techniques et méthodes en usage à la Faculté de Théologie de Paris, au XIIIe siècle," *Archives d'Histoire Doctrinale et Littéraire du Moyen Age* 35 (1968): 65; J. Le Goff, *Les Intellectuels au moyen âge* (Paris: Seuil, 1969); P. Mandonnet, "Chronologie des questions disputées de Saint Thomas D'Aquin," *Revue Thomiste* 1 (1918): 226; G. Paré, A. Brunet, and P. Tremblay, *La Renaissance du XIIe siècle: les écoles et l'enseignement* (Paris: J. Vrin, 1933); J. Verger, *Les Universités au moyen âge* (Paris: Presses Universitaires de France, 1973).

dens. Much like the decision—also a sentence—emanating from the judicial encounter, the *determinatio* marked the formal end of debate.

The search for certainty with respect to the origins of twelfth-century debate literature remains problematic because of the general medieval inclination toward dispute and because of the tendency for all highly developed social bodies—Greece of the City State, Rome, the Carolingian Empire—to make efficient use of verbal disputation. Nonetheless, the Carolingian *conflictus* seems to offer the closest literary analogue to what was a virtual renaissance of the dialogued mode. The *Conflictus Veris et Hiemis* attributed to Alcuin, the *Carmen Nigelli Ermoldi Exulis in Laudem Gloriosissimi Pippini Regis, Ecloga Theoduli,* and *Rosae Liliique Certamen* of Sedulius Scottus furnish the most probable models for the outpouring of Latin debate poems from the mid-eleventh century onward: the Goliardic stanza, *Altercatio Phillidis et Florae, Cardinalis Domina* (Council of Remiremont), *Altercatio Ganymedis et Helenae, Jupiter et Danae*; the debates of winter and summer, old age and youth, wine and water, body and soul, vices and virtues; and even the series of disputes which occupy such a large portion of Andreas Capellanus's treatise on love.[2]

The revival of preexisting patterns of literary dialectic gained further momentum through the interest of vernacular poets in what had been, until that time, a learned form of discourse. Much of the same material, along with an affinity for disputation, became increasingly familiar to Provençal and French poets. Debates between wine and water, body and soul, the upper and lower halves of the lady's body date from this period. The conflict of vices and virtues constituted a genre of its own. Rutebeuf's *Bataille des vices contre les vertus,* Huon de Méri's *Tournoiement d'Antéchrist,* the *Tournoiement d'Enfer, Bataille des sept arts,* and the *Bataille de Caresme et charnage* are, like the *Ecloga Theoduli,* reminiscent of Prudentian conflict and of the early Christian polemical debates. Numerous French versions of the *Council of Remiremont* demonstrate sufficient thematic unity to be considered as a whole.[3]

---

2. See A. Gunn, *The Mirror of Love* (Lubbock: Texas Tech Press, 1952), pp. 457–482; J. Hanford, "Classical Eclogue and Medieval Debate," *Romanic Review* 2 (1911): 16–43; H. Walther, *Das Streitgedicht in der lateinischen Literatur des Mittelalters* (Berlin: Beck, 1920), pp. 144–153; E. Köhler, *Trobadorlyrik und höfischer Roman* (Berlin: Rütten and Loening, 1962), pp. 153–192.

3. See E. Faral, "Les Débats du clerc et du chevalier dans la littérature des XII⁰ et XIII⁰ siècles," *Romania* 41 (1912): 473; C. Oulmont, *Les Débats du clerc et du chevalier dans la littérature poétique du moyen âge* (Paris: Champion, 1911).

Vernacular Debate Forms

There is no genre, lyric or narrative, that is not infused with at least a smattering of formal debate. Yet the uniqueness of twelfth-century debate literature lies in the wealth of fresh dialogued patterns to which it gave rise. It was during this period that hitherto unknown genres based solely upon the alternation of contrasting verbal responses came into their own. *Terminus a quo* of a fundamental formal shift, the appearance of the earliest *coblas*, double *sirventes*, *pastorelas*, *tensos*, and *jocs partits* signalled the beginning of the institutionalization of literary debate, a process that culminated in the sophisticated *ballades dialoguées* of the fourteenth and fifteenth centuries, those of Eustache Deschamps, Christine de Pisan, Jean Régnier, Charles d'Orléans, and Villon.[4]

The *cobla*, a minor dialogued form, contains a one or two strophe exchange.[5] Although closest in structure to the *tenso*, of which it is a reduced version, the *cobla* demonstrates a certain thematic affinity with the *sirventes* as well: its tone is often satirical and filled with personal invective; its theme is sometimes political. The *cobla* appears, in fact, to represent an early prototype of both the *tenso* and *sirventes*, even though the oldest examples—those of Folquet de Marseille, Peire Vidal, and Raimbaut de Vaqueiras—were written around the beginning of the thirteenth century.

The *sirventes*, a satirical poem about any subject but love, enjoyed immense popularity among Provençal poets. A less well-known form, the double *sirventes*, consists of a pair of antithetical lyrics of the same length, schema, and, generally speaking, the same rhyme.[6] It resembles the *tenso* in all respects, except for the fact that each set of strophic exchanges characteristic of the *tenso* has been expanded to the dimensions of a complete poem.[7] Theoretically, each poem within the pair, or the series of pairs, constitutes a response to its predecessor, the original challenge

4. See O. Jodogne, "La Ballade dialoguée dans la littérature française médiévale," in *Mélanges R. Guiette* (Anvers: De Nederlandsche Boekhandel, 1961), p. 71. Although the terms *tenso, joc partit, pastorela,* and *sirventes* refer to Provençal versions of the *tenson, jeu-parti, pastourelle,* and *sirventes*, I have used the Provençal term whenever both Old French and Provençal poems are concerned.

5. See A. Jeanroy, *La Poésie lyrique des troubadours* (Paris: Didier, 1934), p. 275; A. Jeanroy, "La Tenson provençale," *Annales du Midi* 2(1899): 456.

6. For a discussion of the double *sirventes* see: G. Bertoni and A. Jeanroy, "Un Duel poétique du XIIIe siècle," *Annales du Midi* 27–28 (1915–1916): 269.

7. D. Jones considers the double *sirventes*, which he labels *sirventès-tensons*, to represent the original form of the *tenso*; see *La Tenson Provençale* (Paris: Droz, 1934), p. 70.

emanating from an unexplained but preexistent source of personal and professional tension.[8] In an exchange between Marcabru and a certain Audric, for example, the latter accuses his rival of immoderate desire and challenges him to respond (Marcabru 95). Marcabru's reply, a poem of identical schema (seven strophes) based upon different rhymes, blames Audric for miserliness, lust, gluttony, and for "conduct unbefitting a Christian" (Marcabru 101). A similar interchange pits Bertran d'Alamanon against a *jongleur* named Gui. Thanking his rival for teaching him so much about "the various occupations that exist on earth," Bertran denounces him as a *trotiers* (fast liver) and a cattle, goat, kid, and sheep thief; he ridicules his poetic and knightly pretensions. Gui counterattacks with an accusation of stinginess, degeneracy, and cowardice: *Gran maluestat ab croy captenemen, / E gran cors flac farsit d'auol coratie.*[9]

The most celebrated *tenso-sirventes* comprises a series of six attacks and retorts traded back and forth between Sordello and Peire Bremon between 1234 and 1240. The former launches into the fray, suggesting that his rival is cowardly and false-hearted; that he is a liar and a braggart; that women are dishonored by sleeping with him. Sordello invites response, and Peire defends himself by claiming to have been assailed without having first wronged his assailant. Furthermore, everyone knows that Sordello is nothing more than "a tricky and vicious jongleur." Peire's poetic enemy has recently been chased from the court of Lombardy because of his disloyalty. If his own cowardice renders him unfit to consort with women, as Peire concludes, then Sordello must suffer the same fate. The latter claims, in his reply, to be delighted that Peire recognized himself in the original *sirventes*. He repeats the accusation of unmanly weakness while at the same time denying the charge of infidelity: *q'ieu sui leials, et el tant fals.*[10] Peire responds with an allusion to his opponent's imitation of a wolf and, worst of all, with contempt for his poetic skill. Sordello maintains that his mastery of the *sirventes* is adequate

8. See also the exchanges between: Peire Roger ("Seigneir Raimbautz, per vezer") and Raimbaut d'Orange ("Peire Rogiers a trassaillir") (C. A. F. Mahn, *Werke der Troubadours* [Berlin: Dümmler, 1855], 1: 124, 73); a certain Mathieu ("Seigner Bertran per la desconossenza") and Bertran de Gourdon ("Se'm dises mal, Matheus, ni'm moves tenza") (Jones, *La Tenson*, p. 73); Peire Torat ("G. Riquier, si be'us es luen luenh de nos") and Guiraut Riquier ("Sie us es tan luenh, mos cors es pres de vos") ed. C. Chabaneau, *Revue des Langues Romanes* 32 (1888): 117.

9. A vile character and the manners of a boor, / And a great flaccid body, stuffed with cowardice (*Bertran d'Alamanon*, p. 77).

10. I am loyal, and he, on the contrary, is so false ("Un Duel poétique," p. 285).

to destroy his foppish rival and that Peire has not only been expelled from the courts of Provence and Toulouse, but has been rejected by the Templars and Hospitalers as well: *que'l cors a gran e lonc, e'l cor petit e fals.*[11] He adds the charges of dandyism, avarice, cowardice, and cruelty toward his wife to that of pride. Sordello's parting shot looks like a declaration of victory:

> e quar es d'aital pens qu'e re non tem falhir,
> ni Ihesu Crist descreire, ni sagrament mentir,
> ni donas dechzer, ni en luy envelir.

> For he is so prideful that he thinks he can never fail,
> even when he renounces Jesus Christ, breaks his oaths,
> dishonors women, and is himself completely degenerate.[12]

Peire, however, does not admit defeat, pretending that it is he who has won the poetic contest—*pero tuit semblan motz siei dit a prop en cap*—and the amatory contest as well.[13] Thus, from the original challenge to the final declaration of victory, the encounter between Sordello and Peire Bremon has all the earmarks of verbal warfare: a series of reciprocal parries and responses, claims and counter-claims, each intended to inflict injury. The stakes in this war of words are the poet's reputation as knight and lover and, by extension, access to the lady in question. Furthermore, this series of independent exchanges permits an analytic glimpse at the discrete constitutive elements of the integrated dialogued form. In order for the separate poems to be seen as a whole they need only be placed next to one another; this juxtaposition of metrically matched insults and replies shows how easily personal antagonism can be translated into new and meaningful poetic structure.

A more playful brand of antagonism can be found in the *pastorela* (O.F. *pastourelle*), a love debate genre popular in the south as early as the first half of the twelfth century.[14] The *pastorela* depicts, within a rustic setting, the verbal duel between a knight—or poet—and a peasant girl over the latter's virtue; it is, in other words, a combat or *disputatio* in which the girl herself is at stake. Metrically, the *pastorela*, like the *tenso*, contains alternating dialogued stanzas sometimes followed by a short *envoi*. There are three possible outcomes to the rustic drama of seduction. On occasion, the

---

11. He has a large and tall body, but a small and false heart (*Ibid.*, p. 291).
12. *Idem.*
13. For in the final analysis, all his words have neither head nor tail (*Ibid.*, p. 293).
14. See M. Zink, *La Pastourelle: poésie et folklore au moyen âge* (Paris: Bordas, 1972).

girl submits, having been persuaded by her pursuer's argument or by more forceful means. In Gauvadan's "Dezamparatz, ses companho," for instance, a despondent knight offers his love to a shepherdess who refuses at first on the grounds that she is engaged to another.[15] His offer to become her "commended man and servant" causes a shift in her resistance to more abstract ground: even Solomon, she maintains, was tricked by love. Finally, the knight's ironic threat to become a monk if his request remains unfulfilled proves irresistible.

Elsewhere, surrender is the result of more energetic pursuit. Having offered a recalcitrant shepherdess a finely woven blouse and having been rebuffed, Guiraut d'Espanha takes her by force.[16] Most often, however, the knight is obliged to relinquish his suit. The girl sometimes outwits her admirer who, like Marcabru, admits to failure (Marcabru 141). Or, the shepherdess manages to summon her lover, brother, or father; and a fight ensues between her protectors and pursuer. Thibaut de Champagne's poet-knight of "L'autrier par la matinee" is forced to flee:

> Lors la pris a acoler,
> Et ele gete un haut cri:
> "Perrinet, traï, traï!"
> Du bois prenent a huper;
> Je la lais sanz demorer,
> Seur mon cheval m'en parti.

> Then I grabbed her to embrace her
> And she cried aloud:
> "Perinet, betrayed, betrayed!"
> In the forest a cry was raised:
> I left her without delay,
> And departed on my horse.
>   (Champagne 182)

Thus, despite the *pastourelle*'s obvious distortion of courtly etiquette in extolling the love of a woman of lower social standing, the most basic element of the love encounter remains unchanged. The poet or knight still finds himself trapped in a zealous, if sometimes farcical, struggle not only against a clever shepherdess—the degraded image of the courtly lady—but against her guardians—the comic counterparts of the jealous husband or *gardador*.

15. J. Audiau, *La Pastourelle dans la poésie occitane du moyen âge* (Paris: Boccard, 1923), p. 20.

16. *Ibid.*, p. 100.

A third possible outcome of the exchange between shepherdess and knight involves a mediated solution: their difference is submitted to a third party for judgment. In what remains an unusual version of the *pastorela* ("Entre Lerid e Blois"), Serveri de Gerona tells of having witnessed the theft of an indiscreet shepherdess's workhorse while she dallied with her lover. The poet finds the horse, hides it, and extracts a promise of her affection in return for its safe recovery. When he produces it she reneges, reminding the poet that many have fooled him in the past and that, besides, she tricked him gently. He, however, insists so vehemently that she proposes to let the Infanta settle their quarrel.[17] He consents, revealing the arbiter's name as well as her title:

> —"A la Vezcomtesa plazen,
> Na Toza, de Cardona'm ren,
> C'amor no te pro, forçada."
>
> I submit myself to the kindly
> Vicomtess of Cardona, for love
> does not profit at all from constraint.[18]

Although Serveri's variation upon a familiar motif remains unique, it is nonetheless significant. For in the decision to accept the verdict of an outside party of superior authority, the poet upsets the symmetry of the pastoral encounter. He extends beyond its normal limits the exchange which is, as a result, transformed from a quest for victory to a search for adequate independent arbitration. Serveri thus combines the model of warfare with that of the trial.

The Poem as Trial

The *cobla*, double *sirventes*, and *pastorela* are all, in some extended sense, trials: that is to say, arguments, attempts to convince an adversary of the probity of a particular opinion or desire. They are also trials to the degree that they represent ordeals, tests of endurance in which the reader,

17. —"Seyner, caus'es desguiada
   Per forç' ab cut' autreyada.
   No's deu far, per qu'eu m'en repen;
   Pero vuyll n'auzir jutyamen
   De l'Enfan, on pretz s'agrada."

Sire, it is unbecoming that a critical situation has constrained me to bring you to an accord; this must not be, and that is why I refuse; but I would like nonetheless to hear on this subject the judgement of the Infanta, in whom merit is pleased [to reside].

(Audiau, *La Pastourelle*, p. 105)

18. *Idem.* The Vicomtess of Cardona was, in fact, Serveri de Gerona's protectress.

in lieu of God, is called upon to choose between irreconcilable alternatives. The act of judgment remains implicit, however; there are no judges, except in Serveri's unusual case, to whom the parties agree to turn.[19] This absence is especially apparent in light of the debate genres which include, as a matter of course, an official arbiter: the *tenso* and the *joc partit*. The *Leys d'Amors* leaves little doubt concerning the formal necessity of decision, since the *tenso* is, by definition, a discussion followed by adjudication.[20] Similarly, the *joc partit* or *partimen*, which is identical in every respect but the original freedom of the challenged poet to select a defendable position, calls for conclusive pronouncement.[21]

19. A notable exception is Rutebeuf's "Disputaison de Charlot et du Barbier" in which the two interlocutors, after heated debate, ask the poet, who has overheard their conversation, to act as judge (Rutebeuf, *Oeuvres complètes*, ed. E. Faral and J. Bastin [Paris: Picard, 1959], 2: 264).

20. Tensos es contrastz o debatz. en lo qual cascus mante e razona alcun dig o alcun fag. Et aquest dictatz alqunas vetz procezih per novas rimadas e adonx pot haver. XX. o trenta cobblas o may. et alcunas vetz per coblas, et aquest conte de. vi. coblas a. x. am doas tornadas en lasquals devo jutge eligir, lequals difinisca lor plag. e lor tenso. El jutges per aquel meteysh compas de coblas. o per novas rimadas pot donar son jutiamen. Enpero per novas rimadas es huey mays acostumat. En loqual jutiamen alqu volon seguir forma de dreg. fazen mensio davangelis. e dautras paraulas acostumadas de dire en sentencia. laqual cauza nos no reproam pero be dizem. que aysso no es de necessitat. quar abasta solamen quom done son jutiamen. et aquel declare. per aquela maniera que mays plazera a cel ques elegitz per jutge.

The *tenso* is a discussion or debate in which each party maintains and discusses some word or deed. Sometimes the work proceeds by changing rhymes; then it may have twenty or thirty couplets or more; other times there are from six to ten couplets, with two tournades, in which the two parties must select a judge who ends their argument and their *tenso* (or contention). The judge can give his judgment in couplets of the same measure, or in changing rhymes. Some would have the judgment written according to legal form, citing the gospels or other texts which one usually cites in sentences. We do not condemn this method; but we say that it is not necessary: for it is sufficient that the judgment be given; and can be pronounced in the manner which best suits the one who has been chosen as judge.

(*Leys* 1: 344)

The Old French *tenson* or *tançon* was synonymous with the word argument. Eglantine says to Hueline in the debate bearing their name: "Dame, a bon commencement, Puisque avez mené tançon. . . ." "Lady, you have begun well, Since you have opened debate. . . ." (Oulmont, *Débats du clerc*, p. 158); Chrétien equates the term with passion or anxiety: "Amors li est el cuer anclose, / Une tançons et une rage / Qui molt li troble son corage." "Love has inflicted upon her heart, / A dispute and a rage / Which greatly trouble her spirit" (*Cligés* v. 870). While A. Jeanroy believes that judgment was a necessary component of the *tenso*, he also maintains that they were rendered—at the time of the actual poetic performance—in prose. Thus the small number of decisions which have survived ("La Tenson," p. 449).

21. "Partimens es questios ques ha dos membres contraris. le quals es donatz ad autre per chauzir. e per sostener cel que volra elegir. e pueysh cascus razona e soste lo membre de la

The *tenso* and *joc partit* are inherent forms of poetic competition, and the range of possible contestants runs the gamut of courtly struggle. The poet's adversary is sometimes his lady, other times the God of Love, himself, a rival in love, or, simply, another poet. The Countess of Die ("Amics, ab gran cossirier") reproaches her lover for the nonchalance of his attention; he blames the *lauzengers* and promises to love with greater constancy in the future.[22] Maria de Ventadorn ("Gui d'Uissel, be·m pesa de vos") asks her lover Gui if a lady is as bound to obey her admirer as he is to obey her (Nelli and Lavaud 2: 134). Gui maintains that there can be no hierarchy among lovers, while Maria upholds the sovereignty of the lady. Thibaut de Champagne ("Dame, merci! Une riens vos demant") debates with his lady whether or not love will survive their death (164). Elsewhere, Thibaut argues with the God of Love about the source of his suffering ("L'autre nuit en mon dormant") (166). Bernart de Ventadorn ("Era·m cosselhatz, senhor") comes into conflict with himself; after defending both sides of a delicate point of amatory casuistry, he resolves it at the end of the *tenso* (Ventadorn [Lazar] 156). A common theme of contention between competing lovers, the question of whether it is more advantageous to meet one's rival as one leaves one's lady or as one arrives, was debated by Rainaut and Gui d'Ussel ("Segner Rainaut, vos qi·us faitz amoros") as well as by Jehen Bretel and Jehen de Grieviler ("Grieviler, se vous quidiés").[23] Gui and Elias d'Ussel discuss the merits of the role of husband relative to that of lover ("Ara·m digatz vostre semblan"). Elias concludes the husband's case with a humorous attempt to outwit his opponent:

> Per q'ieu am mais, cals qu'en sía lo critz
> Esser martiz gauzens que drutz marritz.
>
> Therefore I prefer—whatever one may say—
> To be a happy husband than a hapless lover!
>
> (Nelli and Lavaud 2: 124)

---

questio. lo qual haura elegit. En totas las autras cauzas cant al compas. e cant al jutiamen. e cant al so. es semblans a tenso." "The *joc partit* is a question with two possible answers, the choice of which is left to another, who supports the one he chooses. Each discusses and supports the side of the issue which he has selected. As for the meter, the judgment, and the rhyme, they are the same for the *joc partit* as for the *tenso*" (*Leys* 1: 345).

22. J. Véran, *Les Poétesses provençales au moyen âge* (Paris: Quillet, 1946), p. 169.

23. *Les Poésies des quatre troubadours d'Ussel*, ed. J. Audiau (Paris: Delagrave, 1922), p. 64; *Receuil général des jeux-partis français*, ed. A. Langfors, A. Jeanroy, and L. Brandin (Paris: Champion, 1926), 1: 133.

Thibaut de Champagne ("Roi Thiebaut, sire en chantant responnez") emphasizes the potential cruelty of the rivalry between competing lovers in arguing with a *trouvère* named Baudoin; the enemy poets dispute whether it is preferable to find oneself forced to carry one's lady around his neck to the house of another lover or to arrange a rendezvous for the couple at one's own house (144).

Despite the relatively small number of judges appointed and the even smaller number of judgments actually rendered at the end of *tensos* and *jocs partits*, there can be little doubt that the purpose of the poetic encounter is the same as that of trial: the nonviolent termination of a potentially violent quarrel. As Thibaut de Champagne's opponent Gui recognizes ("Cuens, je vos part un jeu par ahaitie"), the concluding verdict of the *tenson* produces an end to conflict, a restoration of peace:[24]

> —A Gilon pri qu'il en die le voir
> Qui a tort de la meslee
> Ne qui s'en doit plus doloir,
> Die le por pès avoir.

> —I ask Gilon [le Vinier] to tell the truth
> About who is wrong in our quarrel
> And should grieve the most because of it,
> I say this in order to restore peace [between us].
> (Champagne 137)

In appointing an arbiter to resolve the question of whether one should continue or desist loving the wife of a good friend, Gamars de Vilers and Cuvelier seek to stop their bickering:

> —Cuvelier, de ma partie
> Je preng la dame jolie
> De Fouencamp sans targier
> S'en voelle le droit trïer,
> S'est no tençons apaisie.

> —Cuvelier, for my part
> I choose the lovely lady
> De Fouencamp; if she will
> Without delay decide who is right,
> Our dispute will be appeased.[25]

---

24. Elsewhere, Thibaut gives up in order to cease fighting (152, 165).
25. *Receuil des jeux-partis*, 2: 31.

Likewise, Adam de la Halle and Jehen Bretel designate separate judges "to restore peace between them."[26] The explicitly dialectical nature of the *tenso*—its alternating arguments followed by at least the expectation of resolution—serves to emphasize its basic affinity with both scholastic and judicial debate. Both literary and extra-literary modes of disputation are aimed at the cessation of hostilities between opposing parties through the imposition of a mediated decision.

Whether one traces the origins of the *tenso* and *joc partit* to classical tradition (Raynouard, Galvini), to the dialectical tendency common to every era (Diez), to Arabic debate literature (Fauriel), to the everyday life of the poet (Knobloch), to the Carolingian *conflictus* (Selbach), to improvised poetic contests before live audiences (Zenker), to popular tradition combined with learned convention (Jeanroy), or to actual poetic exchanges similar to the double *sirventes* (Jones), the fact remains that these two literary forms show a marked resemblance to the emergent judicial forms of the thirteenth century.[27] The dialogued poem in which antagonistic interlocutors defend contradictory positions on a given subject in alternating stanzas of equal length and rhyme, followed by a real or assumed determination, shows an implicit structural identity with the procedure of trial by inquest: the presentation of articles and responses before a jury of judges with the goal of eliciting a verdict. Once again, it should be emphasized that such an analogy suggests neither the direct influence of the literary text upon the procedure of trial nor the reverse; rather, the contemporaneous and parallel development of literary and legal institutions signals the emergence of a polyvalent mental structure whose transformational effect was felt in seemingly divergent areas of cultural and social life. Without falling into the trap of *Geistesgeschichte*, we can assume that the emergence of inquest within the secular judicial sphere, and of dialectical patterns within the vernacular lyric, contributed—in different ways, at different times, under different circumstances, and to different degrees—to the substitution of a socially sanctioned verbal

26. *Ibid.*, 2: 79.
27. Raynouard, *Choix des poésies orginales des troubadours*; G. Galvani, *Osservazioni sulla poesia dei trovatori* (Modena: Soliani, 1929); F. Diez, *Die Poésie der Troubadours* (Leipzig: Barth, 1883); Fauriel, *Poésie provençale*; H. Knobloch, *Die Streitgedichte in Provenzalischen und Altfranzösischen* (Breslau: Korn, 1886); L. Selbach, *Das Streitgedicht in der altprovenzalischen Lyrik* (Marburg: Pfeil, 1886); R. Zenker, *Die provenzalische Tenzone* (Leipzig: Vogel, 1888); Jeanroy, "La Tenson"; Jones, *La Tenson*.

ordeal for a more immediate and physical one. The legitimization of a mediated model of human order within the courtly lyric and courts of law gave impulse to the transformation—through pacification—of postfeudal France.

The "Canso"

The medieval debate form in general, and the *tenso* and *joc partit* in particular, are predicated upon the same model of verbal disputation as the trial. Less apparent, but nonetheless crucial to a fuller understanding of the inherently legal character of courtliness, is the dialectical nature of the most popular courtly genre, the love lyric or *canso (chanson d'amour)*.[28]

The *canso*, as an implicit appeal to a lady-judge made in the context of contradictory rival claims, functions, along with the more obviously juridical debate forms and the inquisitory process itself, as a forum for the conversion of the epic ordeal of force into its verbal equivalent. Like the goliardic *invitatio amicae*, the *canso* represents, first and foremost, a love-request: an expressed desire for a glance, kiss, caress, rendezvous, or more complete satisfaction.[29] Bernart de Ventadorn demands a kiss.[30] He asks to watch his lady as she undresses; he seeks her embrace and is sure that he will have "beneath his hand still more" (Ventadorn [Appel] 215).[31] William IX requests a rendezvous and a kiss:

28. The term *canso* denotes any lyric whose subject is love. In fact, almost no genre is more varied in form, and, as the *vida* of Marcabru attests, most lyrics composed before 1150 were considered to be *vers*: "Et en aqel temps non appellava hom cansson, mas tot qant hom cantava eron vers." "In those days one did not speak of 'cansos,' but all that one sang was called 'vers' " (J. Boutière and A.-H. Schutz, *Biographie des Troubadours* [Paris: Nizet, 1964], p. 12. See also P. Zumthor, *Essai de Poétique médiévale* [Paris: Seuil, 1972], p. 158.)

29. See R. Dragonetti, *La Technique poétique des trouvères* (Bruges: De Temple, 1960), pp. 281–283; M. Lazar, *Amour courtois et "Fin' Amors" dans la littérature du XIIe siècle* (Paris: Klincksieck, 1964), pp. 68–71; R. Nelli, *L'Erotique des troubadours* (Toulouse: Privat, 1963), p. 21; P. Zumthor, "Au Berceau du lyrisme européen," *Cahiers du Sud* 326 (1953): 35–37; *Essai*, p. 251.

30. Be for' oimais sazos	It is high time,
bela domna e pros,	o beautiful and noble Lady,
que-m fos datz a rescos	to give me a secret
en baizan guizardos.	kiss for recompense.

(Ventadorn [Appel] 168)

31. "Mas mas jonchas li venh a so plazer, / e ja no'm volh mais d'a sos pes mover, / tro per merce'm meta lai o's despolha." "Hands clasped, I surrender to her will, / and I do not want to budge from her feet, / before she will, by her grace, lead me to where she undresses" (Ventadorn [Appel] 243); see also Ventadorn (Appel) 152, 159.

Si'm breu non ai ajutori,
Cum ma bona dompna m'am,
Morrai, pel cap sanh Gregori,
Si no'm bayz' en cambr' o sotz ram.

If soon I do not obtain the aid
of the love of my good lady,
I will die, faith of Saint Gregory,
unless she kisses me in her chamber or in a bower.

(William IX 20)

Bertran de Born and Marcabru express a similar hope.[32] Arnaut de Maruelh and Raimbaut d'Orange seek "a kiss and more."[33]

Alongside the precise and concrete demands of the troubadours, those of the northern poets often seem vague and pale. Gace Brulé patiently waits for a "glance of recognition" (Gace Brulé 3). Thibaut de Champagne awaits a "kindly look" (Champagne 5). Le Châtelain de Coucy invites Love:

Proi vos, dame, cui drois mostre et valors,
Que vos amez vostre loial ami.
Alegiez moi mes maus et mes dolors.

I pray you, lady, who show yourself true and worthy,
That you love your loyal friend.
Relieve my hurt and my pain.

(Coucy 84)

Though the *canso* usually contains a declaration of love, assurances of the honesty of the poet's intentions, praise of his virtue and of the lady's perfection, it is, above all, a request. All the declarations, promises, praise, and flattery are motivated by the expectation of reward; for despite the necessity of patience, of long periods of waiting and suffering, of fear of failure, the courtly lover is sustained by the hope of eventual satisfaction.

On the surface, the love-request seems to constitute an autonomous demand, a direct communication between two parties, one of whom desires what the other has the power to grant. In fact, the interpersonal dynamic of the love lyric is more complex. The lover's petition is always —

32. *Die Lieder Bertrans von Born*, ed. C. Appel (Halle: Max Niemeyer, 1932), p. 12; Marcabru 121.

33. M. de Riquer, *La Lirica de los trovadores* (Barcelona: Escuela de Filologia, 1948), pp. 141, 466.

submitted with a third party in mind. Behind the insistent calls for a glance, a meeting, a kiss, "and more" lurk the ever-present enemies of gratification, the *lauzengers*. The *canso*, like the *cobla*, *pastorela*, *tenso*, and *joc partit*, exists within the context of an inherent rivalry between a worthy subject who seeks satisfaction and those who work to prevent it. From the perspective of the poet, love represents a triangular relation in which the object of desire, the lady, must choose between two alternatives. More precisely, she must, from a position of moral and spiritual superiority, validate the allegations of either *lauzenger* or lover. The *canso*, regardless of its apparent autonomy, represents a case submitted for judgment against all other conflicting claims. Like the inquisitory plea, its goal is the creation of a coherent argument in defense of the lover in the light of similar contradictory declarations; the love lyric is aimed, ultimately, at convincing the lady of the lover's worthiness despite allegations to the contrary. Marcabru, recognizing the necessity of choice between rival representations of the poet himself, laments that his beloved chooses to believe the accusatory lies of the false flatterers and that their words keep him from her:

> Si l'amia non crezi' enganador
> Lauzengier ni mal parlier acusador,
> Sieus seria, si'm volia, ses bauzi' e ses error.
>
> Puois qu'ieu vei qu'ella non crei castiador,
> Anz de totz malvatz pren patz, cals la groissor
> A la den torna soven la leng' on sent la dolor.
>
> If my friend did not believe a deceiving slanderer or an accuser
> with evil words, I would belong to her, if she wanted me,
> without perfidy and without lies. But I see that she does not
> believe the one who criticizes her and that she makes peace
> with the wicked, just as the tongue often turns to the swelling
> which pains the tooth.

(Marcabru 116)

Le Châtelain de Coucy complains of a similar error of belief but hopes for its eventual rectification (Coucy 66). For Gace Brulé, as for Le Châtelain de Coucy, the probity of his lady's judgment, her innate ability to distinguish falsehood from truth, will prevail in the end despite momentary setbacks (Gace Brulé 68). William IX adopts an explicitly juridical vocabulary in pleading for "justice in his case":

Qual pro y auretz, dompna conja,
Si vostr' amors mi deslonja?
Par queus vulhatz metre monja.
E sapchatz, quar tan vos am,
Tem que la dolors me ponja,
Si no'm faitz dreg dels tortz qu'ie'us clam.

What do you gain, lovely Lady,
If you send me away from you?
You seem to want to be a nun,
But know, I love you so much,
That I fear piercing pain
If you do not do justice in my case.

(William IX 20)

In declaring his love, Thibaut de Champagne also throws himself at the mercy of his lady's judgment:

Dès ore mès vueil prïer en chantant,
Et, se li plest, ne mesera tant fiere,
Car je ne cuit que nus hons qui requiere
Merci d'amors, qu'il n'ait le cuer plorant,
Que, se Pitiez li chiet aus piez por moi,
Si dont je mult qu'ele ne la conqiere.
Ensi ne sai se faz sens ou foloi,
Car cist esgarz va par son jugement.

From now on I will supplicate by singing,
And, if it please her, I will not be so proud,
For I do not believe that any man seeks
Mercy in love, without a sorrowful heart,
So that if Pity fell at her feet on my behalf,
I doubt much that she [Pity] would conquer her.
Thus I know not if I act wisely or foolishly
Since this decision will go according to her judgment.

(Champagne 74)

The decision left to the lady's discretion emphasizes her role as judge within a suppliant situation, a situation subjectively similar to the mediated outcome of the inquisitory trial procedure.[34] From the plethora of

34. Ilse Nolting-Hauff makes a case for a limited number of similar arbitrations within romance: "Da sich ein Roman auf die Dauer nicht mit latenter Spannung begnügen kann, muss das Verständigungsproblem doch schliesslich auf irgendeine Weise seine Lösung finden. Zuweilen geschieht das durch die Vermittlung eines unbeteiligten Dritten, der entweder sozial höher- (die Königin im "Cligés", der Herzog in "Ille et Galeron") oder tie-

potential petitions either for her favor or against the lover's request, she must elect the most compelling demonstration. The test of strength of the epic, like that of the judicial duel, has become a test of truth—a determination of the validity of equally coherent but mutually exclusive propositions. Moreover, since the love lyric is itself the vehicle of presentation, there can be no distinction between literary and amatory competition. The most convincing plea is that which can claim superior poetic merit; and, conversely, that which is superior poetically is the most persuasive. Every attempt to sway the lady's judgment in the poet-lover's favor depends, ultimately, upon the excellence of the *canso* itself.

Because the love lyric is designed, either knowingly or unconsciously, to present the lover's suit as persuasively as possible, it almost always contains an element of self-justification. This is why, within the overall context of the lover's trial, his defense against belligerent *lauzengers*, the oath comes to occupy such a prominent position. In fact, the *Leys d'Amors* designates the vindicatory poem or *escondig* as an independent lyric genre:

Escondigz es us dictatz del compas de chanso, cant a las coblas. et al so. e deu tractar de dezencuzatio. es contredizen se. en son dictat. de so deques estatz acuzatz o lauzeniatz. am sa dona. de oz am son capdel.

The *escondig* is a work with couplets and song in *chanson* measure. It should contain excuses; the author justifies himself in this work for what he has been accused of or blamed for concerning his lady or his lord.

(*Leys* 1: 348)

Only one example of the *escondig* has survived, Bertran de Born's "Eu m'escondisc, domna, que mal non mier." The poet begins by declaring his intention "to plead his case" and thus to clear his reputation besmirched by "treacherous false flatterers."[35] The actual compurgation which follows contains a systematic denial of the liars' accusations: Bertran offers "to ride through a storm with his helmet and hood reversed, with stirrups too long at the side of a nag,"[36] "to sit at a chessboard

---

fergestellt sein muss (Lunete im "Yvain", die vieille im "Eracle")" (*Die Stellung der Liebeskasuistik im höfischen Roman* [Heidelberg: Winter, 1959], p. 82).

35. *Die Lieder Bertrans von Born*, p. 8.

36. This strophe is apocryphal and does not appear in Appel's edition. It does appear, however, in Raynouard, *Choix des poésies originales des troubadours*, 3: 142.

without winning a cent," "to be the lord of a treacherous castle," "to dispute a tower with three other heirs, always lacking crossbowmen, archers, mercenaries, spies, and physicians," if his infidelity to the lady in question can be proved. The poet's willingness to endure physical hardship and to lose at chess and at war, in order to support his refutation of the claims against him, is further strengthened by his parting counter-accusation: *Fals, enveios, fe-mentit lauzengier, / Puois ab midons m'avetz mes destorbier, / Be lauzera que'm laussassetz estar.*[37] Although "Eu m'escondisc, domna, que mal non mier" remains an isolated example of a minor lyric genre, it is nonetheless significant. Bertran demonstrates to an extreme degree what other poets sense to a greater or lesser extent: that the *canso* represents an intrinsic attempt at self-vindication.

Bernart de Ventadorn combines the love-request with an exculpatory oath. Like Bertran de Born, he swears loyalty even at the price of severe physical suffering (Ventadorn [Lazar] 148). The Countess of Die's lover, having been accused of fickleness, rests his defense upon a similar oath of good faith.[38] Thibaut de Champagne repeatedly seeks to convince his lady of the honesty of his intentions through the equivalent of a sworn deposition:

> Mais je l'aim plus que nule riens vivant,
> Si me doint Deus son gent cors enbracier!
> Ce est le riens que plus avroie chier,
> Et, se j'en sui parjurs a escïent,
> On me devroit traïner tout avant
> Et puis pendre plus haut que un clochier.

> But I love her more than anyone alive,
> So may God give me her lovely body to embrace!
> She is the person I hold most dear
> And if I lie about this knowingly,
> I ought to be dragged all around
> And then hanged higher than a steeple.

> (Champagne 19)

In calling God to guarantee the probity of his words and in denying willful perjury—*parjurs a escïent*—Thibaut again insists upon the implicitly dialectical nature of the courtly encounter: to love successfully is to convince one's lady of the righteousness of his suit despite her tendency,

---

37. Ill-bred, traitorous false flatterers, you who have embroiled me with my lady, why have you not left me in peace? (*Die Lieder Bertrans von Born*, p. 9).
38. Véran, *Poétesses*, p. 179.

self-induced and encouraged by the lover's detractors, toward disbelief. Like the oath of compurgation within a purely juridical context, love represents an ordeal to be endured and, hopefully surmounted.

What we are suggesting is that the courtly love encounter is, in many respects, identical to the increasingly important judicial ordeal of trial by inquest. Even within the *canso*, whose competitive format is less apparent than that of the *tenso* or *joc partit*, adversary lovers, or lover and *lauzenger*, struggle against each other under the supervision of an elevated lady-judge. Behind the seemingly nonviolent ordeal of patience, faithful service, and verbal persuasion the courtly lover engages in a fight. The vocabulary of courtly confrontation, especially the terms *joi* and *merci*, barely hides this fact.

More than a meeting, kiss, embrace, or *faît* (consummation), the lover seeks the *joi* of love and the *merci* of his lady. Peire Vidal hopes that his "intelligence, ability, and constance will elicit the only joy that can calm me" (Vidal 35). Bernard de Ventadorn feels "completely transformed by the joy in his heart" (Ventadorn [Appel] 260). That same joy makes Le Châtelain de Coucy feel invincible and Thibaut de Champagne "superior to all other men" (Champagne 5).[39] As Peire, Bernart, Le Châtelain de Coucy, Gace Brulé, and Thibaut suggest, joy and mercy constitute a universal goal, a point of convergence toward which the courtly lover strives and which, if attained, signals the end of striving, a transcendence of desire.

Among the principal terms of the courtly lexicon none has elicited more diverse interpretation than the word *joi*. It has been taken variously as a quasi-mystical exaltation of love, a source of spiritual regeneration, a combination of courtly service and love, the *delectatio* of Augustinian tradition, a synonym of sensual excitement with roots in Greek paganism, a moral climate in which the lover becomes conscious of the erotic meaning of *mesura*, or a metaphor for love and the desire for sexual union.[40] The question of *joi*'s meaning is further complicated by the lack of definitive philological information concerning the Provençal *joi, joy,* and *jai*. Anglade and von Wartburg trace the term *joi* to the Latin

39. Coucy 79; "Mès cil qui sert et merci i atent, / Cil doit avoir joie fine et entïere." "But he who serves well and waits for mercy, / Should expect complete and exquisite joy" (Champagne 73); see also Gace Brulé 2.
40. For a resumé of diverse interpretations of *joi* see Lazar, *Amour courtois*, p. 107.

gaudium.[41] Charles Camproux, in a short article and a book of great interest to the present discussion, derives *joi* from the Latin *joculum* (> *jocum*) meaning game, revelry, or sport.[42] Originally, the term signified a pleasant pastime or light amusement, and only later did it become the equivalent of the Old French *joie.* More important, Camproux equates *joia* with the plural neuter *jocula* meaning gift, reward, or "prize bestowed upon him who has played a game well and won."[43] By extension, *joi* or *joie* can be assumed to refer to a gift or prize conferred by the lady-judge upon the successful lover. Cercamon understood joy to be synonymous with recompense and prize:

> Aquest amor no pot hom tan servir
> Que mil aitans no'n doble'l gazardos:
> Que Pretz e Joys e tot quant es, e mays,
> N'auran aisselh qu'en seran poderos;
>
> This love cannot be served so long that the recompense
> will not be a thousand times greater (than the pain) for
> the Prize and Joy and all things, and still more, will
> come to those who have it in their power.
> (Cercamon 15)

So did Bernart de Ventadorn:

> Mout i fetz Amors que pros,
> car tan ric joi m'a pertraih.
> Tot can m'avia forfaih,
> val ben aquest guizerdos.

Love, this time, has worked well in granting me a joy so exquisite. This recompense repays me well for all the wrong he has done me.
> (Ventadorn (Lazar) 120)

And Guilhem de Cabestany:

41. Von Wartburg, *Französisches etymologisches Wörterbuch* (Leipzig: Teubner, 1922), p. 82.
42. "La Joie civilisatrice chez les troubadours," *Table Ronde* 97 (1956): 64–69; *Joy d'amour* (Montpellier: Causse, 1965).
43. "En réalité, il existe deux mots différents, l'un *gang, jai* avec sa riche dérivation; l'autre, *joi,* qui nous parait représenter non point un emprunt au parlers d'Oïl, mais une forme régulièrment phonétique dans une grande partie des pays d'Oc: *joi* remontant au latin *joculum,* dérivé de *jocum: jeu, badinage, ébats* au pluriel" (C. Camproux, "La Joie civilisatrice," p. 65).

E ges maltraitz no m'en fai espaven,
Sol qu'ieu en cug e ma vida aver
De vos, dompna, calacom jauzimen:
Anz li maltrag mi son joy e plazer

No torment frightens me, when I think
That it might procure for me, in the end, recompense
From you, my Lady; and I love my pains
Which are for me like joy and pleasure.

(Nelli and Lavaud 2: 118)

Both the fourteenth-century Académie des Jeux Floraux and its charter, the *Leys d'Amors*, confirm the explanation suggested by Camproux. The Toulousain Consistoire de la Gaie Science awarded as part of its annual poetic competition a gold or silver laurel—*joie* or *joyau*—to the winner. To this day the prize poems are published under the rubric of the *Joies du Gai Savoir*.[44]

The origin of *merci* is less problematic than that of *joi*; its connotation is the same, however.[45] From the Latin *mercēdem* the term came to mean "prize" or "gift" in Gallo-Romance and "grace accorded by sparing" in Old French. A commonplace of feudal terminology, *merce* or *chauzimen*, the bestowal of favors, was the equivalent of salary. It was not until the fourteenth century that *merci* became a term of politeness.

What this means, again, is that the lover's ordeal—the test of his faithfulness, endurance, and diligence—is closer to a physical struggle against an opponent of flesh and blood than at first seems obvious. While the courtly ordeal does contain an undeniable element of tension between the lady who judges and the lover whose service is measured, its full consequence extends beyond their rapport. For the lover's ultimate goal—*joie* and *merci*, reward and prize—can only be attained, like the preliminary kiss, glance, or rendezvous, against the opposition of the *lauzengers*. In the rivalry for the lady's favor the *gent malparliere* represents the sworn enemy of all possible joy.[46]

44. Jeanroy, *Poésie*, p. 307. The winning entries between 1324 and 1484 have been edited by A. Jeanroy under the title *Les Joies du Gai Savoir* (Toulouse: Privat, 1914).

45. See Dragnonetti, *Technique poétique*, p. 77.

46. "Amicx, fa s'elha, gilos brau
An comensat tal batestau
Que sera greus a departir,
Tro qu'abdui en siam jauzen."

E s'eu consec gelos ni lauzengier
C'ab fals conselh gaston l'autrui sobrier
E baisson joi a presen et a frau,
Per ver sabran cal son li colp qu'eu fier:
Que s'avian cors de fer et d'acier
No lur valra una pluma de pau.

And if I get hold of one of these jealous ones,
of these plotters, who covertly gain
superiority over others, and, both openly
and in secret, bring joy low, truly
will they learn what kind of blows I strike,
for even if their bodies were made of iron or steel, they
would not serve them any more than a peacock's feather.

(Vidal 42)

* * * * *

Tres granz amors ne puet partir ne fraindre,
S'el n'est en cuer desloial, losengier,
Faus, guileor, qu'a mentir et a faindre
Font les loiaus de leur joie esloignier.

Great love cannot be split up or broken
Unless it is in disloyal, lying,
False, deceiving hearts that by lies and deceit
Separate loyal ones from their joy.

(Champagne 86)

In the struggle to achieve what the *lauzengers* try to prevent—the lover's reward—the deepest significance of the terms *joie* and *merci* becomes apparent: they are indistinguishable from the notion of victory. *Joi* accorded by one's lady is, as Arnaut Daniel recognizes, synonymous with triumph over one's enemy (Nelli and Lavaud 2: 122). And as Gui D'Ussel maintains, victory implies a necessary defeat of "those who suffer at the lover's happiness":

Dompn'ab un baisar solamen
Agr'eu tot cant voil e desire,
E prometetz lo-m e no-us tire,
Sivals per mal de l'enojosa gen,

Friend, she (my lady) told me, these vulgar jealous ones have begun such a fight that it will be difficult to settle in such a way that together we will be joyful.
(*Les Chansons de Jaufré Rudel*, ed. A. Jeanroy [Paris: Champion, 1915], p. 8). See also Gace Brulé 10, 32.

Qu'aurían dol, si-m vezían jauzen,
E per amor dels adreitz, cui plairïa;

Lady, with just one kiss
I will have what I want and desire,
Promise it, without getting angry,
Simply to enrage the annoyers
Who would suffer if they saw me happy,
As well as to please those who are kind.
(Nelli and Lavaud 2: 120)

The lover who succeeds in persuading his lady of the righteousness of his plea, in convincing her that the contradictory claims of his detractors are false, has, in effect, triumphed over them. He has emerged victorious from the contest which is the essence of the courtly encounter.

Victory, however, is never very sure or enduring. Behind the *joi* of winning lies the persistent threat of possible loss, the *dolor* ready at any moment to supplant its opposite as soon as the felons gain the upper hand:

Aquest' amors me fer tan gen
al cor d'una dousa sabor:
cen vetz mor lo jorn de dolor
e reviu de joi autras cen.

This love so nobly wounds
The heart with a sweet savor;
one hundred times a day I die of sorrow
and revive through joy another hundred times.
(Ventadorn (Appel) 189)[+]

Far from enduring, the transient joy of victory is interspersed with corresponding moments of suffering. The regularity with which the joy of love alternates with its pain constitutes a uniform cycle of positive and negative value that is the most abiding fact of the poet-lover's existence; Cercamon explains: *Qu'après lo mal me venra bes / Be leu, s'a lieys ven a plazer.*[48] The alternation between necessary suffering and reward emphasizes the fundamental identity of the formalized courtly encounter and the dynamics of extra-literary confrontation. Like the feudal warrior within a system of reciprocal vendetta, the champions in a judicial duel, the

47. See also Champagne 88; Coucy 53, 57; Gace Brulé 31; G. Lavis, *L'Expression de l'affectivité dans la poésie lyrique français du moyen âge (XIIe–XIIIe s.): étude sémantique et stylistique du réseau lexical joie-dolor* (Paris: Belles Lettres, 1972).

48. For after the pain joy will come to me, very soon, if it pleases her (Cercamon 3).

parties in an inquisitory trial, and the disputants in a Scholastic debate, the courtly lover oscillates between the possibilities of winning or losing the contest against an opponent who is his equal. When he wins, the sensation of joy produced reflects the feelings attached to victory: exultation, loss of self, a sense of superiority, even divinity:[49]

> Totz me desconosc, tan be'm vai. . . .
> qu'e re no sen mal que'm dolha.
> sí m'a jois pres e sazit,
> no sai si'm sui aquel que sol!
>
> I do not know myself, I feel so good. . . .
> for I feel no ill that makes me suffer,
> in such a way has joy taken hold of me
> that I know not if I am the person I was.
> (Ventadorn (Appel) 157)

Conversely, the *dolor* that accompanies loss is strongly allied with the notion of defeat and produces feelings of despair, impotence, physical pain, and, according to courtly convention, forebodings of imminent death.[50]

Whether its form is explicitly contentious, as in the *débat*, or implicitly combative, as in the *canso*, the courtly struggle has all the earmarks of immediate physical conflict. Though differences of personal style and literary convention may seem essential to the understanding of individual poets, they are less important to an overall understanding of the phenomenon of courtliness than recognition of its basically combative context.[51] Stated simply, the courtly encounter represents an attempt on

49. Victory for the other side elicits a corresponding sense of elation: "Or seront li li faus losengeor / Cui tant pesoit des biens k'avoir soloie." "Now will the false flatterers be happy / Who were so pained by the delight I used to have" (Coucy 38).

50. Pierre Bec has masterfully categorized the semantic range of negative feelings around the term *dolor* under the headings of: loss of joy, torment, painful thought, martyrdom, sadness, manifest pain, desire, patience, resentment, and death. "La Douleur et son univers poétique chez Bernard de Ventadour," *Cahiers de Civilisation Médiévale* 9 (1968): 545–571; 12 (1969): 25–33.

51. Though the focus and thrust of our argument seem in many ways to contradict recent critical trends, in particular the monumental studies of Paul Zumthor, here we find ourselves in complete agreement with Zumthor's emphasis upon the common elements of a poetic register as opposed to the uniqueness of the individual poet: "Ce qui frappe d'abord, c'est le grand nombre d'éléments communs à tous ces textes. Leur densité diffère d'une chanson à l'autre; mais dans la majorité des cas ils constituent l'essentiel du discours" (*Essai*, p. 219). We might only add that the medieval text's extrapersonal status is further proof of its inherently legal—public and collective as opposed to private and individual—nature.

the part of the poet-lover to establish difference—hierarchy, superiority or inferiority—between himself and a real or imagined opponent. From a position of initial equality he emerges either objectively victorious and subjectively joyous, or objectively vanquished and dolorous. In the latter case his adversary captures the joyous feelings that he would have ordinarily experienced. Even when aware of the cyclical nature of the process in which he is trapped, the alternation of triumph and defeat, the courtly lover remains unable to withdraw from the struggle to maintain or to regain dominance. What this means is that love, as the poets of northern and southern France conceived of it, is never a unilateral attachment; that it necessarily involves a contest against a third party, the *lauzenger* or false flatterer; and that its ultimate object, the joy of triumph, stands, like the inquisitory encounter, as a mask for a more immediate violence that is primary to it.

Here a word is in order concerning the ambiguous nature of both poetic and inquisitory contention. On the one hand, we have insisted upon the combative context of the courtly lyric in order to demonstrate its thematic—but not formal—resemblance to the *chanson de geste*. In many ways the struggle of the lover against an ever-present unidentifiable enemy is not the antithesis but a generalization of epic combat, its extension to every facet of the courtly poet's relation to others. On the other hand, the conversion of this struggle into a battle of words serves to hide—or to minimize—its possible consequences. The assumption underlying the poetic model as we have described it is that words and not deeds are the only acceptable vehicle, the currency, of interpersonal exchange; resort to any force but that of argument is a transgression of the assumed code of courtly (literary), civil (judicial) behavior. The lyric as an ideal model of human conduct thus assures the maintenance of true violence within prescribed limits. It may be argued that epic literature serves a similar purpose. After all, the presence of the text is ample proof of an act of composition which has only the most tenuous relation to the real or imaginary deeds of violence which it portrays. And yet, the existence of the text as *a priori* proof of an act of mediation, a mimetic and therefore unrealized action, is not the same as the promulgation of a mediated model of nonviolent conduct which is the profoundest function of the lyric. The epic is designed to encourage feats of armed valor despite their often obvious futility. The courtly lyric has the opposite effect—to discourage the active expression of a violence that is nonetheless a guiding principle of human relations. Again, like the inquisitory court, the *pastorela*, *tenso*, *joc partit*, and *canso* proffer as a cultural ideal the containment of violent impulses within the bounds of language itself.

Romance: the Text as Deposition

The question of how the courtly narrative fits into our discussion is a difficult one since romance combines the epic ordeal, violence openly enacted, with that of the lyric, violence expressed only through words.[52] The closest analogy to the patterns of lyric exchange is to be found in the inner monologue or debate—violence which, unexpressed, is represented as internal and verbal. Beginning with the *Roman d'Enéas* and the earliest romances, the tendency to portray conflict as internal becomes increasingly apparent. This trend can, in fact, be traced as far back as the final strophe of *La Chanson de Roland* where Charlemagne's weariness and lack of enthusiasm for further crusade provokes what remains the only thoroughly private utterance of the entire poem (strophe 291). Later epics such as *Raoul de Cambrai* or *Les Quatre Filz Aymon* stress the importance of personal, noncommunicative speech intended only for the speaker, a tendency which reaches its zenith with the emergence in the thirteenth century of sustained works of allegory.[53] For Guillaume de Lorris and Jean de Meun the world is no larger than the dreamer's psyche, all conflict having become an inner war of words upon a psychic battleground. Nonetheless, it is really from Chrétien de Troyes onward that the internal monologue can claim to share the stage equally with those elements of the story supposedly occurring outside of the mind.

In Chrétien's novels the true violence of the battlefield and the mimetic violence of the mind exist side by side and even seem to complement each

---

52. For a discussion of the vestigial survival of the epic ordeal within Chrétien see W. Kellermann, *Aufbaustil und Weltbild Chrestiens von Troyes im Percevalroman* (Halle: Max Niemeyer, 1936), pp. 158–160. Eugene Vance has written a more theoretical discussion of the same topic: "Le Combat érotique chez Chrétien de Troyes," *Poetique* 12 (1972): 544–571.

53. For a discussion of the gradual intrusion of personal discourse upon the more collective language of epic see: R. Bezzola, "De *Roland* à *Raoul de Cambrai*" in *Mélanges Hoepffner* (Paris: Belles Lettres, 1949), pp. 195–213; W. C. Calin, *The Old French Epic of Revolt* (Geneva: Droz, 1961), p. 143; D. Kelly, *Sens and Conjointure in the "Chevalier de la Charette"* (Hague: Mouton, 1966), p. 227; P. Matarasso, *Recherches historiques et littéraires sur "Raoul de Cambrai"* (Paris: Nizet, 1962), pp. 170–172; C. Muscatine, "The Emergence of Psychological Allegory in Old French Romance," *PMLA* 68 (1953): 1165–1179; Nolting-Hauff, *Stellung*, pp. 30–66.

other. Erec's mysterious departure and the series of ritualistic combats against increasingly dangerous opponents derives its dramatic effect from the tension between inner and outer narrative perspectives. On the one hand, Erec seems willing to take on all challengers, to devote himself entirely to the realm of pure activity with a corresponding prohibition of speech. On the other hand, Enide, under Erec's interdiction, finds herself confined to the essentially passive realm of dialogue with the self. An entirely self-contained, mimetic, verbal conflict parallels the more immediate contests against robbers, rapists, seducers, and giants. Even the fixity of the prohibition itself becomes a source of doubt, as Enide wonders whether or not to warn her husband of unseen danger, given the prospect of his defeat (*Erec* vv. 2962–2969). The fact of having twice defied Erec's proscription only produces further doubt and self-reproach (vv. 3100–3112, 3715–3735). Enide's fear of betraying her husband's trust at the price of losing him altogether is reminiscent of the lyric poet's fear of speech at the moment when he most desires it.

It is within *Cligés* that the inner debate reaches its fullest development.[54] Soredamors's sense of depersonalization following Love's attack, like Enide's own confusion, is translated into self-doubt. Unable to believe her eyes, she accuses them of treason, of having "tricked and corrupted her heart" (*Cligés* v. 464). Unable to sleep because of the internal strife—*tançons*—that love has caused, Soredamors's uncertainty borders on madness. She too feels torn between the necessity of speech and the risk that speech entails (v. 868). Once she has decided to address Alexander, the choice of words takes the proportions of a major debate (vv. 1369–1382). For Soredamors the psychological dilemma of inhibition stirred by timidity verges upon a more pervasive linguistic crisis: not only does she find herself divided between conflicting perceptions and courses of action, but language has lost the power to resolve them. Like the violence of the lyric that is never resolved, never translated into action, that of the inner monologue serves as a constant brake upon the hero's or heroine's behavior—a means of self-regulation through which impulse is detached from deed.[55] In this way the collective physical violence of the epic is displaced toward a more personal and sublimated violence of the mind; it is neutralized.

What we are suggesting is, of course, hardly original. Students of Old

---

54. See also *Lancelot* vv. 1097–1125, 4197–4244, 4263–4283, 4318–4396; *Yvain* vv. 1432–1435, 1751–1774, 3525–3556.

55. See Nolting-Hauff, *Stellung*, pp. 59–60.

French literature have long taken for granted the mediatory function of romance, even though they have devoted less attention to the theoretical aspects of mediation than have the post-Hegelian critics of the nineteenth-century novel—G. Lukács, R. Girard, or Lucien Goldmann, for example. In any case, there is general agreement among medievalists that the courtly novel furnishes a model of behavior considerably more civilized—that is to say, less conducive to the open expression of physical violence—than its epic counterpart, which is designed, on the contrary, to inspire feats of arms. Wilhelm Kellermann, whose study of the structure and worldview of Chrétien's novels has defined many of the issues of subsequent discussion, recognizes vestiges of the epic ordeal of force in romance and acknowledges that Chrétien does not fully achieve the chivalric ideal. Nonetheless, Kellermann emphasizes that the courtly novel imposes a model of less aggressive behavior based upon self-mastery, the "Zucht der Rede, Zähmung des Trieblebens, gemessene Haltung und Selbstbeherrschung."[56] Jean Frappier's numerous articles and books on romance also stress the presentation of ideal models of conduct—"des exemples de morale pratique aussi bien que des modèles de vie idéale."[57] Frappier insists, as does Kellermann, upon "cette fonction normative de la communauté arthurienne."[58] If Yvain and Lancelot are the "supermen of courtly morality," it is because they know how to act with moderation in the service of just causes: "Le Héros doit fournir sa mesure entière mais en gardant le sens de la modération et le souci des causes justes."[59]

In a recent article on *Yvain* Robert Hanning comes to a similar conclusion: that romance serves as "a guide through the stages of self-control." Its mediatory power is the result of:

an identification of the audience's aspirations and self-awareness with those of the hero whose activities embodied established *courtoise* ideals. In this way the crises of the hero become those of the audience, metaphorically expressed. The crises of the chivalric romance are two: the relationship between chivalry and self-awareness, and the relationship between the chivalric hero and the society which alone can honor him for his deeds.[60]

56. Kellermann, *Aufbaustil*, p. 168.

57. J. Frappier, *Chrétien de Troyes* (Paris: Hatier, 1968), p. 99.

58. *Ibid.*, p. 214; see also Kellermann, *Aufbaustil*, p. 168 and Nolting-Hauff, *Stellung*, pp. 43–44, 59–60.

59. Frappier, *Chrétien*, p. 215; see also J. Frappier, *Etude sur Yvain* (Paris: Société d'Edition d'Enseignement Supérieur, 1969), p. 209.

60. R. Hanning, "The Social Significance of Twelfth-Century Chivalric Romance," *Medievalia et Humanistica* 3 (1972): 3–29.

In stressing the relation between self-awareness, the chivalric hero, and societal legitimization of his deeds, Hanning touches upon one of the essential traits of romance also suggested by Frappier's "moderate service of just causes." For not only does the courtly model work to modulate —regulate and defuse—interpersonal relations, but it is itself predicated upon a model of behavior external to the literary text: the code of chivalry seen as an historical phenomenon.

Scholars have dwelled upon different aspects of the rapport between literary and extra-literary sources of our knowledge about medieval chivalry: Is romance a mirror of actual chivalric practice or an idealized model of sanctioned behavior? Few medievalists would deny, however, the often identical nature of the chivalric principles mentioned in legal documents as early as the eleventh century, expounded in political tracts and books of manners from the twelfth through fourteenth centuries, and put to literary purpose from Chrétien's *Perceval* onward.[61] The striking similarity between these two levels of discourse, one considered historical and the other poetic, has led, in fact, to a certain passivity before the question of their relation, to a willingness merely to acknowledge their rapport without examining the underlying causes and theoretical consequences of what H. Brinkmann termed the "ritterlich-höfische Lebenshaltung."

Erich Köhler has made the most sustained attempt to explain how an historical model of behavior became a literary ideal and how this ideal, in turn, shaped the course of history. According to Köhler, the courtly novel in general, and the themes of adventure and quest in particular, offered, at a critical moment in the development of France's feudal aristocracy, an idealized model for the recuperation of the unfamiliar distance between a world sensed as inner and personal and that perceived as outer and objective (see below pp. 220–223).[62] As an attempt to escape the

---

61. Epic and classical texts from the first half of the twelfth century might also be considered to exhibit chivalric traits; see S. Painter's discussion of feudal chivalric virtues (*French Chivalry* [Ithaca: Cornell University Press, 1957], chapt. 2). Here, however, what is meant by chivalry is a fusion between religious and secular ideals within a unified code, which first received literary expression in Chrétien's *Conte du Graal*.

62. *Aventure* und *queste* bedeuten die angstrengte, von Leben selbst gebotene Bemühung, den fragwurdig gewordenen Bezug zwischen Individuum und Gesellschaft im Sinne eines ontologischen "Ordo", einer Übereinstimmung von Sein und Seienden, wiederherzustellen (*Ideal und Wirlichkeit in der höfischen Epik* [Tubingen: Max Niemeyer, 1956], p. 82).

increasingly problematic relation between individual and society evident in the hero's sense of alienation, adventure holds the key to return to a simpler order of things, the Hegelian "reconstitution of lost ontological unity."

The global social function of romance is thus the accommodation of the socially disruptive desires of individuals with the external demands of the group, a reconciliation only possible according to laws of an extra-literary type:

> Die eigentlich einzig richtig, gleichsam historisch legitime Aufgabe des Ritter-tums in dieser Situation jedoch ist es, zwischen der überpersönlichen Gemein-schaftsordnung, in der es als Stand wurzelt, und der neuen Welt des autonom werdenden Individuums zu vermitteln, und zwar so, dass beide in einer neuen Synthese aufgehoben sind.[63]

For Köhler, both chivalry as an historical phenomenon and the appear-ance of the earliest *romans chevaleresques* are consequences of an evolving class consciousness on the part of an aristocracy "in search of historical models and human ideals" at a time when its own integrity was most threatened.

Though Köhler's analysis of the historical situation and its role in determining literary form is the most rigorous of its kind, his methodo-logical premises do not differ fundamentally from those of Kellermann, Frappier, and Hanning. All assume that the courtly novel functions as a model of normative behavior and that the mediation which it achieves works mimetically: those who listen to or read the literary text encounter ideal examples of heroic action which they then seek to emulate. Literature may be a reflection of social reality. But its power to transform the reality it reflects resides primarily in its potential for presenting models worthy of imitation. With his usual aplomb Frappier phrases the premise underlying all four critical attempts:

> Il va de soi qu'en cette circonstance comme en d'autres le fait social et le fait littéraire ont agi réciproquement: la réalité historique a suscité un besoin d'ex-pression, un miroir où elle put se refléter; l'image poétisée a pris la valeur d'un modèle, imposé des règles de conduite, élevé à une conscience de plus en plus claire des aspirations latentes ou confuses parfois.[64]

63. *Ibid.*, p. 99.
64. J. Frappier, "Vues sur les conceptions courtoises dans les littératures d'oc et d'oïl au XIIe siècle," *Cahiers de Civilisation* Médiévale 6 (1959): 135.

The usefulness of a mimetic view of the mediatory process cannot be denied. The medieval poet, to a much greater extent than his modern counterpart, was explicitly concerned with moral issues; and there is no genre which does not revolve around the polarity of socially sanctioned and socially proscribed values which we must assume had the effect of encouraging or discouraging certain types of behavior among those circumscribed by a particular poetic code.[65] This is not to imply that such values do not vary diametrically within different forms; rather, it is intended as a reminder that the medieval poet was, above all, a creator of clearly distinguishable positive and negative *exempla*, a fact which accounts both for the crudely dualistic appearance of much Old French literature and for the temptation on the part of critics to explain its mediatory effect in terms of an essentially mimetic process.

If few scholars have disputed the role of moral models in the dissemination of behavioral codes, and especially in the imposition of a mediated model of conduct through romance, some critics have nonetheless stressed the importance of an esthetic rather than a purely mimetic mediation. Ilse Nolting-Hauff, for example, speaks of "exemplary normative behavior" within courtly narrative: ". . . die Funktion des 'Individuellen' erschöpft sich darin, das es die exemplarische Bewegung zur Norm hin, also die Überwindung seiner selbst, ermöglichen muss."[66] According to Nolting-Hauff, the novelistic hero only comes to awareness of acceptable modes of action—"Kennzeichen der überpersönlichen, normativen und daher exemplarischen Denkens"—through a process of "distancing" from the self; and this self-distancing, whose chief vehicle is the courtly dialogue or monologue, represents the "Grundmoment höfischen Verhaltens." Under the best of circumstances, once or twice in a text, such a moment takes on an autonomous function which is, for Nolting-Hauff, the basis of the novel's mediatory power.[67] It is then that we are able to see how romance serves to deflect an immediate and potentially violent tension toward its esthetic equivalent:

65. See N. Freeman Regalado, *Poetic Patterns in Rutebeuf* (New Haven: Yale University Press, 1970), pp. 67–68; Kelley, *Sens and Conjointure*, p. 72; Zumthor, *Essai*, pp. 34, 46.

66. Nolting-Hauff, *Stellung*, p. 36.

67. Die Höfische Rede nimmt also die ganze Situation beschreibend in sich auf, sie folgt damit einem ästhetish bedingten Bedürfnis nach Vollständigkeit ohne eigentliche Sinnfunktion und dient in diesem Fall ausserdem ebenfalls der Abschwächung des Engagements" (*Stellung*, p. 81).

Alle Formen höfischer Ausdruckweise laufen, nur durch die Anpassung an die jeweilige Situation unterschieden, letzen Endes darauf hinaus, zwischen menschliche Spannung dadurch zu entschärfen dass ein selfstzweckhaftes Spiel auf ihnen aufbauen, bzw. unproblematische Situation durch Erzeugung einer künstlichen Spannung interessant machen (Konversation).[68]

Peter Haidu carries the principle of esthetic mediation even further. According to Haidu, Chrétien manages to manipulate the reader's response to the text through the use of dramatic irony, parallelism, symmetry, satire, and various rhetorical devices. The courtly poet creates a moral distance between his readers and characters:

In the art of Chrétien de Troyes the reader's imaginative life is expanded in a universe of structural fantasy offered for his delight from a perspective which unites pleasure and moral awareness. The full enjoyment of these romances is savored from a distance which both defines and reaffirms the reader's moral and aesthetic freedom.[69]

The will to be entertained and to judge from a distance thus becomes the means by which the text's mediatory force operates.

On the surface, the notion of esthetic mediation seems to differ qualitatively from its mimetic equivalent since it implies an act of deflection toward pleasurable substitutes for action instead of imitation. In fact, they amount to the same, except that the esthetic conception focuses upon an identification which occurs at a secondary stage in the mediatory process. Those who conceive of mediation as esthetic in nature tend to stress the act of self-consciousness preceding adoption of an appropriate course of action. Nolting-Hauff's "distancing" and Haidu's "moral and aesthetic freedom," both acts of reflection prior to judgment, do not deny the necessity of choice between moral alternatives; they merely leave undefined the substance of such decisions. Herein lies the difficulty with a purely esthetic approach to the problem of mediation: excessive emphasis upon the act of self-consciousness avoids the issue of specific models and, more important, fails to recognize that self-reflection as a literary motif is

68. *Ibid.*, p. 92.
69. P. Haidu, *Aesthetic Distance in Chrétien de Troyes* (Geneva: Droz, 1968), p. 263. Leo Pollmann also insists upon the esthetic component of mediation: "Wir haben gesehen, dass sie in Nordfrankreich trotz des grossen ästhetischen Interesses, das sie weckt, abgesehen von den Trouvères viel Ironie, Kritik und Parodie erntet, daneben einige Bedeutung als Spielelement höfischer Gesellschaft erhält" (*Die Liebe in der hochmittelalterlichen Literatur Frankreichs* [Frankfurt: Klostermann, 1966], p. 341).

itself rooted in a specific historical context with rather special political consequences (see below pp. 228–238). To be satisfied with an esthetic explanation for the early novel's mediatory effect is to assume that man is primarily an esthetic rather than social being and takes us away from our major concern: the assessment of the legal, that is to say both political and social, dimensions of romance.

In determining how romance mediates between individuals and the community to which they belong, it is difficult, if not impossible, to get beyond the notion of mimetic models of socially legitimized and socially censured behavior. It would be a mistake, moreover, to neglect the importance of chivalry as an historical phenomenon at work in the constitution of ideal literary types—an Yvain, Lancelot, Gawain, or Perceval. On the contrary, in order to understand fully the social effects of the courtly novel, we must first place the chivalric model within its proper historical perspective; and, second, we must distinguish the literary appropriation of such a model as an element of theme from its integration upon a deeper structural level.

Most specialists who accept the *a priori* identification of the chivalric novel with chivalry fail to stress that the latter was hardly the non-problematic ideal of an ascendant aristocracy as reflected in Chrétien's early works, but a relatively late development and, in fact, an inhibiting force upon aristocracy's autonomy as a class. More precisely, the rules of chivalry represented a diminution of the nobleman's historical prerogative to make war whenever, wherever, and especially however he liked.[70] Before the twelfth century the term "chevalier" designated either the *de facto* situation of those who enjoyed military dominance or a legal tie between men of disparate economic means. To be a knight meant to fight on horseback, and to be the knight of another man meant to hold land from him in return for military service. There was no mention of the order of chivalry in historical documents prior to the mid-1000s, nor did chivalry constitute an hereditary legal class. It was not until around the time of the First Crusade (1096) that knighthood became mixed with the trappings of religion: the sacred ceremony of dubbing, clerical benediction of weapons, consciousness of a mission in the unfolding of Christian history.

More important, the Church sought through the institution of chivalry

70. Painter, *Chivalry*, pp. 17–18.

to place definite limits upon the right of private war. Ecclesiastical writers from Saint Anselm to Saint Bernard had maintained that the bloodthirsty noble was not a true Christian; chivalry was automatically equated with wickedness: *non militia, sed malitia*. Beginning in the twelfth century, however, a shift in attitude can be detected. The function of those who fought was not condemned unconditionally; rather, only those who violated certain precepts of military conduct were no longer considered to be true knights. The knight was one who made war according to the rules of the Church as outlined in John of Salisbury's *Policraticus*, Etienne de Fougère's *Livre des manières*, Alain de Lille's sermon for knights, the romances of Chrétien, and the thirteenth-century Lancelot Prose Cycle. These rules included: the necessity of generosity, piety, service of worthy causes such as the protection of widows, orphans, the helpless, and the poor; injunctions against slaying a helpless adversary or taking advantage of one's enemy; exhortations to pursue glory and praise rather than profit, to avoid perjury and false counsel.[71]

Knighthood transformed into a moral code meant a substantial modification of the hawkish ideals of an earlier era—war as a prerogative of class justifiable under almost any circumstances and even as a principle of semi-regular economic exchange. From this perspective chivalry seems less an ideal appropriate to the flowering of a warrior caste than a formula for its decline.[72] The rules of chivalric warfare have more in common with the peace movements of the late feudal period than with the ill-defined rules of war—the justifiable causes, means of declaration and termination—by which a fiercely independent aristocracy had settled quarrels and maintained sovereignty since the collapse of the Carolingian state. Thus chivalry can be situated alongside—and not in opposition to—contemporaneous ecclesiastical, municipal, royal, and some seigneurial efforts to regulate private war (see above pp. 108–118).

What this means in terms of our discussion of legal institutions is that the constitution of chivalry as an order goes hand-in-hand with the judicial transformation of the twelfth and thirteenth centuries. Like William the Conqueror's early attempt to curtail private campaigns and the Church's encouragement of the *Pax* and *Treuga Dei*, chivalry as an

71. M. Bloch, *Feudal Society* (Chicago: University of Chicago Press, 1966), 2: 317; Painter, *Chivalry*, chapt. 2.
72. Though Köhler is aware of such a possibility, he passes quickly over it, p. 234; see also Kellermann, *Aufbaustil*, p. 172 and below pp. 250.

ideal represents an intermediate stage in the pacification of postfeudal France: a codification and regulation without elimination of the unrestricted right to fight. The model through which the chivalric model mediates the rupture between individual consciousness and external societal claims has an inherently legal basis, a fact not astonishing in itself, but which must be taken into consideration if we are to appreciate fully the broader social implications—and the ideological impact—of the courtly novel.

We seek then neither to dispute the principle of mimetic identification nor to contest the chivalric character of the model through which the process of mediation operates. The venture into chivalry as a social phenomenon is intended first to emphasize the extent to which romance as a literary mechanism for the modulation of potentially violent action is itself predicated upon an already mediated model of behavior. Second, it is aimed at an awareness of the extent to which both chivalry and the chivalric novel support the main thrust of our argument concerning the imposition of mediated judicial models.

Here, however, we must be careful to distinguish the chivalric values of piety, charity, loyalty, service, and honesty as they are expressed as literary themes—through the triumph of ideal heroic types—from the more implicit integration of a mediatory model at the level of deeper structure. Kellermann, Emmel, Köhler, and Zumthor have all discussed the ways in which the Arthurian court functions as a fixed locus of justice and peace from which the ideal knight ventures in his conquest of himself and of the uncontrolled nonchivalric forces that surround it, all prior to a final reintegration within a strengthened chivalric order at the end of the archetypal quest.[73] The critic thus assumes that because the shared chivalric ideals of Arthur's court seem to motivate action (departure, conquest, and return) and to set the limits of sanctioned behavior, they therefore provide a superstructural framework for the digressive elaboration of a sequence of adventures whose only unifying thread is the hero himself. Once again, without trying to discount the importance of chivalry for the early novel, we are obliged to call into question such easy passage from a set of privileged moral values undeniably chivalric in character to essential literary form. How, for instance, does such a

73. Kellermann, *Aufbaustil*, p. 168; H. Emmel, *Formprobleme des Artusromans und der Graldichtung* (Bern: Francke, 1951), p. 34; Köhler, *Ideal*, pp. 66–88; Zumthor, *Essai*, p. 351.

transfer occur? And if the mechanism is one that we associate with depth psychology—self-regulation according to internalized ideals—what are its social and political implications? Is the translation of chivalric values into adventure sufficient to explain the links between episodes or the overall design of romance? Finally, what is the role within such a process of writing both as theme and as the material basis for the text? In answering these questions we seek a new perspective, for it has become increasingly clear in the course of our research that the mediatory power of the courtly narrative can never be grasped through recourse solely to the chivalric values that both shape it and set its moral tone. This can only occur when the chivalric model is supplemented by a clearer understanding of the implicit legal model underlying romance: that of the inquisitory deposition.

We have seen that the ordeal of battle is reduced within romance to the proportions of a single hand-to-hand combat occurring outside the bounds of the social community (see above pp. 141–143). A knight's prowess, his place within the chivalric hierarchy, is determined by his success in the chance encounters with the daemonic dwarfs, outlaws, and giants who inhabit the forest or with others like himself. Forest and court constitute mutually exclusive moral spaces; one the *locus* of the physical and the chaotic, the other a place of courteous behavior and peace. And yet, there exists a privileged path of communication between the two worlds, a path whose form and mediatory effect tend to confirm our conclusions with regard to the courtly lyric.

If the hero of romance leaves the court to test his knightly valor, he returns victorious or vanquished in order to tell the story of his *avanture*. So important, in fact, is the conversion of the adventure of the forest into a verbal account once a knight reenters the limits of organized society that it can be considered alongside the subliminal substitution in the lyric of a verbal ordeal for a more immediate and physical one.[74] Only this dis-

---

74. Zumthor considers this cycle to constitute the "unique energy of the Arthurian model": "Le chevalier affronte seul les dangers de l'aventure; la cour elle-même n'y prend pas part. Mais la victoire l'y ramène, le réintègre dans cet ordre. Ce schème provient sans doute d'une exigence profonde de la mentalité de ce temps et de la société courtoise en particulier: les valeurs de l'individu n'ont d'existence que reconnues et visiblement manifestées par la collectivité. L'histoire est ainsi moralement finalisée. Cette tendance constitue comme l'énergie propre du modèle arthurien" (*Essai*, p. 351). See also Emmel, *Formprobleme*, p. 35. Neither Zumthor nor Emmel recognize, however, the inherently legal character of the pattern of departure, conquest, return, and report.

tinction pertains: where the lyric functions according to the legal model
of disputation, romance seems to correspond to that of deposition—a
testimonial description of acts which, if carried out within the boundaries
of court, would constitute criminal infraction.

The transfer of the violence of the forest to court and its accompanying
transformation into a verbal report is evident in the romances of Chrétien.
Erec, having vanquished Yders, sends his captive to Cardigan with the
news of his victory (*Erec* v. 1024). Erec's own return to society after the
quest which occupies the center of the novel features the hero's account of
the adventures accomplished since leaving court:

> Quant apeisiez fu li murmures,
> Erec ancomance son conte:
> ses avantures li reconte,
> que nule n'en i antroblie.
> (. . . .) il lor conta et dist:
> des trois chevaliers qu'il conquist,
> et puis des cinc, et puis del conte
> qui feire li volt si grant honte;
> et puis des jainz dist aprés;
> trestot en ordre pres a pres
> ses avantures lor conta.

> When the tumult had died down,
> Erec began his tale:
> He recounted his adventures
> So that none there could forget them.
> (. . . .) he told them of:
> the three knights whom he conquered,
> and then of the five, and then of the count
> who tried to shame him so heinously;
> and then he told of the giants;
> all in order, one after the other
> he recounted his adventures.
>
> (*Erec* vv. 6416, 6429)

Lancelot, upon his return from the Land of Gorre, is questioned concerning his adventures; and like Erec, he obliges with a full account of his
imprisonment, escape, and victory over Méléagant:

> —Certes, fet Lanceloz, biax sire,
> a briés paroles vos puis dire
> tot si com il m'est avenu.

—"Certainly," said Lancelot, "my lord,
I can tell you briefly
about everything that has happened to me."
(*Lancelot* v. 6865)

In *Le Chevalier au lyon* it is Calogrenant's recital of an unsuccessful adventure, the battle against Esclados in the forest of Brocéliande, which lures Yvain from court (*Yvain* v. 59). And in *Perceval* the motif of the chivalric report becomes mixed with that of confession.

Chrétien's exemplary hero responds to the call of a violent and chaotic Other World, triumphs over the disorder that lurks in the forest, and returns bearing the verbal account of his victory.[75] He is a pacifier of the countryside—an avenger of injuries, a liberator, a defender of righteous causes, a paladin whose highest purpose is to bring outlaws under the law. Erec avenges the wound wrongfully inflicted upon Guinevere's hand-maiden by Yder's dwarf; he lures and conquers would-be thieves and thugs, either killing them or dispatching them as reformed members of society to Arthur's court; he liberates the inhabitants of "La Joie de la Cour," those whose captivity was the result of a healthy will to fight (Maboagrain's) carried to the point of obsession. Lancelot, a defender of helpless maidens, rescues the kidnapped Guinevere and frees the prisoners of Gorre as well. In the cause of his own rehabilitation and redemption Yvain saves the desperate Lady of Norison, the embattled lion which becomes his companion, Gawain's sister and nephews, Lun-ete, and the three hundred enslaved damsels of the Castle of Pesme-Aventure. Chrétien's heroes, like the historical *chevalier*, bring the law of Camelot—a sense of justice, prohibitions against senseless killing, theft, and rape—to the forest, a zone governed only by the laws of chance and of the strongest.

The ideal hero is, at the same time, capable of bringing to Camelot a mediated version of his adventures in the form of a verbal record. Thus the passage between both worlds is, in fact, a one way street: movement in either direction serves to keep the violence of the forest from pene-trating the more peaceful universe of the court. And if the knight who ventures forth in order to prove himself worthy dispatches to Camelot the

---

75. See Kellermann, *Aufbaustil*, p. 172; Köhler, *Ideal*, pp. 89–105; Nolting-Hauff, *Stellung*, p. 21.

tamed victims and liberated beneficiaries of his martial strength, his own return is accompanied by the conversion of the potentially disruptive adventure into a *conte d'aventure*. The hero is, in essence, one who becomes capable, through his accomplishments, of telling the tale which we read. The simultaneous transmission and transformation of the epic (physical) ordeal from forest to court and from action to words are central to any analysis of the relation of literary discourse to that of law. A closer look at the thirteenth-century Lancelot Prose Cycle, where this double shift is articulated most clearly, will, I think, prove worthwhile.

A Literary Inquest[76]

The author of *La Mort le roi Artu* frames this final sequence of the Pseudo-Map Cycle within a bivalent narrative perspective that is at once a continuation of a previous text and a return to the moment before the existence of any text. He tells us that when Walter Map had finished writing the *Aventures del Seint Graal* his lord King Henry requested that he continue. Map begins by describing how Boort returned from the Holy Land and how Arthur ordered a record to be made of his exploits while abroad:

Aprés ce que mestres Gautiers Map ot mis en escrit des *Aventures del Seint Graal* assez soufisanment si com li sembloit, si fu avis au roi Henri son seigneur que ce qu'il avoit fet ne devoit pas soufire, s'il ne ramentevoit la fin de ceus dont il avoit fet devant mention et conment cil morurent dont il avoit amenteüs les proesces en son livre; et por ce commença il ceste derrienne partie. Et quant il l'ot ensemble mise, si l'apela *La Mort le roi Artu*. . . .

* * * * *

Quant Boorz fu venuz a court en la cité meïsmes de Kamaalot de si lointeignes terres comme sont les parties de Jerusalem, assez trouva a cort qui grant joie li fist;. . . . Et quant il ot aconté le trespassement Galaad et la mort Perceval, si en furent tuit moult dolent a court;. . . . Lors fist li rois metre en escrit toutes les aventures que li compaignon de la queste del Seint Graal avoient racontees en sa court.

After Walter Map had put into writing the *Adventures of the Holy Grail* as he saw fit, it was his lord King Henry's opinion that what he had done would not suffice if he did not recall the end of those he had mentioned before and how those whose feats of prowess he had depicted in his book had died; and for this reason he began this last part. And when he had put it together, he called it *The Death of King Arthur*. . . .

* * * * *

76. Parts of the following section appeared under the title "The Text as Inquest: Form and Function in the Pseudo-Map Cycle," *Mosaic* 8 (1975): 107–119.

When Boort returned to Camelot from such distant places as Jerusalem, he found many at court who welcomed him with great rejoicing;. . . . And when he had recounted the death of Galahad and Perceval everyone at court was very sad; . . . . Then the king ordered a record to be made of all the adventures that the companions of the Holy Grail Quest had recounted at his court.

(*La Mort* 1)

In Henry II's invitation to record the tragic "end of those already mentioned" and in Arthur's command to put into writing the "adventures recounted by the companions of the Holy Grail Quest," we detect the basic formula of inquest: the commission by a ruler in a position of legal authority to transcribe the reality of the past. The casual blending of the historical king and a member of his court with the figures of Arthurian romance tends to minimize the distinction between fiction and historical fact. In the first instance, a real king orders a literary production; in the second, a fictional king orders a supposedly historical transcription.[77]

The interpenetration of history and narrative serves to obscure the qualitative difference between an act of legal documentation and one of mimetic creation. Both are defined by the ordering of inchoate elements of memory or imagination into credible written form. In essence, the author of *La Mort* performs a task analogous to that of the royal inquisitor, the compiler of customals, and the early recorders of verdicts and laws—that is to say, the gathering and structuring of fragmentary testimony, legend, or procedure into a sustained narrative whole. The dossier, a collation of the circumstances surrounding a particular infraction, and the customal, a comprehensive collection of usage pertaining to all such situations, share with the romance a common linguistic ground. The inquisitor's attempt to capture the facts of criminal wrongdoing coincides with the author's effort to register the truth of the tale that constantly escapes him: *Mes atant lesse ore li contes. . . . En ceste partie dit li contes.*[78]

77. The author's choice of king and scribe is particularly significant. Henry II was responsible, in large part, for the transformation of English law and judicial procedure from a feudal to a national system. Walter, a member of Henry's court, was himself a jurist and man of letters. Scholars have tended, since Ferdinand Lot's study (1918) of the Lancelot Prose Cycle, to discount the possibility of Walter's authorship and Henry's patronage. Despite Henry's historical interest in the Briton king and the fact that he pretended to have discovered Arthur's and Guinevere's graves, the Angevine ruler had been dead for thirty or forty years by the time *La Mort Artu* was written; Map died in 1219—that is to say, ten to fifteen years before its composition.

78. But now the story leaves off. . . . In this part the story says (*La Mort* 19); see also pp. 39, 55, 65, 75, 78, 81, 92, 97, 119, 127, etc. T. Todorov has written an article relevant to the present discussion: "La Quête du récit," *Critique* 262 (1969): 195–214.

[203]

Both recognize the possibility of a logical ordering of objects and events, the existence of a rational human truth separable from the immanence of divine truth, upon which the legal and literary discourse of the postfeudal world depends.

Throughout the Pseudo-Map Cycle the *greffiers* and *sages clercs* of Camelot find themselves perpetually cast in the dual role of author and judicial scribe. Like the royal officers of justice who were responsible for the compilation of written testimony from the mid-1200s on, the Arthurian scrivener was charged with recording the sworn depositions of those who had actually participated in the adventures of the Round Table. Their inquiry points in the direction of an oral account situated midway between a lived but unverbalized experience and its representation in the text that we are reading. Arthur, like both the English Henry II and the late Capetian kings of France, summons his knights to testify under oath before the official court stenographer:

a. Et li roys li coniure sour son sairement qu'il le die, oiant la compaignie, lez aventures qui auenues li estoient puis qu'il estoit partis de laiens. Il en reconut grant partie; et grant partis lor en cela. Si les oy moult volentiers li roys et la royne. si les fist li roys mettre en escrit. por ce que apres lor mort fuissent ramenteues.

a. And the king begged him by his oath to tell, in the hearing of all, the adventures that had happened to him since he had left. He acknowledged most, but hid a great proportion of them. The king and queen listened willingly. The king had them put into writing so that they might be remembered after their death.

(Sommer 4: 227)

* * * * *

b. Et quant cil orent manjé. si fist li roys uenir avant ses clercs si mist on en escrit les auentures si com lancelot les conta. Et par che les sauons nous encore.

b. And when they had eaten the king summoned his clerks and had them put into writing Lancelot's adventures as he told them. And that is how we know them still.

(Sommer 4: 296)

* * * * *

c. Celui iour apres disner fist li roys uenir tous lez compaignons de la table roonde. Et quant il furent tout uenu deuant lui. Si les fist asseoir ou renc. Lors apela ses clercs qui metoient en escrit lez aventures de laiens & toutes les auentures qui auenoient as cheualiers errans.

c. That day after dinner the king convoked all the companions of the Round Table. And when they were all before him he had them sit down in rows.

[204]

Then he called his clerks who put into writing the adventures of those there and all the adventures that happened to wandering knights.

(Sommer 5: 190)

* * * * *

d. Or dit li contes que lendemain de pentecuste fist li rois artus uenir deuant li tuz les compaignons de la queste & quant il furent a[s]sis deuant li lun lez lautre si apela li roiz les hauz homes de leanz que il uenissent oir les auentures que li compaignon auoient troue tant cum il orent este en la queste. . . . Quant il auoit tut conte se [le]s fist li rois mettre les auentures lancelot par eus.

d. Then the tale says that the day after Pentecost the king summoned before him all the companions of the quest and when they were seated before him, one beside the other, the king called his noblemen to come hear the adventures that the companions had undertaken during their quest. . . . After they had told all the king had Lancelot's adventures placed among the others.

(Sommer 5: 332)

* * * * *

e. Ensint cunta missires Gauain tutes les auentures qui li estoient auenues. apres ceste cunta tutes les autres. si furent tutes mises en escrit. Apres li conta hestor & puis lyonel & puis misire yvain & puis Gaheryes.

e. Thus Sir Gawain recounted all the adventures that had happened to him; then he told all the others which were put into writing. Afterwards, Hector, Lionel, Sir Yvain, and Gaheriet told of theirs.

(Sommer 5: 333)

Arthur's goal in convoking his vassals and committing their testimony to writing is the fixing of the truth of the past so that it may be remembered in the future: *si les fist li roys mettre en escrit. por ce que apres lor mort fuissent ramenteues . . . Et par che les sauons nous encore.*[79] In fact, Lancelot's

---

79. An even more systematic treatment of the theme of Arthurian deposition can be found in the Huth *Merlin*, ed. G. Paris and J. Ulrich (Paris: Firmin-Didot, 1886). Merlin orders Arthur to have the adventures of Logres put into writing "in order that after our death our heirs, both poor and rich, can know the truth of the adventurous king" (*Merlin*, 2: 100); see also 1: 174. Shortly after Arthur receives the Round Table Merlin makes him promise to force every knight to take an oath " '. . . si tost coume il (a knight) s'en partira de court qu'il dira voir au revenir de toutes les choses qui li seront avenues et qu'il avra trouve en sa queste, ou soit s'ounour ou soit sa honte. Et par chou porra on connoistre le proueche de chascun; car je sai bien qu'il ne se parjurront en nulle maniere.' 'En non Dieu,' fait li rois, 'Merlins, vous m'aves bien enseigniet. Et je vous creant que ceste coustume sera tenue en mon ostel tant coume je vivrai.' 'Encore vous di jou plus,' fait Merlins: 'se li chevaliers ne jure au mouvoir de sa queste, se le faites jurer au revenir, 'Si ferai je,' che dist li rois.'' ''. . . as soon as he leaves court that he will tell the truth, upon return, about all the things that have happened to him and that he will have found in his quest, whether they be to his honor or shame. And in this way one can know the prowess of each one; because I know truly that they would not perjur themselves for anything.' 'By God,' said the king, 'Merlin, you

exploits have been conserved in the royal archives—*l'aumaire du roy Artu*—where they were supposedly discovered after his death (Sommer 5: 332).[80] Similarly, Boort's account of the Grail Quest has been preserved in the abbey at Salisbury:

> Quant il ot mangié, li rois fist uenir les clercs qui metoient en escrit les auentures as cheualiers de laiens. Et quant Bohort ot contées les auentures del saint graal teles comme il les auoit ueües, si furent mises en escrit et gardés en l'abeie de Salisbieres, dont maistre Gautiers Map les traïst a faire son livre del saint Graal por l'amor del roi Henri, son signor, qui fist l'estoire translater du latin en franchois.

When he had eaten the king summoned his clerks who put into writing the adventures of the knights present. And when Boort had recounted the adventures of the Holy Grail as he had seen them, they were put into writing and kept in the Abbey of Salisbury whence Master Walter Map retrieved them in order to write his book about the Holy Grail, for the love of his lord Henry, who had the story translated from Latin into French.

(Sommer 6: 198)

The Lancelot Prose Cycle has a genealogy all its own: the exploits of the Knights of the Round Table were, shortly after their occurrence, recorded in Latin by the stenographers of Camelot. The transcribed testimony was deposited in the archive and abbey whence Walter Map, at Henry's behest, translated the Latin manuscript into French.

What looks, then, like a simple attempt to bolster romance with realistic detail corresponds to a double linguistic movement: from the lived experience perceived at the ontological level of gesture, ritual, and vision to the oral account raised to documentary status through transcription, and, finally, to literary status through "translation": a process which Paul Zumthor has treated at some length in terms of a "monumentalization" of language, its elevation from a primarily communicative to a generative function.[81] Within a broad cultural context, the author, or

---

counsel me well. And I promise to uphold this custom as long as I live.' 'Furthermore,' said Merlin: 'if the knight does not swear when he leaves on his quest, make him swear upon return.' 'I will do it,' said the king" (*Merlin*, 2: 98).

80. See F. Lot, *Etude sur le Lancelot en Prose* (Paris: Champion, 1918), p. 126. The word *aumaire* connotes the earliest archival arrangement which was, in fact, a closet-like series of shelves intended for the deposition of evidence, records, and any other material relevant to inquest.

81. "On constate un *effet structural* qui, s'exercant à travers un état de langue primaire plus ou moins anarchique, l'émende et le modifie, y ajoute et surtout en transpose des

authors, of the Pseudo-Map Cycle define a general linguistic shift that might be reconstructed as follows: at a primary stage an oral or previously unrecorded utterance is transcribed. Through an operation analogous to a change in chemical valence, a personal or collective memory is endowed with tangible written status: it is elevated to the level of document. This may involve the transformation of either real or legendary material into its documentary form—the chronicle or pseudo-history, of which Geoffrey of Monmouth's or Nennius's *Historia* are both particularly relevant and archetypal examples.[82] It may also entail the transcription of traditional everyday usage into its documentary form, the customal; or, of personal narrative into its documentary equivalent, the dossier. In each case, the movement from oral to written discourse through the interrogation of legend, communal opinion, or individual memory corresponds to the recurrent Arthurian motif of the sworn deposition—the translation of *aventure* into an official record.

At a secondary stage the preexisting documentary formulation is reworked—mixed with similar material, combined with imaginary or personal elements—to produce the literary text. The process may be a translation such as Wace's French version of Geoffrey's *Historia*, a re-working closer to Layamon's *Brut*, or, as is the case at hand, a combination of the two accompanied by a translation from verse to prose. This second revision, a qualitative shift in linguistic valence, implies a true process of edition, an ordering of the inchoate elements of imagination along with those of the received text within a sustained narrative framework. The Lancelot Prose Cycle is, at bottom, the literary form of pseudo-history, integrating as it does a wealth of prior Arthurian material: Geoffrey, Wace, Béroul, Layamon, Chrétien, and Robert de Boron.

It is within the context of transcription and translation that the pseudo-historical records of the marvels of Arthur's court begin to take on added meaning. One begins to suspect, in fact, that the collection, stor-

---

éléments de manière à porter le discours à un état second, où il mêle moins le flanc aux forces de dispersion naturelles. Peut-être cette structuration, à haute époque, aura-t-elle un caractère provisoire, ne durera-t-elle que le temps d'un exposé particulier. Du moins cet exposé aura-t-il posédé virtuellement, une valeur éternelle" (P. Zumthor, *Langue et technique poétiques à l'époque romane* [Paris: Klincksieck, 1963], p. 37). See also p. 33 and *Essai*, pp. 76–77.

82. For an excellent discussion of the relation between medieval novelistic and historical discourse see Zumthor, *Essai*, pp. 178, 346–370.

age, and revision of chivalric testimony which follows so closely the emerging judicial model—the quest which becomes the pretext for in-quest—betrays a common function: that the transcription of lived *aventure* into document and document into romance represents a way of speaking about a more fundamental shift in the relationship of writing to both individual experience and that of the community as a whole. For if the net result of the hypothetical genesis of the Pseudo-Map Cycle is the con-version of immediate experience into first verbal, then written, and in both cases mediated form, then it must again be stressed that the *aventures* of the Arthurian world are never very far from the immediacy of physical violence. That which Lancelot, Boort, and Gawain recount before the royal *greffiers* has more to do with killing than with anything else. Their story is one of ambushes, judicial duels, tournaments, ordeals, and wars of vengeance; of challenges, threats, insults, and boasts; of errant knights, gate keepers, guardians of passes, thieves, and abductors who struggle continually against one another. Between the successive tellings of the tale, which is recorded periodically at important assemblies of Arthur's court, stand the long and tiresome series of physical confrontations that occur as soon as the Knights of the Round Table venture from Camelot.

Lancelot's deposition upon his first return from Gorre (p. 204, ex. a) includes all that has happened to him since he was last at court: *les auentures qui auenues li estoient puis qu'il estoit partis de laiens*; it contains, therefore, no less than sixteen separate violent encounters. Lancelot has done battle with Méléagant and his men (Sommer 4: 161), two giants (169), a knight guarding a pass (171), a damsel's suitor (177), two knights protecting a pass (178), the four knights of the *pas des perrons* (180), the ambushers of the *pas de la petite forest* (181), a knight who insults him at dinner (196), an entire ambush party (199), two lions (200), Méléagant (204), Baudemagu's men (207), one of his captors (208), Méléagant (211), the Senechal of Claudas (220), and, finally, Méléagant again (225). The period between his departure and the completion of the adventures of Gorre (p. 204, ex. b.) encompasses a series of eight conflicts against: Margondes (Sommer 4: 228), ten knights of the pavillion (230), Melyadus (231), the Knights of the *chastel as puceles* (234), the five armed knights guarding Galehot's body (278), the knight escorting Méléagant's sister to the stake (280), the Red Knight and his men (284), Argonadras (291), and a knight who insists on kissing the damsel escorted by Lancelot (294).

The sworn deposition (p. 204, ex. c) following Lancelot's visit to Corbenic comprises, along with the description of the Grail Castle, the story of how he: (1) fought Boort, *Si lor conte tout premierement de bohort comment il iousta a lui* (Sommer 5: 190); (2) assisted the sons of Calles against their enemies and unknowingly defeated Agravain, Gaheriet, and Guerrehes, *Apres lor conta de la guerre as enfans au duc Kelles. Et comment il desconfi lez trois freres Gaheriet & Guerrehes & Agrauain*; (3) participated in the tournament between Baudemagus and the King of Norgales, *Apres lor conta comment il auoit este au tornoiement que li roys baudemagus auoit pris encontre le roy de norgales*; (4) aided in the vendetta against Calles's nephews, *Apres lor conte comment il ocist tous ceuls de laiens quil y auoit troues.*

During an absence of several years, counting the year and a half spent in Morgain's prison, Lancelot was involved in no less than eighteen encounters. His testimony before the court gathered at Whitsuntide (p. 205, ex. d) should have included an account of his struggles against: sixty of Maten's men (Sommer 5: 197), Terrican (206), a robber-knight (211), a peasant (213), two giants (213), Marabron (231), Boort (238), two lions (244), an errant knight (250), Belias (253), the Black Knight (263), two knights (278), the Knights of Galehodin (286), the kidnapper of Maranz (292), two brothers (305), the Black Knight (306), Kay's assailant (306), four more of Kay's attackers (308), and Gawain, Yvain, Hector, and Sagremor (309).

To extend the above examples any further would only serve to belabor an already tedious point that seems abundantly clear. The pseudo-genealogy of the Lancelot Prose Cycle illustrates systematically that which is merely suggested in the romances of Chrétien: that for the knights of Arthur's realm killing is as basic an activity as love or the pursuit of spiritual perfection; that in order for such acts of physical violence to assume significance within a social context they must first be recounted publicly; that the process of transcription which remains implicit to earlier romances—we do, after all, read at length the tales that Erec, Lancelot, and Perceval tell in brief—is sufficiently like that of inquest to assume a common purpose. Both judicial and literary inquest, that of the courtroom and of the courtly novel, function to assure the displacement of the physical ordeal of battle toward a verbal and, eventually, written equivalent. Proof of criminal infraction, once the object of the judicial duel, depends within the inquisitory court upon debate concerning the testimony transcribed and assembled into a legal dossier. Similarly, the lived *aventure* synonymous with actual combat is, through the periodic testimony of Arthur's knights, converted in a written form indistinguishable from the text itself. If it seems that we have skipped a step, we need only remember that the Pseudo-Map Cycle is presented as a translation of the original depositions of the knights of the Round Table and that the procedure of transcription inscribed in it is but a reduced image, a *mise en abyme*, of the whole.

Numerous scholars have emphasized the connection between the dialectical patterns of the medieval lyric and contemporaneous judicial (as well as scholastic) institutions. What I am suggesting, in contrast, is that both narrative and lyric courtly genres achieve in different ways a related end which both also share with the inquisitory court. The profoundest effect of even the earliest romance is the displacement of the *aventure* or ordeal toward its verbal counterpart—the conversion, according to the model of legal deposition, of a physical struggle against a flesh and blood opponent into a tale of adventure. The courtly lyric contributes, in turn, to the substitution of a mediated model of social conduct, that of disputation, for a directly confrontive one.

Finally, both literary types demonstrate a further resemblance to inquest: a tendency to obscure their origins in a violence—that of the epic and of the judicial duel—which is nonetheless primary to their design. Romance works to hide its true subject—a contemporary crisis of values and institutions (not unlike that reflected in the epic)—behind a seemingly distant temporal and spatial setting: the fairylike world of a mythic king. Lyric, on the other hand, conceals an analogous subject—the omnipresent threat of violence among the members of a warrior aristocracy—behind the obsessive veil of strong emotions: the deceptive *joi* and *dolor* of the lover. Thus the function of each is double and involves both an act of displacement and a dissimulation of the dislocating process. Like the inquisitory court, which can function only under the assumption that verbal violence is the only permissible form of exchange between opposing parties, courtly literature achieves its implicit social effect by always pretending to be other than it is. This trend reaches fullest expression in the allegorical texts of the thirteenth century. There the violence which is overt within the *chanson de geste*, hidden in courtly poetry and romance, surfaces intact. *Le Roman de la rose*—with its mixture of military and amatory vocabulary, its extended series of vindictive exchanges between the partisans of the rose and of the lover, its wounds, betrayals, and sieges—duplicates the reciprocal violence of the epic. In allegory, however, the vendetta principle becomes masked by the level of its abstraction; the mechanism of reciprocity, which is that of the *psychomachia*, remains unrecognized in order that it may serve its preventive, mediatory, and, inevitably, legal function.

Andreas Capellanus leaves little doubt that courtliness served to minimize the danger of violent confrontation between those who historically had enjoyed the right to war and who were also eligible to participate in the ritualization of passion. As a code of social conduct, courtly love worked, again like an inquisitory legal system, to deter rivalry between those who desire the same thing and who might come to blows as a result. Andreas prohibits intrusion upon a love affair already in progress (*Courtly Love* 81) and includes, among the Rules of Love, specific provisions governing double amatory allegiance: "A true lover does not desire to embrace in love anyone except his beloved"; "A new love puts to flight an old one" (184). While admitting the likelihood of conflicting attachments, a natural result of desire which works independently of moral constraint, Andreas encourages the avoidance of excessive contention whenever possible. Thus the preoccupation with opposing claims to the same lady or lover, and thus the appropriateness of the discussion between the woman of middle class and the man of nobility concerning the rights of rival hunters:

Woman: But doesn't a wild beast who has been wounded by the spear of one hunter and then is later taken by another, belong to the man who got her?
Man: What you said about hunting cannot stand in my way, because we know that this applies to a particular practice, unfair enough, of certain people. But the usual rule throughout the world is that if anyone starts a wild beast from her lair and follows her, even though someone else takes her, custom reserves her for the first man. Therefore, since my suit came before that of the other man, you cannot with justice deprive me of your love.

(*Courtly Love* 89)

Through the rules which forbade disruption of preexisting relationships and through the imposition of precedence where the legitimacy of conflicting claims was not apparent, the courtly apparatus functioned, like a civil judicial system, to diffuse potentially explosive situations before they could erupt into violence. Its purpose was at least partially preventive.

The *Art of Courtly Love* proposes, in addition, a model for the resolution of disputes which either cannot be prevented or which have evolved beyond the contestants' capacity to achieve an adequate solution. In such cases the metaphor is not that of the hunt, but of the judicial court. For example, the dispute between the man of high nobility and the woman of simple nobility concerning the status of love in marriage is settled through the arbitration of the Countess of Champagne. Like the *tornada* of certain *tensos* and *jocs partits*, their agreement to abide by the ruling of a third party represents a trial of sorts (*Courtly Love* 105). More important, chapter VII of Book II consists entirely of similar decisions. The twenty-one verdicts of the Countess of Champagne, Eleanor of Aquitaine, and Hermengard of Narbonne transform the irregular procedure invoked by the quarreling lovers into a regularized institution. Again, the mechanism of decision is designed to resolve potentially destructive rival claims between: two men of equal worth, birth, and morals, but of unequal means (169); two men of equal worth in every respect (169); a young man and an older man who both love the same woman (170, 176); a good man who loves a lady first and a better man who comes along later (171); a lover and an indiscreet confidant (174).

In cases of excessive tension between lovers or between rivals Andreas establishes a procedure of mediation applicable to a wide range of situations:

Love may be revealed to three people besides the lovers themselves, for the lover is allowed to find a suitable confidant from whom he may get secret comfort in his love affair and who will offer him sympathy if things turn out badly; the woman may choose a similar confidante. Besides they may have one faithful intermediary, chosen by common consent, through whom the affair may always be managed in secret and in the proper fashion. These two confidants are bound, when both of the lovers wish it and the occasion demands, to go before the ladies and tell them what has happened but without giving any information as to the identity of the lovers concerned in the case.

(*Courtly Love* 165)

Whether or not the court of ladies of which Andreas speaks ever actually existed—and there has been much debate—the fact remains that he suggests a strategy for the settlement of conflict between individuals which is substantially the same as that of the inquisitory court, that is to say, a system of advocacy, negotiation, and arbitration. Through the confidants who counsel the lover, the intermediary who communicates between them, and the ladies who render judgment, the potential stalemate of the argument over love in marriage and the potential violence of the conflict of rival hunters comes to a satisfactory mediated, and verbal, solution. This does not mean that Andreas believes in the efficacy of the historically problematic Love Court. Few are willing to take seriously the allegorized laws of love that he mythologizes elsewhere. Nonetheless, the system which he proposes as an ideal method for the resolution of differences between members of France's chivalric nobility poses, at a time when the privileges of private armies and trial by combat were increasingly contested, an alternative to the violence which was traditionally a noble prerogative.

At an extreme, the love court poem of the same period makes the identity of inquisitory and courtly models explicit by dissolving all distinction between legal and literary modes.[83] The troubadour Monk of Montaudan, for example, combines judicial and poetic disputation in three playful poems set in God's own court. In "Autra vetz fui a parlamen" and "Quam tuit aquist clam foron fat" a dispute between the holy statues of the earth and courtly ladies over the price of facial makeup is settled through the intervention of Saints Peter and Lawrence (Nelli and Lavaud 2: 826). A third poem, "L'autr'ier fui en paradis," recounts the story of the Monk's own trial and condemnation.[84] In Raimon Vidal de Besalu's *Judici d'Amor*, the most fully developed Provençal version of the love court motif, a ticklish quarrel between a lady, her ex-lover, and her young niece is submitted to the arbitration of Uc de Mataplana. Acting as judge, Uc quotes Peire Vidal on the subject of *mezura* and thus puts an end to the potentially violent drama of jealousy (Nelli and Lavaud 2: 180). The anonymous thirteenth-century *Judici d'Amor* is primarily a manual of courtly conduct, an allegorized art of love similar in many respects to *Le Roman de la rose*. Its author insists upon the submission of amatory disputes to the Bailiff of Love (*Baillessa d'Amor*) for formal legal resolution.

For the poets of northern France, the love court theme was synonymous with the numerous versions of the debate between knights and clerics. A common Latin source, the *Council of Remiremont*, combines exemplary canonical procedure with a less than doctrinal discussion of the

---

83. For a resumé of the scholarly debate concerning the question of Love Courts in the Middle Ages see Lafitte-Houssat, *Troubadours et Cours d'Amour* (Paris: Presses Universitaires de France, 1966).

84. K. Bartsch, *Chrestomathie Provençale* (Marburg: Elwert, 1904), col. 143.

sexual merits of those who pray versus those who fight.[85] The Old French *Jugement d'Amours* presents essentially the same issue within a distinctly secular setting. Unable to convince her adversary Blancheflor of the superiority of clerics, Florence summons her to the God of Love's court. He agrees to hear her case before the barons of the realm, a parliament of fowls, as the poet's initial concern for psychological and legal detail yields to allegory and satire. The author of manuscript D of *Florence et Blancheflor*, another version of a similar story, considers the outcome of ornithological combat to constitute a triumph of bookish learning over physical might. The cleric whom Blancheflor loves is, above all, a man of law: *Maistres estoit de lois, de plais.*[86]

If we have introduced the love court poem into our discussion, it is because these works serve to exaggerate the homological identity of judicial and literary models. The love court poem is, however, at once the quintessential and the least successful of courtly forms. Because of the overtness with which it exposes its true subject, the legal function of courtliness itself, the *Judicia amoris* flounders on a tedious no-man's land between pseudo-document and literary text. The displacement achieved in the more successful courtly genres depends, like the justice of the inquisitory court, upon the subliminal substitution of an attenuated verbal ordeal for one that is potentially more physical and immediate—an implicit masking of the violence inherent to both the feudal and the epic ordeal of combat. We turn in our conclusion to the common ideological basis of trial by inquest and courtly literature.

85. C. Oulmont, *Débats du clerc*, p. 94.
86. He was a Master of Laws and of pleas (*Ibid.*, p. 143).

CHAPTER V

The Ideology of Courtly Love

Out of the critical chaos surrounding courtly love—what it was, where it came from, if it existed at all as a social phenomenon—there is general agreement on only four points. First, the love lyric of the troubadours and *trouvères*, as well as the novel of chivalry, originated in the seigneurial courts of Champagne, Flanders, Normandy, Aquitaine, and Anjou. The soil in which courtly literature first took root included the courts of great feudatory princes along with the entourages of lesser lords. Although it may also have encompassed the territory under the direct control of the French king, the Ile de France, this area is not considered to have been the cradle of emerging courtly forms.

Second, social conditions in the Midi and north were generally favorable to the development of a literature of love alongside the epic types which had flourished, at least in Anglo-Normandy, from the beginning of the twelfth century. Among these it is customary to cite: the relative refinement of life at southern courts; the role of women in the shaping and support of an artistic climate appealing to both sexes; a general relaxation of feudal organization as evidenced in numerous *alleux* or free holdings, the demographic signs that the fief had ceased to fulfill a purely military function; the limited influence of an open-minded clergy over the southern magnates; a waning of enthusiasm for the Crusades after the defeats of the 1140s; and, finally, the revival of a money economy along with the reopening of trade routes to the east. These factors, combined with a *prise de conscience* on the part of the northern secular clergy of its historical mission in the continuation of classical

culture, give the impression of a time and a place ripe for the crystallization of what one critic has termed "la scholastique de la vie mondaine."

Third, scholars have insisted, since Raynouard's publication of the
lyrics of the troubadours (1818) and the first modern edition of Andreas
Capellanus's *De amore* (1892), upon the subversiveness of courtly love.
This insistence has led in two directions. On the one hand, courtliness has
been considered subversive because of its tendency to isolate the love
couple from the rest of society and thus to discourage their participation
in and responsibility to the community as a whole. Here one thinks
immediately of the Tristan legend—the seclusion of the lovers in exile,
their deception while at court.[1] And yet, love represents an equally
isolating force in the *fin' amors* of the troubadours even though its effect
upon the nature of the human community is less apparent. Nor is the
social subversiveness of courtliness limited to the realm of adulterous
passion. The threat of Erec and Enide's or of Yvain and Laudine's
excessive preoccupation with each other, their dual narcissism, is as real as
that of Tristan and Iseult or the *fin amador*.

The doctrine of courtly love has also been judged morally subversive
because it glorifies, against the teachings of the Church, the practice of
adultery. It is a commonplace of medieval studies to point to the relaxed
moral climate of the southern clergy as opposed to the ascetic reform-
minded Cluniac or Cistercian spirit of the north; so too has it become
practically a matter of course to acknowledge the possible influence of the
heretical movements of the twelfth and thirteenth centuries—Cathar,
Averroist, Pictish, mystical—upon the spiritualization of romantic passion. Leaving the question of heresy aside, the fact remains that the
Church maintained throughout the Middle Ages the doctrine of indisso-
luble, life-long marriage. According to early Christian writers, adultery
constitutes a mortal sin; only later was it reduced to the status of venial
offense. This is why literary specialists have so readily associated courtliness with doctrinal heresy. For A. Jeanroy, glorification of the love of
another man's wife represents "une explosion d'esprit païen dans un pays
et un siècle si profondément christianisés."[2] J. Frappier considers the

1. Jean-Charles Payen has even gone so far as to suggest that a substantial portion of
courtly literature represents an attempt to come to terms with this aspect of the Tristan
story. See "Lancelot contre Tristan: la conjunction d'un myth subversif (Réflexions sur
l'idéologie romanesque au moyen âge)" in *Mélanges LeGentil* (Paris: S.E.D.E.S., 1973):
617–632.

2. A. Jeanroy, *La Poésie lyrique des troubadours* (Paris: Didier, 1934), p. 88.

"religion of adultery" to be "l'élaboration la plus audacieuse et la plus hérétique d'un paganisme mondain."[3] A. J. Denomy, who has devoted a small volume to courtliness's "variation with Christian morality," deems it "impossible to reconcile the tenets of Courtly Love with the commandments of God, with the divine Will as interpreted by Saint Paul, with the teachings of Christ and his Church."[4] This impossibility is further complicated by the dogma governing sexual love even in marriage. According to the celebrated letter of Paul (I Cor. 7. 32ff), love within marriage is preferable to love out of wedlock even though abstinence is preferable to both. Later ecclesiastical doctrine holds intercourse to be lawful only for the purpose of procreation. As Peter Lombard specifies, "the passionate love of one's wife is the equivalent of adultery."[5]

Finally, ever since Eduard Wechssler demonstrated the similarity

---

3. J. Frappier, "Vues sur les conceptions courtoises dans les littératures d'oc et d'oïl au XII⁰ siècle," *Cahiers de Civilisation Médiévale* 6 (1959): 143.

4. A. J. Denomy, *The Heresy of Courtly Love* (New York: McMullen, 1947), p. 27.

5. As cited in C. S. Lewis, *The Allegory of Love* (Oxford: Clarendon, 1936), p. 15. The difficulty of reconciling adulterous love and ecclesiastical precept has produced the most extreme explanations for the appearance and for the social significance of courtly literature. It has led, at least on this side of the Atlantic, to the attempt to minimize the conflict by emphasizing one of its terms to the exclusion of the other. D. W. Robertson and his followers have mounted in the last twenty years an impressive campaign against the sensual nature of courtly love. Robertson seeks to demonstrate that adultery is either condemned outright or treated in an ironical, humorous, or satirical fashion (see *A Preface to Chaucer* [Princeton: Princeton University Press, 1963]). More recently, John Benton has shown with considerable rigor the paucity of information suggesting courtliness to be other than a literary phenomenon (see "Clio and Venus: An Historical View of Medieval Love" in *The Meaning of Courtly Love*, ed. F. X. Newman [Albany: State University of New York Press, 1968], pp. 19–42).

European scholars have tended since the publication of C. S. Lewis's *Allegory of Love*, to place the conflict of secular and Christian conceptions of love at the center of any explanation of courtly literature. For Lewis, "This erotic religion arises as a rival or parody of the real religion and emphasizes the antagonism of the two ideals" (*Allegory of Love*, p. 18). Robert Briffault's discussion of the troubadours picks up the thread of Lewis's thought, shifting its historical focus toward the south. According to Briffault, deception functions in the place of parody. And if courtly love represents "an expression of opposition between two converse orders of sexual morality," it emanates from the deliberate attempt of a "licentious Germanic aristocracy," under pressure from the Church, to cloak its traditional *mores* behind a cultivated spiritual ideal (see *The Troubadours* [Bloomington: Indiana University Press, 1965], p. 96). Reto Bezzola treats the question of influence in a more even-handed manner. Neither a "parody of the real religion" nor an illusion promulgated by a "licentious" aristocracy, courtliness reveals the struggle of lay society in southern France to liberate itself from clerical tutelage. Courtly love represents a synthesis of clerical and secular ethos, a merging of the ideal of the convent with that of the military court (see *Les Origines et la formation de la littérature courtoise en Occident: 500–1200* [Paris: Champion, 1958], pt. 2, vol. I, p. 311).

between lover-lady relationship and the feudal bond of homage, there has been a tendency among medievalists either to avoid entirely the question of literature and ideology or to assume that courtliness represented an expression of the ideological interests of the class for which it was intended.[6] This assumption is based partially upon linguistic considerations. For the poet of the twelfth century, writing in the vernacular was itself an ideological gesture. To choose the language of everyday speech instead of Latin—the artificial vehicle of universal culture, the language appropriate to the expression of philosophical truth, poetic beauty, and judicial right—was to opt for that which is most restricted temporally and geographically, the linguistic medium most attached to a specific time and place.[7] The particularist quality of the dialects of *langue d'oc* and *langue d'oïl* was, moreover, a reflection of the particularist tendencies of feudalism itself. According to Reto Bezzola, who has written the most comprehensive study of the origins of courtly literature, the medieval vernacular poet automatically affirmed the preeminence of that which is local. Within the political context of the twelfth century he supported, consciously or not, the sovereignty of aristocracy as opposed to the centralizing thrust of monarchy, empire, and Church: *Rien d'étonnant donc que les troubadours assimilent la vassalité à l'amour courtois.*[8] The movement away from Latin, away from Dante's *grammatica*, was, in essence, an abandonment of the hope of restoring Rome, an endowment of the diverse, historically corruptible vernacular with a claim to permanence equal to that of the universal and eternal *lingua romana*.

The correlation of courtly literature and the ideological interests of France's feudal nobility is also founded upon the little we know about the economic relation between poets and patrons during the High Middle Ages. For if the effort to link the social origins of individual poets to the milieu of literary performance has thusfar proven fruitless, it is still difficult to deny the influence of the medieval audience upon the per-

---

6. E. Wechssler, "Frauendienst und Vassallität," *Zeitschrift fur französische Sprache und Litteratur* 24 (1902): 159–190.

7. See P. Zumthor, *Langue et technique poétiques à l'époque romane* (Paris: Klincksieck, 1963), p. 30.

8. Bezzola, *Origines et formation*, pt. 2, 2: 240. Charles Camproux maintains, on the other hand, that the troubadours were ideologically engaged on the side of the emperor against the King of France: "L'Inspiration générale de la politique du Saint Empire était plus conforme aux aspirations du Joi d'amour" (*Le Joy d'Amor des troubadours* [Montpellier: Causse et Castelnau, 1965], p. 196).

former.[9] Alfred Jeanroy attributes the rise of courtly literature to the economic dependence of the Provençal singer/writer. The art of the troubadours, he maintains, originated in the collaboration between a "public de grands seigneurs" with newly acquired literary tastes and a class of jongleurs with traditions dating back to the Roman Empire.[10] H. Brinkmann had already insisted upon an assumed "Verbundenseins von Verfasser und Hörer."[11] Others will adopt the metaphor of the "courtly mirror." According to H. Emmel, Chrétien "hält seinen Hörern einen Spiegel vor."[12] W. Kellermann refers to romance as the "Spiegelung der höfischen Kultur"; I. Nolting-Hauff, as the "wahrheitsgetreue Spiegelung historischer gesellschaftlicher Lebensformen."[13] Jean Frappier, whose treatment of the conditions which produced the chivalric novel varies little from Jeanroy's discussion of the southern lyric, situates the social component of romance in the desire of poets to flatter, as through a "magnifying mirror," those who paid their wages.[14]

Marc Bloch's sensitivity to the economic factors affecting both social and artistic forms leads him to conclude that courtliness's profoundest effect lay in the "spontaneous expression of class consciousness to which it gave rise."[15] The exclusiveness of courtly literature, its presence as a "class code of noble and 'courteous' people" which the *vilein* could neither join nor understand, had the global social function of assuring the cohesiveness of the community to which it was addressed. More recently, Paul Zumthor, whose monumental studies of medieval literature dis-

9. Some of the names associated with courtly tradition belong to great feudatory families (e.g., Guillaume IX, Thibaut de Champagne), others to the lineages of lesser lords, still others to the bourgeoisie (e.g., Aimeric de Peguillan, Foulquet de Marseille). For a discussion of the question of the social origins of courtly poets see P. Zumthor, *Essai de Poétique médiévale* (Paris: Seuil, 1972), p. 67.

10. *Poésie lyrique*, pp. 61–100; see also E. Faral, *Les Jongleurs en France au moyen âge* (Paris: Champion, 1910), pp. 119–123; P. Gallais, "Recherches sur la mentalité des romanciers français du moyen âge," *Cahiers de Civilisation Médiévale* 7 (1964): 479–493; 13 (1970): 333–347.

11. H. Brinkmann, *Zu Wesen und Form mittelalterlicher Dichtung* (Halle: Max Niemeyer, 1928), p. 24.

12. H. Emmel, *Formprobleme des Artusromans und der Graldichtung* (Bern: Francke, 1951), p. 12.

13. W. Kellermann, *Aufbaustil und Weltbild Chrestiens von Troyes im Percevalroman* (Halle: Max Niemeyer, 1936), p. 7; I. Nolting-Hauff, *Die Stellung der Liebeskasuistik im höfischen Roman* (Heidelberg: Winter, 1959), p. 9.

14. J. Frappier, *Le Roman Breton* (Paris: C.D.U., 1949), p. 5.

15. M. Bloch, *Feudal Society* (Chicago: University of Chicago Press, 1966), 2: 317.

courage the facile assimilation of poetic text and historical context, has insisted upon the ideological complicity built into the performative process: *Le vouloir-chanter, le vouloir-dire procède d'un accord profond et d'une unité d'intention avec le vouloir-entendre du groupe humain. . . .*[16]

The most rigorous studies of the relation between literary form and ideology during the period under consideration are, once again, those of Erich Köhler, for whom the key to courtly literature is to be found in its appearance at the very moment at which the class for which it was intended became most threatened by those it excluded: threatened from above by an ambitious monarchy; threatened from below by the rise of an urban bourgeoisie—a class of literate bookkeepers, merchants, manufacturers, and jurists often allied with royalty; threatened, above all, from within by a split in its own ranks (see above pp. 98–99).[17]

According to Professor Köhler, courtly literature is at once an idealization of the deteriorating situation of aristocracy and a forum for the resolution of intraclass tension. Both the lyric and the early novel of chivalry satisfy the aspirations of upper and lower nobility. To the great feudatory princes, themselves still powerful enough to rival the Capetians, Arthurian romance offered an ideal image of a feudal king who maintains traditional rights and obeys customary laws, but who does not seek to extend his own prerogative or power. Thus, as a "corrective mirror" held up to the increasingly assertive Louis VII and Philippe-Auguste, Arthur stands not above his vassals, but among them, *primus inter pares*. To lower nobility Arthurian romance offered the possibility of attaining a measure of lost prestige through the myth of an aristocracy of soul rather than birth. It functioned, moreover, to guarantee the material maintenance of the dispossessed knight by transforming the traditional

16. Zumthor, *Essai*, p. 42.

17. E. Köhler, *Ideal und Wirklichkeit in der höfischen Epik* (Tubingen: Max Niemeyer, 1956); *Trobadorlyrik und höfischen roman* (Berlin: Rütten and Loening, 1962); "Observations historiques et sociologiques sur la poésie des troubadours," *Cahiers de Civilisation Médiévale* 7 (1964): 27–47; "Les Romans de Chrétien de Troyes," *Revue de l'Institut de Sociologie de Bruxelles* 36 (1963): 271–284; "Narcisse, la fontaine d'amour et Guillaume de Lorris" in *Humanisme médiévale dans les littératures du XIIe au XIVe siècle*, ed. A. Fourrier (Paris: Klincksieck, 1964): 147–164. Our insistence upon Köhler's dominance of the question of Old French literature and ideology is not based upon neglect of Leo Pollmann's impressive *Liebe in der hochmittelalterlichen Literatur Frankreichs* (Frankfort: Klostermann, 1966). Here we must distinguish, however, between Pollmann's thesis, which, in seeking to determine the cultural origins of courtly love, remains genetic in nature, and that of Köhler, which seeks to determine the indigenous social roots of courtliness.

feudal contract into the moral value of obligatory *largesce* and by transforming the degrading search for financial profit among those whose
"raison de vivre" was a right of birth into the ideal of *aventure*, a tangible
sign of personal grace. The ideal protector is, like Arthur, one who
distributes gifts generously; and the model knight is, like Perceval, Lancelot, and Gawain, one who willingly answers the call to adventure. Thus
the precarious position of both segments of an endangered chivalry
produced a consciousness of their mutual class interest—the courtly literature which, in turn, prevented the internal tension between them from
assuming the proportions of open conflict: *Artursreich und Arturs-
königtum erweisen sich als dichterisch sublimierte Wunschbilder der feudal-
höfischen Welt, und zwar als Wunschbilder, die die disparaten Interessen
der verschiedenen adligen Schichten in sich aufzunehmen geeignet waren.*[18]

The limited cast of characters within the lyric serves to reduce the
problem of romance to its most basic elements. The triangle of lover
lauzenger, and lady is, again, both the reflection of intraclass tension and a
formula for its resolution.[19] The uniformity of the *canso* is designed, like
the myth of the Round Table, to project the illusion of equality among all
levels of courtly society. Every poet has an equal chance to gain his lady's
favor, since poetic skill is not a function of rank or wealth. And if in
romance the unity of the community is sanctified by the cycle of departure and return implicit to adventure, the same result is achieved in the
lyric through the lover's voluntary submission to the ideals of *obediensa*
and *mezura.*

For Köhler, courtly literature represents a daydream conceded by
upper aristocracy to its less fortunate supporters, an illusion which allowed the dreamer to participate vicariously in a tension-filled existence
where feats of arms still have a meaningful place and where loyalty in love
will be justly rewarded. Yet, at the same time, courtliness serves to
disguise the true material situation of those most attracted to it. As a
crystallization of the aspirations of France's dispossessed *hobereaux,* the
doctrine of gentle love permitted ideological access to the prestige of the
powerful while limiting any more tangible access to genuine political
power. By also encouraging the economic maintenance of a caste of poor

18. *Ideal,* p. 38.

19. ". . . les trois personnages de la chanson et les relations caractéristiques qui les
unissent en les opposant reproduisent fidèlement la structure de la société féodale en voie
d'intégration et ses contradictions internes" ("Observations historiques," p. 45).

but worthy knights, it redounded to the advantage of all the members of a class in transition.

The historical significance of the tension between high nobility and squireen cannot be ignored. Köhler's explanation of the origins of court-liness in terms of a mechanism for the regulation of a potentially violent intraclass struggle accounts for a number of the essential characteristics of medieval love literature. And yet, the ideological differences separating upper and lower echelons of aristocracy were less important than the ideological gulf separating both from the ambitions of monarchy, on the one hand, and those of bourgeoisie, on the other. Köhler himself admits that the integrating power of the courtly ethos was short-lived indeed. The triumph of high nobility over squireen was a fact of life by the last quarter of the twelfth century; and the triumph of royalty over both was assured by the second quarter of the thirteenth. The love which served to socialize the individual in the troubadour lyric and in Chrétien's early novels (*Erec et Enide* and *Cligés*) becomes problematic in his middle works (*Lancelot* and *Yvain*).[20] Pushed beyond reasonable limits, love as obsession assumes the status of destiny; and the power of Guinevere and Laudine over Lancelot and Yvain not only menaces the independence of the lover, but negates the autonomy of feudal nobility as well. *Perceval*, the swan song of chivalry, carries to completion the trend begun else-where. In Chrétien's last and unfinished romance the noble ideal which endowed existence with meaning is situated beyond love. Perceval's mysterious and irrecuperable sin is a symptom of the failure of chivalric and courtly values; the unresolved quest for the Holy Grail, a sign of the failure of chivalry's historical mission. Guillaume de Lorris transforms nobility's former claim to hegemony into an introspective journey via the dream into the self. As an aristocratic memory from beyond the tomb, the first part of the *Roman de la rose* displaces the ideal world of chivalric adventure—that of Chrétien and of the Grail novels—toward an entirely internal space outside of historical time.[21] In this way aristocracy relin-quished all hope of playing a meaningful historical role.

Köhler's reading of *Perceval* and *Le Roman de la rose* is laden with paradox. How, for instance, can a literary form which works "sublimi-

---

20. *Ideal*, pp. 163–180.

21. "L'Univers chevaleresque idéal a perdu toute chance de réalisation historique; c'est justement à cause de cela qu'il connaît sa plus haute spiritualisation profane, bien entendu dans une poésie de rêve, dans la révélation d'une réalité supérieure, qui, paradoxalement, renonce à priori à toute réalisation" ("Narcisse," p. 163).

nally" to ease intraclass tension also serve to express the impossibility of such a gesture? How does the dynamic relation of textual idealization to social reality become, within a space of twenty years, a mere reflection of the futility of idealization? How, in short, can the text seen as compensatory daydream (the troubadour lyric, *Erec et Enide, Cligés*) be reconciled with the text viewed as a cathartic effusion of the hopelessness of dreams (*Lancelot, Yvain, Perceval*) and with the allegorical superdream (*Le Roman de la rose*), which, in "revealing a superior reality, renounces all possibility of fulfilment?"[22] Köhler shifts his basic assumptions regarding the social function of the courtly text: from an organically integrating force holding nobility together to a mirror of its critical situation. That such a shift is necessary is itself indicative of a willful blindness to the contradictions inherent to courtliness from the beginning, though more pronounced in later works. The twisting of method to fit the literary evidence and to accommodate a foregone conclusion about the political role of the courtly text can, I think, be avoided by a fresh look at the ideological implications of the courtly/inquisitory model as we have defined it.

Consciousness against Class

On the basis of our discussion of literary forms and judicial institutions we are tempted, even obliged, to reopen the question that has been closed for as long as scholars have wrestled with the social backgrounds of the early French text—namely, the assumed identity between courtly literature and the ideological aspirations of feudal nobility. From what we have learned about the transformation of epic and courtly types along with the shift in trial procedure, it is possible to understand the subversiveness of courtliness in a way that reaches beyond the subversiveness of the hermit couple or the doctrinal problem of adultery. Stated simply, both the lyric and romance promulgate an implicit model of relation between individual and community similar enough to that of inquest to assume a common ideological effect which is just the opposite of that which scholars have traditionally—and perhaps too readily—acknowledged.[23]

22. *Idem.*
23. Zumthor is somewhat of an exception to the above generalization. Though he insists upon the importance of tradition in the constitution of medieval form, he also acknowledges the transformational power of the text: "Le texte, en principe, est dérèglement, transgression; mais dans un univers où les changements de toute nature s'étalent sur de très longues périodes, la transgression est pour ainsi dire récupérée par la règle, à l'instant même qu'elle se produit" (*Essai*, p. 32). See also p. 114.

Inquest transformed trial, the mediatory locus of violence within any society, from a test of physical strength implicating the warrior group as a whole into an abstract, verbal encounter between the individual and the state. Similarly, courtly literature served to transform the collective violence of the epic into the alienating, abstract, and verbal violence of the lover. The image of human society that can be extrapolated from the reduced representational range of the lyric is one of individuals isolated from and in constant conflict with each other. The poet struggles against beings of flesh and blood—his lady, the *lauzengers*, other poets—as well as against abstract allegorical principles such as Love, and, most important, against himself. As in the inquisitory court, the only acceptable vehicle of conflict is language itself. Whether its form is explicitly dialectical, as in the *tenso, joc partit*, and *pastorela*, or implicitly dialectical, as in the *canso*, the verbal violence of debate represents the structuring principle of the lyric, the poetic equivalent of an inquisitory *disputatio*. Within romance the individual again constitutes an autonomous social unit. But where the lyric lover is summoned to convince his lady of his worth through his powers of persuasion and against his detractors, the chivalric hero must prove himself through deeds of prowess accomplished while in the forest, through his ability to live up to the ideals of loyalty to lady and community, and, above all, through the obligation to tell his adventures upon return to court. The structural model of romance is that of the inquisitory deposition, a transcribed eyewitness account of that which has occurred in the realm beyond the law.

As we have seen, the procedure of inquest was designed to serve the political interests of those who sought its imposition—that is to say, the large feudatory states before their annexation, the Church, the inhabitants of towns, and, in particular, the kings of France. It is impossible, in fact, to separate the mechanism by which a political body judges those under its jurisdiction and the form of the state itself. And though trial by combat may have been adequate to the relatively modest needs of local, territorial, feudal states, inquest fulfilled the more elaborate purposes of the amalgam of territories ruled by feudal kings, the ecclesiastical hierarchy (a vestige of Roman organization), and the municipalities which sought in civil trial the public order necessary for the conduct of commerce. Most of all, inquest furthered the political ambitions of monarchy against its chief rival, aristocracy. What this suggests is that courtly literature, because of its affinity with inquest, served to affirm an implicit social model at variance with the long-range interests of the class for which it was intended. Here it is meaningless to distinguish ideology from form, the text as a vehicle for the articulation of a specific set of ideals from its presence as a set of formal relations. More precisely, there can be no distinction between courtliness as a code of conduct and the ways in which courtly poetic patterns worked to achieve their deepest effect. We shall explore, in the remainder of this book, some of the ways in which the courtly/inquisitory model and the "code of courtesy" functioned to undermine the sovereignty of nobility: how, in other words, France's military aristocracy came to embrace the very ideals which assured its own decline—the ideal of individualism, the right of the individual to self-determination according to abstract moral principles, and the ideal of peace itself.

There is no problem more confusing than the relation between the concept of individualism and the forms of social organization that have tended historically to accompany its repeated disappearance and revival. Nonetheless, the twelfth century is generally considered to be one of the great eras of liberation of the individual, the first in a series of steps leading to Renaissance humanism and to the democratic revolutions of the eighteenth century. The literary legacy of that liberation is, however, unclear. On the one hand, the freedom of a knight to leave the community in search of adventure, to act as the defender of mankind against the dark forces lurking in the forest, and to return a more fully integrated member of an enriched society seems to establish the autonomy not only of the individual, but of the entire chivalric class.[24] The power of the lyric lover to transform the pains of love into an attribute of class, the privilege of noble souls, reinforces a similar claim to moral superiority and to dominance. Courtly literature thus appears to serve the ideological interests of aristocracy by proclaiming the independence of each of its members along with the exclusiveness of the courtly community. And yet, the individualism of both adventurer and lover is, at the same time, perfectly consonant with the political strategy of monarchy and bourgeoisie.

Without opening a new area of inquiry at this late stage, I would like to suggest that there exists a much closer connection between the appearance of courtly literature and the revival of a money economy in

24. *Ideal*, p. 81–95.

twelfth-century France than is generally recognized.[25] By connection I refer neither to the economic tie between patron and poet, nor to the demand for refined amusement on the part of a class with increased leisure, nor to the incorporation within the courtly lexicon of terms ordinarily associated with the circulation of goods and money.[26] Rather, I would like simply to draw the reader's attention to the resemblance between the relative autonomy of the courtly lover and the extreme independence of the individual in more recognizably popular forms. The pattern of departure, adventure, and reintegration common to romance and the lyric pattern of constant conflict between poet, lady, *lauzengers*, and other poets represents an important step in the direction of the individualistic and materialist vision of human nature characteristic of Old French satire—a vision based upon the assumptions that man is by nature motivated by self-interest; that the spectrum of human responses can be reduced to the level of acquisitive, sexual, or gastronomic appetites; that everything sublunary is perishable; and that the rewards for human striving are therefore to be found in a personal here and now. The essential threshold in the emergence of the vicious individualism of the *Roman de Renart*, the fabliaux, or Jean de Meun's portion of the *Roman de la rose* is not situated between courtly and satirical genres, but between epic and the sometimes recuperable (Chrétien), periodically recuperable (lyric), or the irrecuperable (*Tristan*) breach between individual and community within courtly literature.

The vision of individuals beholden to no one but themselves first appears in the *Renart* cycle where the fusion between human and animal worlds underscores the futility of living according to chivalric and courtly ideals. It receives its most systematic elaboration in the second half of the *Roman de la rose*. In Jean de Meun's empirically oriented universe men no longer aspire to live according to the exemplary model of conduct outlined by Guillaume's God of Love (vv. 2023–2180); they are guided instead by their own experience and, more important, by their own

---

25. For a discussion of courtly literature and the rise of the twelfth-century southern bourgeoisie see Camproux, *Joy d'Amor*, pp. 35–38; for more recent discussions of poetics and money in medieval France see E. Vance, "Love's Concordance: The Poetics of Desire and the Joy of the Text," *Diacritics* 5 (1975): 40–52; B. Fitz, "The Prologue to the *Lais* of Marie de France and the *Parable of the Talents*: Gloss and Monetary Metaphor," *Modern Language Notes* 90 (1975): 558–596.

26. See R. Dragonetti, *La Technique poétique des trouvères dans la chanson courtoise* (Bruges: De Temple, 1960), pp. 72–113.

interests. For Guillaume, the possibility of life in human society represents "a restoration of all things"—a state of undifferentiated harmony from which conflict is not wholly excluded, but in which all tensions are ultimately resolvable by following the precepts of Love. Jean, on the other hand, equates man's social existence with the prospect of perpetual warfare between individuals. Where Guillaume's lover is assured of triumph through patient submission, he can only survive in the human jungle surrounding Jean's rose through recourse to wit, cleverness, and trickery. Jean de Meun's world is one of individualistic tricksters whose success in love is heightened by their skill at dissimulation. Ami advises the lover to use flattery, deceit, false promises, false tears, and bribery in rusing for the rose (vv. 7333–7718). Even opposing "military" chiefs—Malebouche and Fausemblant (along with Bien Celer)—are allegorical figures strongly rooted in the notion of linguistic deception.

To posit any direct connection between works as divergent as the courtly novel and lyric, on the one hand, and the *Roman de Renart*, the fabliaux, and the *Roman de la rose*, on the other, is to risk the most absurd *contresens*. Yet the gulf between them is not so broad as one might imagine, especially with respect to the question of the autonomy of the individual. When compared to the epic hero's minimal freedom to set the limits of his own relation to society, that of the courtly lover is great indeed. And though this freedom is carried to its logical conclusion only within specifically satirical works, the selfish individualism of rapacious animals, promiscuous wives, luxurious priests, and deceptive suitors is nonetheless latent in the alienation of the chivalric hero and lyric lover. The difference between courtly and popular forms is more one of degree than of kind: While in romance the rupture between individual and community is presented in terms of separation and reintegration and in the lyric it takes the form of a cyclical oscillation between unfulfilled expectations and short-lived satisfactions, the key concern within the explicitly bourgeois genres has to do with extracting the maximum of profit from the liberties that this peculiarly modern schism affords. What this means is that the courtly text can be situated somewhere between the collectivism of the epic and the ardent individualism of satire. It does not conflict, but rather coincides, with the ideological interests of a nascent bourgeoisie: the ethos of one against all within a natural social order in which the economic rights of individuals, as opposed to those of the ecclesiastical community or the clan, begin to come into their own.

If the designation of the individual as an independent social, and hence economic, unit suited the ideological needs of bourgeoisie, his constitution as an independent legal entity also served the long range political interests of monarchy. Monarchic policy was directed, during the period under consideration, toward weakening the unity of the feudal clan through destruction of its legal autonomy (see above pp. 128–141). Chief among the tactics of the Crown was the imposition of direct ties of dependence between each of the inhabitants of the royal domain and royalty itself, thus circumventing the intermediate jurisdiction of aristocracy. Beginning in the twelfth century the individual assumed a distinct legal personality by which he became less and less responsible to the clan, which was, in turn, less liable to and for him. Where the warrior group was once responsible for fighting for the rights of each of its members, avenging their deaths, making sure they were not involved in faulty causes, and paying reparation when they were, the individual grew increasingly accountable to the state only for himself. The fragmentation of legal responsibility, its focus upon the individual, was thus designed (intentionally or not) to undercut the power of nobility by encouraging loyalty to a higher and more central authority.

One of the most important aspects of monarchic policy was, as we have seen, the adoption of an inquisitory trial procedure. With the advent of inquest and appeal, along with the emergence of the office of public prosecutor, the dynamics of the judicial encounter shifted from a conflict between opposing families to a contest between the individual and the broader body politic. The object of criminal infraction was also displaced away from the family or warrior group toward the abstract notion of state, subsumed under the rubric of public peace, public order, or commonweal. In this way, monarchy assumed responsibility for the regular punishment of infractions that would have formerly been "righted" by recourse to vendetta.

Here a word is in order concerning ecclesiastical attitudes governing the role of the individual within the Christian community, for they underwent a parallel evolution at about the same time. The question of individualism cannot, of course, be isolated from the Nominalist controversy, which raised the issue of relation between the whole and its parts, the particular and the universal, on a number of levels—linguistic, social, theological. Nonetheless, it suffices within the scope of the present dis-

cussion to point to some of the similarities between the monarchic individuation of criminal responsibility, contemporaneous notions of sin and
penance, and the emergence of individualistic courtly types.

Beginning in the twelfth century there occurred a movement away
from the solemn penance invoked only once in a lifetime under special
circumstances—after serious wrongdoing or before death—toward the
regular remission of sins at periodic intervals.[27] The Fourth Lateran
Council (1215) declared it the duty of every Christian to attend confession once a year. Hence, the collective public expiations of the early
Christian era, which were still very much a reality at the time of the
Crusades, came to exist side by side with more private and individual
forms of confession conducted, as Gregory VII had prescribed and the
Lateran formula later confirmed, by the local parish priest. As a result,
excessive emphasis upon the act of transgression itself (*operatio mali*)
tended to yield to doctrines stressing the intention behind the act (*intentio
mala*) and, with it, the individual's responsibility for wrongdoing. According to Abelard, the temptation to do evil (*vitium animi*) only becomes sinful when it submits to consent. And whereas human justice is
competent to judge the acts of men, God alone can judge their intentions.

Intention as the foundation of ethical theory served to individualize the
notion of sin itself. The numerous penitentials which appeared in the
twelfth and thirteenth centuries (Bartholomew of Exeter, Roger de
Saint-Pair, Alain de Lille, Robert of Flamborough) focus upon the particular nature of every act of transgression. For example, Alexander of
Stavensby, Bishop of Coventry from 1224 to 1237, outlines a methodical
series of questions—*quis, quid, ubi, quibus, auxiliis, cur, quomodo, quan-
do*—to be used in the assessment of each infraction. The penalties affixed
to sin were also "personalized." The twelfth century was, in fact, a period
of transition from the fixed penances of an earlier era—the tariffs of
punishment which, like the *wergeld*, consisted of codified sanctions
strictly applied in order to produce automatic absolution—to more individual sanctions prescribed according to the age, sex, and social status of
the sinner and according to the circumstances of the sin. Absolution was,
in the latter case, not automatic, but depended upon the offender's ability

27. The following paragraphs are based largely upon Jean-Charles Payen's masterful
study, *Le Motif du repentir dans la littérature française médiévale* (Geneva: Droz, 1968), pp.
1–93.

to offer signs of inner contrition as well as to prove to the confessor's satisfaction that confession was freely given.

The necessity of offering external proof of inner repentance culminated in the twelfth century with an explicit doctrine of Contritionism. For Abelard, Saint Bernard, and the Victorines, the remission of sin occurs once the sinner has agreed voluntarily to receive divine grace, which causes tears of contrition. The tears are a visible sign that God's pardon has been granted. According to Hughes of Saint Victor, repentance represents a two-phased process: an exterior penance which, through the affliction of the flesh, absolves the sinful act; and an internal penance which, through contrition of the heart, absolves the intent behind wrongdoing.[28]

The regularization of private confession along with the insistence upon intention and inner repentance created the conditions under which self-examination could become an everyday practice not only of the clergy, but of the entire Christian community. Self-knowledge as a path to God was, in fact, one of the dominant themes of the age.[29] Augustine had maintained that "the soul cannot succeed in finding God except by passing through herself."[30] Abelard, almost seven centuries later, equated Christian morality with self-knowledge in a work entitled *Ethics: or, Know Yourself* (1135). Saint Bernard, who, in contrast with Abelard, minimized the significance of intention behind wrongdoing, also maintained that because self-knowledge was essential, ignorance constituted a sin.[31] William of Thierry adopted the Delphic dictum "Man, know thyself" in the prologue of his treatise on the nature of body and soul.[32] Aelred of Rievaulx asked rhetorically "How much does a man know if he does not know himself?"[33] And John of Salisbury offered in the *Policra-*

---

28. J.-P. Migne, *Patrologia Latina* (Paris: Garnier, 1879), 176: col. 554. It is worthy of note in passing that the individuation of the notions of sin and repentance were accompanied by the tendency for collective representations of eschatology to yield to a more personal one. The vision of a final redemption of mankind as a whole tended to be replaced by increased emphasis upon the individual fate of each Christian, a shift which is evident in the *Queste del Saint Graal* and which receives its most systematic expression in Dante's *Commedia*.

29. See C. Morris, *The Discovery of the Individual: 1050–1200* (New York: Harper, 1972), pp. 65–70.

30. Migne, *Patrologia*, 37: col. 1712.

31. *Ibid.*, 182: col. 836.

32. *Ibid.*, 180: col. 695.

33. *Ibid.*, 195: col. 683.

ticus what would have been an appropriate answer: *no one is more contemptible than he who scorns a knowledge of himself.*[34]

If we have introduced ecclesiastical notions of sin and repentance within our discussion of judicial institutions, it is, first of all, because of the collaboration during the twelfth and thirteenth centuries between canonical jurists and the secular personnel of the *Curia regis*. It is, second, because the personalization of atonement through private confession and the personalization of criminal responsibility through inquest were part of a global social transformation by which the individual became a self-governing legal entity responsible to God through his confessor, but directly responsible to the state. More precisely, emphasis upon intention, inner contrition, and self-examination established a spiritual link between the sinner and God that was, *mutatis mutandis*, analogous to the legal tie between each inhabitant of the royal domain and an increasingly theocratic monarchy. Finally, the internalization and individuation of criminal responsibility, which favored the interests of monarchy and which cannot be separated from contemporaneous ecclesiastical precept, has important repercussions for our understanding of a similar trend toward consciousness of self within courtly tradition.

Courtliness is, in many ways, synonymous with the psychologizing of social reality—the conversion of a set of reciprocal social relations, sensed as external and objective, into moral values. The courtly lexicon represents a virtual inventory of feudal terminology whose meaning has shifted toward the designation of an internal quality or state: terms associated with economic exchange—*salaire, saisine, guerredon, heritage, droit oir, don, rente, loier, raençon*; terms having to do with legal procedure—*seurté, gage, garantie, plevir, ostage, justisier, clamer, mesfez, traïson, damages, arrêt, baillie, jugement, droit* and *tort*; terms pertaining to military and social organization—*traité, accord, seigneurie, honor, foi, servise, vassalage, homage.*

As an example of the displacement of the feudal lexicon toward its internalized courtly equivalent, the objective obligation of the feudal lord to provide his vassal with material support as well as protection becomes associated, within the semantic range of romance, with the virtue of generosity or *largesce*.[35] Similarly, the expressions *pretz* and *valor*, which,

34. John of Salisbury, *Policraticus*, ed. C. C. J. Webb (Oxford: Oxford University Press, 1909), 1: 19.
35. Köhler, *Ideal*, pp. 11–36.

though economic in nature, once designated a fighter's prowess in battle, come to represent the social reputation and moral worth of the courtly lover.[36] And the terms *joven* and *jeunesse*, which once referred to the social status of a knight who was unmarried and unattached to a fief, become the equivalent of youthfulness, generosity, honorableness, courage, and loyalty—the opposite of *vielh*, which refers not so much to a person's chronological age as to his stinginess, propensity for evil, and scorn of courtesy.[37] *Cortezia* and *courtoisie*, which sometimes designate an independent moral quality and at other times are used as all-inclusive generic terms for the entire spectrum of courtly qualities, originated in the demographic description of "one who lives at court."

The internalization of objective social relations, their transformation into psychological qualities, is symptomatic of an investment of the courtly individual with a moral responsibility for the governance of himself in accordance with his changing relationship to the monarchic state. Without exhausting the complex issue of free will and determinism in Old French literature, we have seen that the epic hero enjoys a relatively small margin of freedom to fix the limits of his own relation to the warrior community. He is, to a varying degree, the triple prisoner of an inflexible set of extrinsic obligations, of his own character, and of the circumstances of which he often finds himself the victim. Though the hero of romance is just as often a prisoner of passion, and therefore no freer in any absolute sense, he is, to a much greater extent than in the epic, obliged to make meaningful choices between a variety of possible responses to his objective situation. Where institutions limit the power of the Charlemagne of the *Chanson de Roland* and that of *Les Quatre filz Aymon*, where character determines the fate of Roland or of Raoul, where the force of circumstance restricts the freedom of Renaud and of Ogier, the chivalric hero finds himself morally responsible as an individual for the crucial choices affecting his own destiny. However helpless

36. M. Lazar, *Amour courtois et "Fin' Amors" dans la littérature du XIIe siècle* (Paris: Klincksieck, 1964), p. 32; A. H. Schutz, "The Provençal Expression Pretz e Valor," *Speculum* 19 (1944): 493.

37. A. J. Denomy, " 'Jovens': The Notion of Youth among the Troubadours, its meaning and Source," *Medieval Studies* 11 (1949): 1–22; G. Duby, "Les 'Jeunes' dans la société aristocratique dans la France du Nord-Ouest au XIIe siècle," *Annales: ECS* 19 (1964): 835–846; E. Köhler, "Sens et fonction du terme 'jeunesse' dans la poésie des troubadours," in *Mélanges R. Crozet*, ed. P. Gallais (Poitiers: Société d'Etudes Médiévales, 1966): 569–583.

love renders an Erec, Lancelot, Yvain, Tristan, or Iseult, each is none-theless liable for resolving the conflicts which love engenders and for achieving—in distinct ways and with varying success—a viable balance between personal desire and social necessity.

The autonomy of the chivalric hero is nowhere more apparent than in the internal monologue or debate, the numerous episodes of self-interro-gation through which he or she comes to a decision concerning a partic-ular course of action (see above pp. 189–191).[38] The decision-making process most characteristic of the epic is the public *concilium* which serves as a forum for the resolution of matters of both personal and collective concern (see above pp. 104–107). In romance, however, the locus of choice is internalized. Instead of the recurrent questions debated be-fore the epic council—whether to make peace or war, whether to grant clemency or extract vengeance, whom to select as ambassador or battle chief—the chivalric hero or heroine asks himself, like Enide, "Wretch, what shall I do?", like Soredamors, "Mad that I am, what shall I do?", or like Lancelot, "God, what shall I do?" (*Erec* v. 3715, *Cligés* v. 889, *Lancelot* v. 1097). And though the issues and responses differ in each case, the fact remains that the individual, and not the assembled community, bears the sole responsibility of choice.

If the inner debate is the most evident sign of the hero's personal responsibility, its most tangible effect upon the formulation of character and upon the overall design of romance can be seen in another and related motif—the *prise de conscience* as a necessary component of self-gover-nance. Erec, for instance, awakens from a long period of sexual indul-gence following marriage to discover his own chivalric negligence (vv. 2476–2572). His decision to right the imbalance between sexual desire

---

38. Ilse Nolting-Hauff has masterfully described the process of sublimation implicit to the inner monologue and has rightly sensed the social, though not explicitly legal, implica-tions of the mechanism of self-governance and adaptation: "Die exemplarische Wirkung des Monologs liegt also nicht in einem etwaigen Sieg des Willens über den Affekt—ein solcher wird ja wenigstens innerhalb des Monologs kaum dargestellt—sondern vielmehr in der Tatsache, das eine Willensposition überhaupt zur Geltung kommt und alles Handeln—jeden falls fur die Dauer des Monologs, oft auch daruber hinaus-suspendiert. Der Monolog kann nur insoweit exemplarisch sein, als er exemplarisches Handeln, das meistens eher Nichthandeln ist, vorbereitet oder doch das Unexemplarische als solches bewusst macht. (. . . .) Der Held erscheint von Anfang an als exemplarisch, seine affektischen Überwind-ung innerhalb der Handlung zu ermöglichen. Im Grunde wiederholt—und steigert—der höfische Roman nur einen Sublimierungsprozess, der seiner eigenen Enstehung schon zu-grunde liegt" (*Stellung*, p. 59). See also pp. 36, 67, 75, 78.

and social obligation becomes the motivating force behind an equally unbalanced demonstration of knightly prowess.[39] Only after Erec rescues Maboagrain, an image of his former self trapped in a similar state of erotic enslavement, does he manage to establish an equilibrium between duty to the community of which he is now the head and satisfaction of his love for Enide. Yvain undergoes a comparable evolution in achieving a similar balance.[40] A period of lapsed chivalric duty as a result of marriage is rectified by sudden departure, an excessively long absence, banishment, and, eventually, madness, accompanied by a series of expiatory adventures prior to repentance and reconciliation with Laudine. Perceval, on the day after his visit to the Grail Castle, learns of the mysterious sin which has caused his mother's death (v. 3593); he too repents, vowing to accept all adventures, fight the bravest knights, and not to sleep more than one night in the same place until he returns to Corbenic. And Tristan and Iseult, freed from the effects of the love potion, awaken literally from sleep and from exile to the conscious decision to return to Tintagel (see below pp. 244–247).

The *prise de conscience* of the romance hero sometimes occurs within a formal religious context.[41] Perceval's Good Friday visit with his hermit uncle takes place five years after the Grail vision and echoes the earlier episode of consciousness and compunction (v. 6364). Tristan and Iseult twice visit the hermit Ogrin who elicits a confession and urges repentance (vv. 1361, 2266). The Lancelot Prose Cycle is filled with examples of confession, repentance, and conversion. In the Lancelot Propre, which is generally less religious in tone than the *Estoire del Saint Graal* or the *Queste*, Arthur confesses publicly and under the supervision of his "archbishop and bishop" to having forgotten both God and his duty as king (Sommer III, p. 216). *L'Estoire del Saint Graal*, which is the story of the evangelism of Britain, features the conversion of Evalac, his wife Sarracinte, Ganor, and Label—as well as the repentance of Josephe, Nascien, and Chanaan. And in *La Queste del Saint Graal* Lancelot,

---

39. Oddly enough, it is Enide who accuses herself throughout the first half of the work; see especially vv. 2492–2501, 3097–3112.

40. See R. Hanning, "The Social Significance of Twelfth-Century Chivalric Romance," *Medievalia et Humanistica* 3 (1972): 3–29, J. Frappier, *Etude sur Yvain* (Paris: Société d'Edition d'Enseignement Supérieur, 1969), p. 201.

41. See Payen, *Le Repentir*, pp. 365–403.

Gawain, Perceval, and Galaad repent numerous times in preparation for the final Grail adventure.

Both the spontaneous *prise de conscience* and its religious counterpart involve some degree of self-accusation, an admission of guilt along with the recognition of responsibility for its expiation. Though Erec never formally verbalizes his role first in neglect of knightly duty and then in its excess, the confession of Maboagrain, the hero's *alter ego*, applies just as well to Erec himself (vv. 6048–6052).[42] The Guinevere of Chrétien's *Lancelot*, upon hearing the false news of Lancelot's death, blames herself and repents (vv. 4180–4243); the Guinevere of the Lancelot Propre acknowledges her own guilt in betraying Arthur: *Je sui departie del roi mon seignor par mon mesfait, jel connois bien. . . .*[43] Yvain accepts the blame for Esclados's death (v. 1994), just as he will later accept full responsibility for breach of his promise to Laudine (v. 2792). Perceval's Good Friday confession begins with the knight's recognition of his own role in "neither loving nor believing in God" and in "only doing evil" (v. 6366).

Though the motif of repentance is common enough within the *chanson de geste*, there it remains generally closer to the once-in-a-lifetime acts of contrition of an earlier historical era. Isembard's conversion, Vivien's repentance (*Chanson de Guillaume*), Raoul's call for divine aid all occur *in extremis*. William's (*Moniage Guillaume*) and Girard de Roussillon's withdrawal from the world are carried out with death in mind. For the romance hero, on the other hand, self-awareness is both a reversible and a more general process.[44] It is assumed that every choice is open to revision. And while a major step in consciousness of the self and the reform that such a breakthrough implies may not represent everyday events, they do mark the critical thresholds in the development of the hero—necessary stages in Erec's and Yvain's isolation and reintegration, Perceval's dedication to the Grail Quest, Tristan and Iseult's decision to return to court. The reversibility of the process of self-discovery, the fact that every choice can be rectified by a subsequent one, means that the individual is, to a much greater degree than his epic counterpart, free to make the

---

42. Maboagrain's sin is, in fact, an amalgam of Erec's double excess, first in the direction of sexual obsession and then in that of obsessive killing.

43. I betrayed the king my lord through my own fault, I recognize it fully. . . . (Sommer IV: 53).

44. The conversions of *L'Estoire del Saint Graal* are, of course, exceptions.

crucial choices which determine his relation to others and, as a consequence, responsible for them.

Within the Provençal lyric the necessity of self-governance is synonymous with the ideal of measure.[45] Among the attributes of the worthy lover none is more central than that of *mezura*, the cardinal courtly virtue which determines both the lover's relation to others and to his innermost self. As Folquet de Marseille notes, "courtliness is nothing more than measure": *cortesia non es als mas mezura*.[46] Unlike the *joi* of the troubadours, the significance of *mezura* leaves little room for discussion. The term implies, first and foremost, a limitation of outward conduct, an avoidance of extremes. For Marcabru, the principle of *mezura* represents the antithesis of gluttony; courtliness entails the "reduction of surplus in everything" (Marcabru 62). Andreas Capellanus praises the value of reason and proportion in every aspect of the lover's comportment. The woman of high nobility advises her middle class suitor to be "moderate about his laughter," "moderate about indulging in games of dice," "to devote only a moderate amount of care to the adornment of his person"; he should take care "not to talk too much or to keep silent too much." The perfect lover avoids prodigality while practicing generosity (*Courtly Love* 31, 60). In lovemaking he remains attentive to the demands of his partner, gauging his advances according to her wishes: *In giving and receiving love's solaces let modesty be ever present* (*Courtly Love* 81). Andreas's concept of measure implies a harmonious balance between the dictates of head and heart, intellect and passion; between negligence and excess in the conduct of everyday affairs; between the desire of lover and lady.

45. And is linked, as F. Goldin has shown, to the theme of the mirror as the *locus* of self-perception, *The Mirror of Narcissus* (Ithaca: Cornell University Press, 1968). Emile Benveniste, who has devoted a chapter of his *Vocabulaire des institutions indo-européennes* to the concept of measure, shows that the root *med-* has historically had a legal significance and that it refers not so much to the physical dimensions of things as to the moral dimension of an individual's conduct: "Partons du latin *modus*. C'est la 'mesure', mais non une mesure qui soit une dimension propre des choses; pour 'mesurer' le latin emploie un verbe distinct, *metior*. Par *modus*, on exprime une mesure imposée aux choses, une mesure dont on est maître, qui suppose réflexion et choix, qui suppose aussi décision. Bref, ce n'est pas une mesure de *mensuration*, mais de modération, c'est-à-dire une mesure appliquée à ce qui ignore la mesure, une mesure de limitation ou de contrainte. C'est pourquoi *modus* a plutot un sens moral que matériel; *modestus* est dit 'celui qui est pourvu de mesure, qui observe la mesure'; *moderari*, c'est 'soumettre à la mesure (ce qui y échappe)'" (*Vocabulaire des institutions indo-européennes* [Paris: Editions de Minuit, 1969], 2: 127).

46. *Le Troubadour Folquet de Marseille*, ed. S. Stronski (Crakow: Académie des Sciences, 1910), p. 59.

THE IDEOLOGY OF COURTLY LOVE

The equilibrium established in relation to others also assumes a personal equilibrium achieved in relation to the self, an internally based act of will. *Mezura* automatically means self-control, discipline, the domination of antisocial instinct through the repression of immoderate desire.[47] *Cortesia* is equivalent to self-mastery, self-possession. The necessity of patience and humility on the part of the lover emphasizes the importance of caution and reflection as a prerequisite to action. According to Peire Cardenal, "he who succeeds in mastering himself has conquered more than a hundred cities."[48] Marcabru identifies the moral aspect of *mezura* —*dreitura*—with wisdom; the wise man freely determines the object of desire:

> —"Don, oc; mas segon dreitura
> Cerca fols sa follatura,
> Cortes cortez' aventura,
> E'il vilans ab la vilana;
> En tal loc fai sens fraitura
> Ou hom non garda mezura,
> So ditz la gens anciana.
>
> Sire, yes, but according to natural law
> the fool pursues his folly and the courteous,
> courtly adventure: let peasant stay with
> peasant. Where measure is not observed, wisdom
> is lacking, so said the ancients.

(Marcabru 141)

More than a simple code of gentlemanly etiquette, a *savoir-vivre* assuring social success, the principle of measure presupposes a voluntary renunciation of excessive desire for the sake of the common social good.

The internalized normative ideal of measure, together with the displacement of the locus of moral decision away from the public *concilium* and toward the chivalric hero, is but one aspect of the historical development that we have encountered elsewhere, that is to say, the designation of the individual as an autonomous legal entity. In contrast with Erich Köhler, who equates the independence of the individual with that of an entire class, we find that the Old French romance and lyric promulgate an inferred model of social order that not only conflicts with the clannish interests of feudal nobility, but that is perfectly consistent with the

---

47. See Lazar, *Amour courtois*, pp. 29–33; J. Wettstein, *"Mezura," Idéal des troubadours: son essence et ses aspects* (Zurich: Leeman, 1945).
48. K. Bartsch, *Chrestomathie Provençale* (Marburg: Elwert, 1904), col. 191.

political strategy of monarchy—the creation of a nation of self-governing individuals responsible for themselves to the state as opposed to a federation of clans accountable to each other.[49] The ideological implications of courtliness will, I think, become even clearer when considered in the light of its most extreme narrative rendering—the Tristan story.

Tristan and the Myth of the Modern State[50]

That the Tristan myth both inaugurates and defines the dynamics of Western romantic love is a likely supposition with a rich and respected tradition. The conjunction of boundless but unmediated passion within the perimeters of suffering and death has become at once the synonym and paradigm of problematic desire. Love represents but one absolute among several; and like all absolutes, it displays a common contrariety to the notion of human will. Within the myth there is no possibility of escaping the nature of passion, no possible margin for personal freedom to assert itself against the universal desire that becomes the equivalent of fate. Unfortunately, excessive emphasis upon *Tristan* as the specific form of a more general striving for transcendence relegates the legend to the realm of static myth and tends to obscure the ontological and social roots of Béroul's poem. For it is also likely, though not generally recognized, that the legend embodies another important myth of origin: the birth of subjective conscience and the foundation of the modern state. A fresh look at the social and psychological elements of the Tristan story reveals much that is misleading in an archetypal interpretation of the romantic myth *par excellence*.

Any reading of *Le Roman de Tristan* as a parable of impossible progression—inescapable anguish until death—focuses, inevitably, upon the ambiguous episode of the sleeping lovers in Morrois Forest (vv. 1774–2132). This is the scene in which Marc, informed of the exiled couple's whereabouts, hesitates to kill his wife and nephew because of the presence of Tristan's sword between the two sleeping bodies. According to those who view the legend as myth, the sword that lies between Tristan and the queen offers certain proof of unconsummated passion.[51] The

---

49. See Köhler, *Ideal*, pp. 70–71.

50. Parts of the following discussion appeared under the title "Tristan, the Myth of the State and the Language of the Self," *Yale French Studies* 51 (1975): 61–81.

51. See D. de Rougemont, *Love in the Western World* (New York: Fawcett, 1956), pp. 31–43.

lovers do not care for one another physically; they are more in love with the idea of love itself than with each other. If their passion fixes autonomously upon its human object, it does so only as a metaphor for pervasive metaphysical desire, which cannot be satisfied by any being of flesh and blood. Self-imposed chastity represents a form of symbolic suicide masking the as yet unrecognized desire for death. By the same token, Marc's refusal to grant the lovers what they secretly and ardently desire—oblivion—serves to perpetuate and reaffirm the cyclical dynamics of hopeless love. His compassion, combined with the ritual exchange of ring, glove, and sword, re-establishes the marriage bond between Marc and Iseult as well as the king's authority over the couple.[52] What amounts to a civilized code of gentle conduct has triumphed over the brutal instinct towards vengeance. In essence, Marc allows the lovers to return to Tintagel without fear of reprisal. He creates the conditions under which passion, having abated during the long exile in Morrois, will be nourished once again by the difficulties inherent to life at court. The dilemma of unfettered possession while in the forest and that of thwarted possession in the company of others are but two phases of a single metaphysical desire.

Marc's discovery of the adulterous couple falls into a special category under medieval law. Ordinarily, any slaying carried out without challenge or open confrontation constituted what today would be called first-degree murder. As we have seen in our first chapter, the essential legal distinction between homicide and murder hinged, up until the fourteenth century, upon the idea of open as opposed to hidden misdeed (see above pp. 34–40).

Glanvill defines *murdrum* as a "killing seen by none." The *Très Ancien Coutumier de Normandie* classifies murder among the unamendable crimes occurring under the cover of night. The *Livre de Jostice et de Pletz* maintains that any slaying committed at night automatically constitutes murder. And for the author of the *Etablissements Saint Louis*, murder was synonymous with "death in bed or in any way that does not involve an open fight."

As we have also seen, medieval law did provide for two cases in which the normal procedure of challenge and struggle might be waived in favor

---

52. J. Marx, "Observations sur un épisode de la légende de Tristan" in *Mélanges Brunel* (Paris: l'Ecole de Chartes, 1955), p. 265.

of a more expeditious slaying (see above pp. 53–58). The first involves the murder of a man who was himself an outlaw—who was not, in other words, entitled to the protection against surprise attack that the law ordinarily afforded. A felon at large was, in effect, at war with the community; and it was the right and duty of others to pursue him and kill him wherever and however possible. The victim's family was, in turn, prohibited from protecting the criminal and from avenging themselves upon his killers once he had been captured.

A second case in which the normal rules of challenge might be suspended involved the entrapment of an offender in the act, especially in the act of adultery. According to medieval custom, if a man captures his wife in a compromising situation with another man, he has the right to slay both wife and lover, again without risk to himself. In contrast to the elaborate procedure governing all other hand-to-hand struggles, the regulations affixed to the slaying of adulterers in *flagrante delicto* are minimal. Thus, through the special procedure governing the entrapment of lovers in the act, the law formally sanctioned what in any other context was defined as premeditated murder: slaying without challenge or warning, without quarrel or equality in the means of confrontation.

As escapees from the king's justice and as discovered lovers, Tristan and Iseult fall into the double jeopardy of outlawry and adultery. Marc's obligation to slay them is compounded by their double transgression against himself as husband and against the community in which the law resides:

> De la cité s'en est issuz
> Et dist mex veut estre penduz
> Qu'il ne prenge de ceus venjance
> Que li ont fait tel avilance.

> From the city he went out
> Saying that he would rather be hanged
> Than not avenge himself upon those
> Who offended him so grieviously.
>
> (v. 1953)

Yet when it comes to the slaying itself, Marc finds himself in the paradoxical position of a well-armed Hamlet in front of a praying Claudius. With sword raised, reflection intrudes upon action. Inhibition at the motor level, internalization of all possibility of action—sublimated instead into thought—provokes the exchange of ring, glove, and sword, the symbolic reinvestiture aimed at inducing awareness of the king's presence in the forest that day (vv. 2020–2024).

In a very real sense the fate of the feudal world hangs in the balance of Marc's raised sword. His hesitation, reflection, and eventual sublimation of the physical vengeance to which he was entitled brings with it an essentially altered notion of kingship and statehood.

The first half of *Tristan* is defined by the barons's pursuit of the lovers, an endeavor to which Marc is forced to consent and in which he participates actively. According to the contractual nature of feudal kingship, the monarch was compelled to follow the dictates of the community whose collective will he expresses (see above pp. 21–22). Unlike the modern state, whose corporate personality determines its ultimate end, feudal polity represented a series of innumerable subjective rights.[53] In this respect it cannot be distinguished from the separate ties of fealty contracted independently between specific men. And, as such, there can be no distinction between private right and communal law. Heavily oriented toward the preservation of private privilege, feudal polity stressed the duty of the state to its members instead of the responsibility of each individual to the political community. The feudal monarch swore, as part of the coronation ceremony, to uphold the customary law of the land and to protect the rights of individuals. Swearing actually preceded anointing. As the guardian of custom and privilege, the king represented a passive figure destined to maintain the status quo rather than extend his land and power. The notion of public sovereignty which transcends private right was foreign to the feudal concept of statehood.

The obligation of the feudal ruler to respect the will of his barons accounts for Marc's weakness in dealing with the situation at court. He is well aware that the counsel of one's vassals is the determining factor in any policy of state:

> —Seignor, vos estes mi fael . . .
> Conseliez m'en, gel vos requier.
> Vos me devez bien consellier,
> Que servise perdre ne vuel.

53. See O. Gierke, *Political Theories of the Middle Ages* (Boston: Beacon, 1960), p. 34; F. Kern, *Kingship and Law in the Middle Ages* (Oxford: Blackwell, 1956), p. 73.

—Lords, you are my vassals . . .
Counsel me, I beg of you.
You must advise me well,
For I do not wish to lose your service.

(v. 627)

Theoretically the barons owe Marc fealty and not unqualified obedience. Feudal sovereignty entails a reciprocal rapport between ruler and ruled, both of whom are bound by communal law. The monarch who failed to recognize the practices of the past abrogated the contractual agreement between himself and his vassals. He forfeited the obedience of his subjects who were then entitled to exercise the medieval Right of Resistance and Principle of Self-Help, to take the law into their own hands in order to obtain redress. Ultimately, the barons of Tintagel had the right to declare war upon Marc for not following their advice in the drive to oust Tristan.[54] It is, in fact, Marc's basically feudal relation to the vassals that shapes Béroul's poem up to and including the scene of the sword. Their insistence upon pursuit of the lovers engenders the episode under the pine tree as well as the entrapment, condemnation, and exile. The repeated sequence of denunciation, verification, and discovery is, furthermore, symptomatic of a state in which there is no distinction between private and public acts, a state in which adultery, the secret deed *par excellence*, automatically becomes a matter of public policy.

The tension between Tristan and the barons can be reduced to a conflict between true paternity, Tristan as nephew, and fictive paternity, or vassalage, the basic elements of the global warrior group. At bottom, they hate each other because they desire the same thing, a privileged rapport with Marc. In this respect the adultery becomes the wedge by which the barons are able to share the king's favor. Each time they manage to convince him of the couple's guilt they rise in his estimation; and with each discovery of their innocence Tristan regains the upper

54. | A la cort avoit trois barons, | At court there were three barons, |
Ainz ne veïstes plus felons;	Never were more felonious ones seen.
Par soirement s'estoient pris	By oath they had agreed
Que, se li rois de son païs	That if the king did not
N'en faisot son nevo partir,	Make his nephew leave his lands,
Il nu voudroient mais soufrir,	They would not support him.
A lor chasteaus sus s'en trairoient	To their castles would they withdraw,
Et au roi Marc gerre feroient.	And make war on King Marc.

(v. 581)

hand (e.g., vv. 287–291). The king, in turn, seeks the lovers not because he wants to, but because his vassals push him to it and because he is compelled by feudal law to comply. If anything, Marc, like Arthur of *La Mort Artu*, resists the truth of adultery and reproaches the barons for their insistence:

> —Seignor, vos estes mi fael.
> Si m'aït Dex, mot me mervel
> que mes niés ma vergonde ait quise.

> —Lords, you are my vassals.
> So help me God, I would be much amazed
> If my nephew had sought my shame.

(v. 627)

In the king's willingness to pursue the adulterers because of the barons' persistence and despite his own reluctance or indifference, we detect the basic pattern of a shame culture, a society in which men act less according to their own feelings than according to what others will think.[55] The feudal warrior group functioned under the assumption that men are motivated to action out of a concern for personal reputation, the classic example being Roland's refusal to sound his horn at Roncevaux for fear of how others, both present and future, will view a call for help. The archetypal epic hero is an externally oriented being, attached to the judgment of his peers: in short, a conformist next to the more problematic hero of romance. This is why Marc, in refusing to slay the couple and in disregarding the wishes of his barons, both of which would have further bound him to the feudal past, lays the foundation of a modern notion of state based upon guilt rather than shame.

It is assumed within a guilt culture, that men act according to an internal sense of what is right as opposed to the fear of any specific sanction. Herein lies the meaning of the exchange of ring, glove, and sword. While the investiture ceremony attached to fealty is, by definition, a contractual agreement by which one party pledges protection and economic support for military aid and counsel, Marc's reinvestiture of the

---

55. For a discussion of feudal warfare in Tristan see A. Várvaro, *Il "Roman de Tristan" di Béroul* (Torino: Erasmo, 1963), pp. 147–160. For a discussion of shame and guilt cultures in medieval epic see W. C. Calin, *The Old French Epic of Revolt* (Geneva: Droz, 1961), p. 152; E. Vance, *Reading the "Song of Roland"* (New Jersey: Prentice-Hall, 1971), p. 36. See also J. Benton, *Self and Society in Medieval France: The Memoirs of Guibert de Nogent* (New York: Harper, 1970), p. 23.

[243]

sleeping couple occurs unilaterally. It represents a one-sided gesture of possession much closer to the notion of generalized social contract than to vassalage. Imposed from above rather than reciprocally, Tristan and the queen's altered rapport with Marc has not been contracted at a specific moment between particular parties. Unlike homage, it is based upon tacit consent, an implicit contract to ally personal desire with common need. The king's rejection of the vengeance prescribed by feudal custom marks the beginning of the fictive corporate state, the abstract amalgam of assumed ties that will henceforth determine all relations between individual and community.

With the intrusion of reflection upon action conscience is born. Guilt as a self-generating internal deterrent to transgression supplants the vendetta ethic characteristic of all shame cultures. The fear of reprisal inherent to the feudal doctrine of Self-Help and private war has been transformed, in the moment that Marc decided to leave a sign of his presence in Morrois rather than slay the sleepers, into a fear of violating that which is right. Hereafter, Tristan, like the citizen of the modern state, will respond not only to that which is overtly dangerous, but also to that which makes him feel uncomfortable. In sparing the couple Marc opens the floodgate of boundless personal guilt. Significantly, his own conscience finds an analogue in that of Tristan who has felt, up until Marc's visit, that something awful has happened to him and who subsequently senses, for the first time, that it is he who has done something wrong:

> Dex! tant m'amast mes oncles chiers,
> Se tant ne fuse a lui mesfez!

> God! my uncle would love me so dearly,
> If only I had not so wronged him.
> (v. 2170)

If the sublimation of violence brings a necessary transformation of shame into guilt, it also entails, as its most immediate consequence, the reconciliation of consciousness and being. Upon awakening, Tristan and Iseult become aware, again for the first time, of the paradox of a queen and royal nephew exiled in the forest. They suddenly discover the autonomous social identity by which the individual within a guilt culture measures himself against the internalized ideal. First Tristan, who, feeling guilty at not having played the knightly role, adds personal doubt to guilt:

Oublĩé ai chevalerie,
A seure cort et baronie.
Ge sui essilié du païs,
Tot m'est failli et vair et gris,
Ne sui a cort a chevaliers.
Dex! tant m'amast mes oncles chiers,
Se tant ne fuse a lui mesfez!

I have forgotten knighthood,
I no longer lead a life at court.
I am exiled from the realm.
I am wretched, unclothed and without furs.
I am at no knightly court.
God! my uncle would love me so dearly,
If only I had not so wronged him!

(v. 2165)

And then Iseult, whose guilt is tempered by a keen sense of what she is missing at court:[56]

Je suis roïne, mais le non
En ai perdu par la poison
Que nos beümes en la mer. . . .
Les damoiseles des anors,
Les filles as frans vavasors
Deüse ensenble o moi tenir
En mes chanbres, por moi servir,
Et les deüse marïer
Et as seignors por bien doner.

I am queen, but the name
I have lost because of the poison
That we drank at sea. . . .
Demoiselles and honors,
Daughters of rich vassals
I should have by me now
In my rooms to serve me,
And I should marry them
To worthy lords.

(v. 2205)

Whereas obligation to the warrior clan produces mandatory vendetta within the shame-oriented culture of the feudal era, an intrinsic sense of responsibility to an ideal model of conduct defines the mode of self-

56. See P. Jonin, "Le Songe d'Iseut dans la forêt de Morois," *Le Moyen Age* 64 (1958): 113.

regulation—the mechanism by which the individual conforms to an internalized social norm—within the modern state.

Iseult's reminder of the love drink at the very moment of self-perception points to a subtle balance between potion and conscience. With awareness of an imperative social ideal the effects of the "lovendrins" automatically subside (vv. 2138–2140). The potion that is sometimes accepted as an "alibi for passion," othertimes as an objective correlative of the wish for death and transcendence, becomes an even more potent symbol of personal and social transformation. It represents the common denominator of all external causality, a global homology both of the couple's love and of their relation to the community. As a principle of causality alien to those it possesses, the "philtre" serves two functions: it both engenders desire and eliminates psychological suffering. While it works, Tristan and Iseult are liberated from the internal conflict that becomes apparent only after their awakening. Although they are able to perceive that something unfortunate has beset them—in the flour scene, condemnation, and exile, they remain untroubled by self-doubt until the "lovendrins" wears off. Only then does the feeling of having transgressed, of having actively sinned, replace the more passive sense of simply finding oneself in a difficult situation. The potion functions as an antidote to interiority in general and to negative interiority, or guilt, in particular.

What we are saying, in essence, is that potion and conscience are mutually exclusive ontological principles and that they imply radically different notions of social organization. The "lovendrins" as an autonomous determinant of love corresponds structurally to fealty, the organizing principle of the shame-based feudal age. Etiologically, it structures the rapport between lovers in a fashion analogous to the bond of homage. Established at a definite moment between specific parties, the "philtre" obligates its partners to a feudal brand of submission and mutual protection. There is, moreover, nothing implicit in Iseult's mother's brew. The effects of passion are not *a priori* to any individual passion. Like homage, the love between Tristan and the queen represents a personal tie that links the couple but fails to link either to the community. It defines their relationship to each other independently of any more comprehensive notion of social rapport. Here the balance between potion and conscience becomes clear: the abatement of the love brew coincides with and is indistinguishable from the moment in which an external structuring principle, like fealty, becomes internalized. In the instant of awakening from both "lovendrins" and sleep, the social fabric of Tintagel is no longer defined by specific obligations between individual men, but by a generalized social contract whose collective quality surpasses the sum of its individual parts. Simultaneously, the mechanism of inhibition and guilt, as opposed to the fear of reprisal and vendetta, becomes a self-generating principle of sexual and social morality.

Thus, with the emergence of a divided guilt-ridden self that has disassociated itself from the integrating effects of the potion, Béroul manages to sever his own attachment to the feudal world. As noted earlier, the first half of *Tristan* is defined to a large extent by the lack of distinction between private and public domains: adultery automatically becomes a matter of state because of the reciprocal obligations between Marc and the barons. The taming and elimination of the barons seem, then, like a rejection of the dilemma besetting all feudal monarchs with the reconstitution of national polity: namely, how to distinguish the personal relation of lord to vassal from the public relation of a chief of state to his subjects.[57] For Béroul, the barons of Tintagel are no longer necessary because the threat of their prohibition has been internalized. Accordingly, Marc looks less and less like the feudal ruler bound by contractual kingship to express the will of the community and more like the aggressive national monarch whose "will," in the phrase of Justinian's *lex regia*, "constitutes living law."[58] He begins, in the trial scene, to resist the barons:[59]

> Se il aprés les escondiz
> En disoit rien se anor non,
> Qui n'en eüst mal gerredon.

> He who after the ordeal
> Utters any but honorable words
> Will have a cruel reward.
>
> (v. 4176)

However feeble Marc's warning, it does represent a return to Roman instead of feudal origins. Regardless of his vassals, he asserts a basically theocratic notion of active kingship in which power descends from above

---

57. For a remarkable general study of this problem see E. Kantorowicz, *The King's Two Bodies* (Princeton: Princeton University Press, 1957).

58. Quod princi placuit leges habet vigorem (Justinian, *Corpus Iuris Civilis: Institutiones*, ed. R. Schoell [Berlin: Weidman, 1912], p. 1).

59. For a more comprehensive discussion of the trial scene see P. Jonin, *Les Personnages féminins dans les romans français de Tristan au XIIe siècle* (Aix-en-Provence: Orphys, 1958), pp. 59–108.

through the monarch to the community and in which the king is at once above positive but below natural law.[60] In founding the civil state based upon implicit contract and guilt rather than specific obligations and shame, Marc becomes its first monarch, "the prince who is king in his own domain" (Beaumanoir 2: 1103: 63).

Leaving aside the obvious differences between Béroul's poem and the more "courtly" *Tristan* of Thomas or the more "chivalric" romances of Chrétien, what is to be learned from our analysis? First of all, that the delegation to the individual of a moral responsibility for the decisions that determine the course of his own existence cannot be separated from the designation of the individual as an autonomous legal entity. Nor can that designation be divorced from twelfth-century political reality. The choice of Marc not to slay, the choice of Tristan and Iseult to return to society are, of course, moral options; but it must be remembered that the notion of morality as an internalization of social obligations was itself rooted in the monarchic thrust toward personalization of criminal responsibility. Historically, the concept of morality, which assumes the existence of a nation of self-governing citizens, forms the basis of a social contract which, unlike that of the feudal state, preexists and survives the individual; it raises the possibility of a system of political allegiance— through moral allegiance to a prevailing ethical code—independent of specific duties of counsel and defense. The fact that vassal and lord were theoretically obligated only to each other is one of the often cited reasons for feudalism's failure to adapt to the broader political needs of a succeeding age. In contrast, the internalization of the values by which the individual directs his own behavior, of which courtly literature is but one expression, favored the creation of lateral social ties, mutual obligations, between even the most distant members of a large body politic—as opposed to the local, personal ties of dependence between lord and vassal or between the members of the same warrior group. Once again, the assumption that every individual possesses an inner code of ethics for which he is morally and legally responsible served the cause of political centralization.

---

60. See W. Ullmann, *Principles of Government and Politics in the Middle Ages* (New York: Barnes and Noble, 1961), pt. 2, chapt. 1.

Conclusion

Our discussion of the political implications of courtly individualism and of the Tristan legend in particular has led to a paradoxical conclusion—that courtliness as the most enduring modern formulation of the myth of interiority did not further the ideological interests of the class for which it was intended. On the contrary, courtliness seems to have contributed, despite its origins, to the creation of the type of mental structure that favors the growth of large political bodies. It appears to have encouraged—against the particularist tendencies of feudalism—the expansion of the late Capetian monarchy.

This conclusion is confirmed by what we have learned about the role of courtly literature in the limitation of the physical violence that was such a fundamental feature of the feudal era and whose suppression was so intimately connected to the reconstitution of the judicial state. To sum up, the epic ordeal of battle is, in romance, relegated outside of the courtly community whence it returns only in the form of a verbal report (see above pp. 199–210). The knights of Arthur's realm enjoy a peace that is continuously reaffirmed by the triumph over the forces of disorder that lurk in the forest, beyond the pale of a law synonymous with civil order. Similarly, in Old French and Provençal love poetry the reciprocal violence of the feudal epic is transformed into a verbal violence coterminous with the major lyric forms (see above pp. 167–189). Both courtly types promote the sublimation—through verbalization—of a violence generative of their distinctive structures. The novelistic cycle of departure, adventure, and the "telling of the tale" assumes the obligatory conversion of the violence outside of the law into the raw material, the *conte*, from which the literary text derives. And the dialectical patterns of lyric promulgate as the only acceptable medium of interpersonal exchange a verbal violence which, because it has been divorced from its representational role and because it exists wholly in language, minimizes the risk of becoming overt.

Thus courtliness's deepest social function resides in the displacement of an inferred model of human order characteristic of a warrior society and predicated upon the principle of direct physical violence toward a more mediated model typical of the modern state. The courtly text is built upon the implicit concealment of the physical ordeal of the warrior behind the verbalized ordeal of the lover, a process that is only partial in the chivalric novel, but that is complete within the lyric. One of the unwritten rules of the love song is, in fact, that the violence primary to and disguised by it should never be recognized as such (see above pp. 210–211). In order for the displacement to achieve its full effect the genuine hostility underlying the lover's encounter with his lady, the God of Love, other poets, his detractors, and, finally himself must always appear to be other than it is. Marcabru's sense of transgression in exposing the destructive potential of adultery stems from the poet's uneasy awareness that in revealing the contagious, vindictive, and retributive nature of sexual desire, its identity with the principle of vendetta, he risks upsetting the illusion that courtesy is designed to maintain:

> Moillerat, per saint Ylaire,
> Son d'una foldat confraire,
> Qu'entr'els es guerra moguda
> Tals que cornutz fa cornuda. . . .
> Si l'us musa, l'autre bada
> E ieu sui del dich pechaire.

Husbands, by Saint Hilaire, share a single madness for such a war has erupted between you that the one who wears horns makes his wife wear them; the cuckold cuckolds his wife, and thus stops braying. . . . While he dallies, she receives, and I sin in saying it.

(Marcabru 20)

Bernart de Ventadorn, in contrast, recognizes the advantages of not saying what he means, of disguising behind lofty words the hostility which his rivals provoke:

Doncs lor deuri' eu be servir,
pois vei que re guerra no'm vau
que s'ab lauzengers estau mau,
greu'm poiria d'amor jauzir.
Per leis es razos e mezura
qu'eu serva tota creatura;
neis l'enemic dei apelar senhor,
c'ab gen parlar conquer om melhs d'amo
tot lo pejor ad ops de ben volen.

I ought therefore to serve them (the slanderers), since it does me no good to wage war with them; and if I am nasty with the slanderers, it is hard for me to enjoy love. To please her, it is fitting and just for me to abase myself before everyone; even my enemy I ought to call "my lord," for with noble language love's adversaries are more easily converted to desire the good.

(Ventadorn (Lazar) 110)

In the renunciation of direct confrontation—*pois vei que re guerra no'm vau*—and in the appropriation of a language which contrasts with what it seems—*neis l'enemic dei apelar senhor*—Bernart has absorbed the basic lesson of courtliness: that anger, verbalized, is potentially a more effective weapon than war.

While verbalization works to hide and thus to mediate the ordeal that is presented as immanent and concrete in the *chanson de geste*, the courtly ideals of gentleness, love, courtesy, civility, and urbanity, which are synonymous with life in the modern state, discourage the open expression of physical violence within the community of noble souls. In particular, the principle of measure, which serves to focus responsibility for self-regulation upon the individual, also stands as the pacificatory value *par excellence* (see above pp. 236–237). The love bond requires, as Andreas specifies, a moderate degree of uncertainty and jealousy. The lover's lack of assurance produces a necessary tension which causes passion to prosper in a dialectical fashion, gaining momentum through constant threats to its continued existence. The struggle between poetic and amatory rivals, between lover and lady, contains, by definition, an element of active aggression. It revolves to some degree around the principle of retort and, when appropriate, retaliation. Under normal circumstances, the reciprocity of the tie may dictate feigned indifference, refusal of the love-request, purposeful absences, or a more formal test like the *assay*.[1] Pushed beyond

---

1. The *assay* (*asag, asais*) refers to a formal test which, as René Nelli maintains, required the lover to promise not to seek complete satisfaction but to restrict himself to embraces,

the prescribed limits of moderate behavior, however, the natural give-and-take of courtly struggle leads to extreme consequences. Once either partner has exceeded the boundaries of reason and measure, the violence underlying courtliness risks becoming overt; for the mediation that is its chief function is, ultimately, reversible. Behind courtly measure lies the violence of epic struggle ready to erupt when its boundaries have been transgressed. As Peire Vidal observes, "love and ire do not go well together":

> A drut de bona domna tanh
> Que sia savis e membratz
> E cortes e amezuratz
> E que no si trabalh ni's lanh.
> Qu'amors ab ira no's fai ges;
> Amors es mezur' e merces,
> E drutz que a bon cor d'amar
> Deu ab gaug l'ira refrenar.

The lover of a noble lady should be wise and prudent, courteous and measured, he should neither get angry nor complain. For love and ire do not go well together; love is measure and pity; and the lover with the proper desire for love should restrain his vexation with joy.

(Vidal 138)

Perfect love—Peire's *bon cor d'amar*—is a mixture of negative and positive elements held in check by each other. It is, again, a delicate balance between impulse and willpower, personal desire and social necessity—in other words, a repression of anti-social and, implicitly, of violent, instinct. To be "courteous and measured" means, among other things, to be divested of one's own violent tendencies—to be pacified, "civilized" in the original juridical sense of the term. It is in this sense that we must understand the contradictory nature of the *De Amore*.

Readers of Andreas's treatise on love have, since its rediscovery in the nineteenth century, been puzzled by the author's seeming incoherence. On the one hand, he extols the virtues of love, its ennobling power and

---

caresses, and kisses (*tener, abrasar, baisar*) for as long as the couple lies naked together. Nelli bases his discussion of the ritual love-ordeal upon the Comtesse de Die's "Estat ai en gran cossirier" and Azalais de Porcairargue's "Ar em al freg temps vengut" (see R. Nelli, *L'Erotique des Troubadours* [Toulouse: Privat, 1963], pp. 199ff). Andreas also mentions, in treating the difference between "pure" and "mixed" love, a procedure of this type (*Courtly Love* 122).

beneficent influence; on the other, he proclaims love's potential for destruction. Book III of the *Art of Courtly Love* stands as a palinode to love's glorification, an abrupt recantation in which Andreas counsels the neophyte lover Walter to reject the experience altogether: he who loves defies divine prescription and runs the risk of losing salvation (*Courtly Love* 187). From the apparent contradiction between Christian love and its carnal equivalent stems an even more compelling reason to shun the latter: love alienates men from each other: *by it one friend is estranged from another and serious unfriendlinesses grow up between men, and these lead to homicide or many other evils* (188). According to Andreas, rivalry is inherent to desire. To enter the "lists of love" is to accept the prospect of perpetual competition, *for in the business of love all men are rivals and are very jealous of each other* (113). Nor is contention restricted to men alone. If women are, as he concludes elsewhere, lustful, indiscreet, gluttonous, fickle, wileful, arrogant, spiteful, superstitious, and unfaithful, they are just as susceptible to competitiveness as men (202). Because of the jealousy which love engenders, he who "serves in Love's army" indulges in "criminal excess" and contributes potentially to the dissolution of social order. Jealousy spawns violence (193). Where love flourishes peace gives way to "deadly inescapable warfare":

Love, moreover, regularly leads men to deadly, inescapable warfare and does away with treaties of perpetual peace. Often, too, it overthrows great cities and mighty fortresses and the safest of castles and changes the good fortune of wealth into the evil fortune of poverty, even though a man may not give away anything that he has; and it drives many to commit crimes that they must atone for, but of which neither they nor their relatives are by any means guilty.

(*Courtly Love* 196)

Andreas points to the examples of David, Samson, and Eve—all well known in the Middle Ages for the degradation to which love led them—in order to illustrate the destructive power of immoderate passion.[2]

Andreas is not guilty of bad faith in his repudiation of love; nor is he trying, as has been suggested, to protect his own clerical status through the pious espousal of chastity. The apparent contradiction between the apologia of passion and the condemnation which follows represents less of

---

2. Among the lyric poets Marcabru was the most concerned with the potential chaos engendered by love. A state of perpetual violence, the equivalent of Andreas's "inescapable warfare," rages between jealous husbands and lovers, threatening the principle of virtuous order, or *Joven* (see especially Marcabru 20, 34, 45, 73, 147, 166, 185).

a true opposition than an attempt to come to terms with love's destructive potential. It is, in essence, both a recognition of the latent violence of the courtly encounter and a plan for its containment. Aware of the ease with which love gives way to jealousy and jealousy to violence, as well as of the consequences of general social conflict, Andreas seeks to reconcile the dangers of excessive desire with transcendent social order. Rather than deny all that has preceded Book III, he has merely reversed the logic of his argument. The prescriptions for success in love contained in Books I and II stand, in relation to this final admonition, as a satisfactory solution. What the author seems to suggest is that love's power, uncontrolled, poses the threat of chaos and dissolution. Therefore, if one chooses to love, he should, for the sake of the community as a whole, regulate his conduct according to certain well defined rules which render love less perilous, laws that are indistinguishable from the code of courtliness.

As a legalization of desire, its charter, the *De Amore* stands, in much the same way as a civil judicial system, as a model for the mediation of any desire which may lead to the kind of violence described in Book III. Andreas's approach to the repression of socially disruptive instinct is, moreover, twofold. He both advances a series of regulations governing potentially violent rivalries and extends the precepts covering specific cases to the proportions of a model for the settling of all such disputes (see above pp. 211–212). And while we can neither verify nor deny the existence of the historically problematic Love Court, we can take its fictitious character as a further sign of the homological rapport between courtliness *per se* and the emerging judicial institutions of the late Capetian state. The system which Andreas proposes as an ideal method for the resolution of differences between the members of France's chivalric nobility and, more generally, as a paradigm for all interpersonal relations, offers, at a time when the privileges of private armies and trial by combat were increasingly contested, an alternative to the violence that was traditionally a noble prerogative.

In making explicit the link between Love Court and law court, Andreas merely confirms that which we have observed with respect to other poetic forms. To the extent to which both the courtly narrative and lyric foster the subliminal displacement of the epic ordeal toward verbal substitutes, they perform an implicit social function analogous to the judicial inquest. In the recounting of the knight's adventures before King Arthur's court we recognize the literary equivalent of an inquisitory deposition; and in the debate of the poet with real or assumed interlocutors we discern a verbalized version of the inquisitory disputation. Put another way, trial by combat as a means of terminating wider armed conflicts stands in relation to trial by inquest as the epic ordeal stands in relation to the verbal tests of the more courtly genres.

The political implications of this analogy are rich indeed. Prohibition of private military campaigns and substitution of inquest for battle were, along with an aggressive economic policy and pursuit of royal wars, two important aspects of the monarchic attempt, beginning in the twelfth century, to usurp the sovereignty of nobility. For the Crown's chief rival, war represented the principal cause and the sustaining basis of its own position of dominance. Even in the postfeudal era the right of a military aristocracy to rule still depended upon its right to rule by armed force just as its ability to resolve the differences within its ranks depended, as an anonymous thirteenth-century lyric attests, upon the corresponding procedure of judicial combat:

> Gent de France, mult estes esbahie!
> Je di a touz ceus qui sont nez de fiez:
> Si m'aït Dex, franc n'estes vous mès mie;
> Mult vous a l'en de franchise esloigniez,
> Car vous estes par enqueste jugiez.

> Gentlemen of France, now you are confounded!
> I am speaking of all those born to fiefs:
> So help me God, you are free no more;
> You have been relieved of your free rights,
> For you are now judged by inquest.[3]

The autonomy of nobility was, above all, a military autonomy; and any impingement upon the free exercise of arms was an impingement upon political power as well.

Courtly literature, both because of the formal resemblance between its dominant types and inquest and because of its presence as a courteous, measured, nonviolent ideal, seems, from this perspective, to violate the ideological premises of a warrior society at the end of a profoundly military age. The chivalric Other World in which the law of the strongest prevails is, in fact, closer to an archaic feudal order than the peaceful *ordo* of Arthur's court. It is the civil peace of Camelot that threatens the

---

3. Leroux de Lincy, "Chansons Historiques des XIIIe, XIVe et XVe siècles," *Bibliothèque de l'Ecole de Chartes* 1 (1839–1840): 372.

traditional "raison de vivre" of aristocracy more than the daemonic *inordinatio* of the forest. Here we touch upon the paradoxical nature of the ultimate chivalric adventure: Completion of the Grail Quest, which holds the eschatological promise of an era of universal peace, spells the end of the historical role of knighthood.[4] Despite the demystification of the millenial myth at the end of the Lancelot Prose Cycle, most Arthurian literature written between Chrétien's *Perceval* and *La Mort Artu* looks forward to the advent of a universe in which nobility's claim to supremacy, based upon the necessity of military protection, becomes an empty daydream. Likewise, the ideal social community that can be extrapolated from the reduced representational range of the lyric has been pacified through the mediating principles—of measure, patience, humility, obedience—characteristic of the worthy lover.

What this means is that courtly literature can most appropriately be situated alongside the peace movements of the tenth through thirteenth centuries: the ecclesiastical *paix* and *trêve de Dieu*; municipal efforts to curtail bloodshed among the members of the "urban friendship"; some seigneurial limitations upon combat within the larger feudal states; and, most important, royal prohibitions of private war culminating in Louis IX's universal interdiction of the 1250s (see above pp. 120–121). Like the inquest, the judicial means by which monarchy sought to bring a bellicose chivalry under its control, courtliness relegates the violence that once belonged to all who were noble beyond the realm of aristocratic privilege. Except for a few especially powerful monarchs, the majority of knights had little to gain from either the suppression of private war or from the codification of the "rules of courteous behavior." Their resistance to the former is chronicled in the epic of revolt. Their appropriation of the latter remains, however, somewhat of a mystery. For in embracing both the egalitarian and the pacifist ideals of courtliness, France's feudal aristocracy renounced voluntarily the means of preserving its own military and political autonomy. Courtly literature was from the beginning a literature of decline because the ethic which it glorifies conflicts with the long range interests of a warrior caste. Just as the earliest *chansons de geste*—the *Chanson de Roland*, *Chanson de Guillaume*, and *Gormond et Isembard*—begin at the point at which war has become problematic—respectively, in

---

4. See E. Köhler, *Ideal und Wirklichkeit in der höfischen Epik* (Tübingen: Niemeyer, 1956), pp. 106–116; W. Kellermann, *Aufbaustil und Weltbild Chrestiens von Troyes im Percevalroman* (Halle: Max Niemeyer, 1936), p. 172.

the middle of a prolonged siege, a difficult local incursion, and rebellion—
the novel of chivalry and the love lyric were born out of the impossibility of their own ideological project.

At the outset of the present study we suggested that the similarity
between the techniques of medieval poetic performance and those of trial
justified a more general exploration of the relation between contemporaneous literary and judicial institutions. Aural, public, and originally
formulaic like the feudal trial, the literary performance represented a
forum for the communication of an acknowledged social code. Although
the early text may have fulfilled the need for diversion on the part of a
society increasingly given to leisure pursuits, it was at the same time a
repository of its most sacred laws. In recitation was ratification. This is
why so many works belonging to the period either revolve around legal
issues (disputed heritages, retribution, the limits of sovereignty); contain
scenes of actual trial (by combat, oath, and ordeal); or, upon a deeper
level, are structured according to formal principles identical to concur-
rent judicial procedures.

The circumstances of composition and diffusion in the High Middle
Ages give the impression that literature played an essentially conservative
role during a period of intense social transformation. As a locus for the
public affirmation of shared values among those with common ideological
interests, the "performed text" seems, at first, to have acted as a brake
upon change, a vehicle of resistance to the tangible historical forces
threatening the supremacy of aristocracy at the dawn of a new era. And
yet such a perception could not be further from our findings; for we have
seen that while the Old French epic appears to glorify the endeavor of
war and to justify aristocracy's claim to hegemony, it also serves as an
expression of a profound tension in the institutionalized forms of violence
characteristic of the "first feudal age." The epic of revolt in particular
chronicles the tactical difficulties and the human tragedy attached to the
aristocratic rights of vengeance and private war at a time when, for
technological and political reasons, the viability of a warrior society was
thrown into question. The epic, however, only articulates a military crisis
with far-reaching political implications. The possibility of resolution remains implicit to a genre which is itself deeply rooted in a strategy of the
past.

Courtly literature, in comparison, is future-oriented and responds in
unsuspected ways to the unresolved issues of epic. Though the courtly

text does not seem to reestablish aristocracy's prior claim to dominance based upon the exercise of arms, it points in the direction of new possibilities of human order which conflict with rather than support nobility's traditional function. In this, courtliness appears to have been neither the last ideological stand nor the swan song of a clannish military caste, but the literary code by which it dismantled its most cherished values and ideals: the unrestricted use of force by which it maintained supremacy; the preeminence of the warrior group over each of its members; a disregard for the self-imposed restraints—the inherent social contract—which create the possibility of a state independent of personal ties of dependence. Such a conclusion calls for a revised concept of the dynamics of medieval literary creation, a concept in which the "performed text" is seen less as a mechanism by which aristocracy affirmed its own solidarity and resisted change than as a forum for adaptation to the political realities of the postfeudal world. As a locus for the public exploration of alternatives to a defunct order, Old French literature was the stage upon which a class in transition struggled—against deep-seated historical interests—toward a new definition of itself.

Index